Constant Delights

Rakes, Rogues and Scandal In Restoration England

GRAHAM HOPKINS

ROBSON BOOKS

First published in Great Britain in 2002 by Robson Books,
64 Brewery Road, London N7 9NY

A member of **Chrysalis** Books plc

British Library Cataloguing in Publication Data
A catalogue record for this title is available from the British Library.

ISBN 1 86105 509 9

Typeset in 11/13pt New Baskerville by FiSH Books, London WC1
Printed by Creative Print & Design (Wales), Ebbw Vale

Contents

For Conor, Maisie and Ella...

but not yet

Introduction

Rude, Rough, Whoremongers

He spends all his Days In runing to Plays,
When in his Shop he shou'd be poreing;
And wasts all his Nights
In his constant Delights
Of Revelling, Drinking and Whoreing.
  – 'Upon his Majesties being made free of the City',
                Andrew Marvell[1] (1621–78)

In the above doggerel verse the republican, politician and poet Andrew Marvell bites at the ankles of the king, snarling that, rather than dutifully attending to business, he is given over to the pursuit of personal pleasure, as would an apprentice. The interregnum had been puritan, austere and moral-driven. The Restoration basically gave its children the keys to the sweet shop. Along with their king, all those frowned-upon antics such as drinking, gambling, playgoing, horseracing and sex were restored to the people. And how they made up for lost time. As one Restoration drinking song had it:

A hound and a hawk no longer
Shall be tokens of disaffection;
A cock-fight shall cease
To be a breach of the peace
And a horse race – an insurrection.

In the hierarchy of pleasure, as with the social order, all flowed from the king – hence Marvell's distaste at the example Charles II set. His courtiers, 'in whose company he took too much delight', given such lengths of rope did not hang fire. One disgusted contemporary recorded the doings of the court on a progress to Oxford: 'Though they were gay and neat in their apparel, yet they were very nasty and brutal, leaving at their departure their excrements in every corner, in chimneys, in studies, coalhouses, cellars. Rude, rough, whoremongers; vain, empty, careless.'[2]

At the court of Charles II's 'virtue was a worthless commodity'. Francis North, Lord Guildford, a dignified and temperate lawyer, was carefully advised to 'keep a whore' or else be 'ill looked upon for want of doing so' by the court. Pepys recorded on 21 February 1665 that 'my Lady Castlemaine will in merriment say that her daughter (not above a year old or two) will be the first mayde in the Court that will be married.' A letter from John Wilmot, Earl of Rochester, to his friend Henry Savile, dated 21 November 1679, emphasised the nature of the day:

> The Lowsiness of Affairs in this place is such (forgive the unmannerly Phrase! Expressions must descend to the Nature of Things express'd) 'tis not fit to entertain a private Gentleman, much less one of a publick Character with the Retaile of them, the General Heads, under which this whole Island may be consider'd, are Spies, Beggars, and Rebels, and the Transpositions and Mixtures of these, make an agreeable Variety; Busie Fools, and Cautious Knaves are bred out of 'em, and set off wonderfully; tho' of this latter sort, we have fewer now than ever, Hypocrisie being the only Vice in decay amongst us. Few men here would dissemble their being Rascals, and no Woman disowns being a Whore.[3]

Such an environment bred, suckled and nurtured the rake: idle, dissipated and immoral. A man driven by relentless pursuit of sexual pleasure whose personal history is plotted by the number and names of conquests. For the first time, sex for its own sake became a desirable commodity. The need for a deep, passionate spiritual love – as a prerequisite for the physical outcome, as in Elizabethan and Jacobean drama – was old hat for this deeply fashion-conscious society. These men were not transported by the higher plane of discourse on morality, principle and conscience: they knew what moved them and it was earthly, tangible and obtainable:

> *Let us indulge the Joys we know*
> *Of Musick, Wine and Love.*
> *We're sure of what we find below,*
> *Uncertain what's above.*[4]

Court life – centred on Whitehall Palace, London – was an eclectic cauldron in which to overheat your senses and stoke the fires of influence. Conversely, the country was bumpkins-ville. Or, at best, a safe, quiet place to retire to recharge the batteries, recuperate from illness or a haven away from the fray. Rochester said the country was 'where only one can think; for you at Court think not at all; or, at least, as if you were shut in a drum; you can think of nothing, but the noise that is made about you.' The country also provided an alternative address for enduring an appropriate period of banishment after such times when even those liberally drawn lines of court were overstepped.[5]

Sir Robert Bulkeley in a letter to Rochester remarked that whenever having cause to leave London it is compared to 'a sort of dying'. The Comte de Gramont labelled the country 'a young person's gibbet and galleys.' Stanford, a character in Thomas Shadwell's *The Sullen Lovers* is told that the country is a place where he could be free. 'Free!' he cries, 'yes, to be drunk with March beer, and wine worse than ever was served in Pye-corner at the eating of pigs; and hear no other discourse but of horses, dogs and hawks.'[6]

Lampoons, libels or satires captured, pilloried and lamented the times. Their authors were the gossip columnists of their day, sometimes wide of the mark, sometimes hypocritical, sometimes bitter, always a read. They were always issued anonymously to protect their names from libel suits and their hides from beatings. Of course, it being such a male-dominated literary pastime, women were targeted remorselessly, having the added attraction of being less likely to draw a sword on you.

It was, unsurprisingly, a man's world. George Savile, the first Marquis of Halifax has been called 'one of the outstanding figures of the century', a man of 'piercing wit and pregnant thought.' But he personified the girdling patriarchal attitude. In 1688 he published his *Advice to a Daughter*. In the chapter 'Husband' he pontificates:

> You must first lay it down for a foundation in general that there is inequality in the sexes, and that for the better economy of the world the men, who were to be the lawgivers, had the largest share of reason bestowed upon them; by which means your sex is the better prepared for the compliance that is necessary for the better performance of those duties which seem to be the most properly assigned to it.[7]

More timely advice centred on the role of a wife to endure the unfaithful husband.

Remember that next to the danger of committing the Fault yourself, the greatest is that of seeing it in your husband. Do not seem to look or hear that way: If he is a Man of Sense, he will reclaim himself, the Folly of it, is of itself sufficient to cure him: if he is not so, he will be provok'd, but not reform'd.[8]

Thankfully there were any number of women willing to commit 'the Fault' themselves and scandalise society. The two champion 'Faulters', Barbara Villiers, king's mistress and ultimately duchess of Cleveland, and Anna Maria Brundenell, the Countess of Shrewsbury, are worthy of their own chapters. They knew how to operate in a man's world:

> *No ways to vice does this our age produce*
> *But women with less shame than men do use;*
> *They'll play, they'll drink, talk filth'ly and profane*
> *With more extravagance than any man.*

And they knew how to seize the day, and wouldn't be victims as those depicted in Rochester's 'Phyllis be gentler I advise', which concludes:

> *Then, if to make your ruin more,*
> *You'll peevishly be coy,*
> *Die with the scandal of a whore*
> *And never know the joy.*[9]

The book opens with the king himself because, as stated above, all flowed from him. However, Charles's sexual history is hardly unexplored territory and we will therefore study his initiation into sex and his experience in exile so we get a picture of the man who rode triumphantly into London on his thirtieth birthday once more the father of his people. Indeed, George Villiers, Duke of Buckingham, given the number of the king's acknowledged offspring, on one time proclaiming Charles to be indeed the father of his people, added under his breath, 'Well, of a good many of them, anyway'. The king's less exposed and failed sexual relationship with Frances 'La Belle' Stewart will also be explored. With the exception of Barbara Villiers, Charles's main mistresses will not be covered other than in passing through our various stories. I have written about Louise de Keroualle, Duchess of Portsmouth, Hortense Mancini, Duchesse Mazarin, and the delicious orange-seller-cum-actress-cum-mistress in *Nell Gwynne – A Passionate Life*, also published by Robson Books.

Given his distaste for the Restoration court, the abstemious and upright James, Duke of York, is perhaps an odd choice. But his roving eye and sauntering libido marked him out as truly the king's brother. The other rakes to warrant their own (albeit shared) chapter are John Wilmot, Earl of Rochester, and Sir Charles Sedley. They were undoubtedly scandalous. However, history has dressed them up as rake-hells in league with the devil. This study illustrates their antics but equally attempts to draw a calmer, more realistic image than that so lazily handed down. It is a similarly sympathetic approach that is adopted for our two female 'rakes'. The other person to capture his own chapter is the rogue known to every schoolboy – 'Colonel' Thomas Blood, crown stealer.

The general, catch-all chapters include one that concentrates on those whose profession was reborn at the Restoration – actors and, for the first time on stage in England, actresses. The other chapters skim over those perennial vices – drink, sex and violence.

Dividing the book in this way, it's clear that the subjects struggle to fit into neat, distinct, stand-alone chapters. Inevitably they overlap, merge and unleash hostile takeover bids. The lives of the main characters necessarily cross over and openly lack consistency about what or who goes where. Indeed, how do you split up sex, violence and drink when more often than not sex and violence (combined or singularly) are often the outcome of drink, and drink the satisfying after-result of sex or violence? Or both?

Restoration England is one of the most remarkable and fashionable periods in English history. Peopled with names such as Milton, Newton, Pepys, Dryden, Halley, Purcell, Bunyan, Wren, Lely and Kneller, it was a time of innovation, creativity and beauty. It also had more than its fair share of rakes and rogues who burned scandal at both ends. This book unashamedly seeks out the incorrigible, the notorious, the infamous, the shameless. It has them all: the blades, the fops, the rakes, the rogues, the whores, the slatterns, the bitches. And that's just the men.

1

Old Rowley: the Private Life of Charles II

'...and can hope for no good to the State from having a prince so devoted to his pleasure.'
                              – Samuel Pepys's diary, 11 January 1668[1]

That Charles II was a very human king endeared him to and infuriated his subjects (and historians) in equal measure. Lord Halifax wrote that Charles's 'inclinations to love were the effects of health and a good constitution...His [passions] stayed in the lower regions.' Pepys's colleague, Thomas Povey, complained to the diarist of the king's obsession with women, in that he 'doth spend most of his time in feeling and kissing them naked all over their bodies in bed – and contents himself, without doing the other thing but as he finds himself inclined; but this lechery will never leave him.' While the other famous diarist, John Evelyn, told Pepys that the king cared for little 'but his lust'.[2]

It was his cared-for lust that spawned his nickname 'Old Rowley'. This was the name of one of Charles's favourite stallions – both, it seemed, covered their duties well. Charles adored horses and for a month in spring and autumn would decamp government to Newmarket for the races. It was Charles's royal patronage that earned the sport the sobriquet of 'the sport of kings'. Charles enjoyed his nickname (he was also known as 'Charlemagne' and, even though this was a tongue-in-cheek swipe at his kingship qualities being less than great, he enjoyed that, too). 'Old Rowley' also became the title of a popular (if lewd) song. A story runs that Charles, overhearing a maid of honour singing it in her room, knocked on her door. 'Who's there?' she called out. ''Tis Old Rowley himself,' replied a smiling monarch.[3]

Charles arrived triumphantly into his capital city (and now home) on his thirtieth birthday. And his infamous reputation was already well established. Unmarried, he is highly likely to have spent the night of his return to London with a married woman, Barbara Villiers. But she was not his first mistress. Not by some distance. The restored king's life in exile was no sexual sabbatical, although possibly neither was it as abandoned as sometimes thought.

Eleanor, daughter of Robert Needham, Viscount Kilmurry, was second wife of John, Lord Byron, and had been one of Charles's mistresses while abroad. On 26 April 1667, Pepys met with John Evelyn ('Mr Eveling') and together they bemoaned 'the badness of the government, where nothing but wickedness, and wicked men and women command the King'. Evelyn described Lady Byron as being 'the King's seventeenth whore abroad'. However, such a number may have been exaggerated.[4]

The image of the king in exile philandering his way across mainland Europe in fully undressed rehearsals for when he might come home is somewhat misplaced. Certainly the Parliamentary propagandists portrayed Charles as a profligate and licentious man corrupt beyond all redemption. But then they would, wouldn't they? Antiroyalist scandal-soaked ammunition whistled about the nation's ears like volleys of musket fire, causing the truth to dive for cover. Nonetheless, it was a time when Charles swapped the armour for amour and left his heart hopelessly unprotected.

However, his thriving career in copulation began modestly enough in 1645 with the Civil War still puncturing Britain, in the market town of Bridgewater, Somerset. It was here that Charles met again his childhood nanny, the 'celebrated beauty and an opulent heiress' Christabella Wyndham, whose husband was the town's governor. And it was here that she nursed the fourteen-year-old prince of Wales through his first sexual experience. And, at that age, he was considered a late starter.[5]

A similar introduction to the world was experienced by Charles's cousin, Louis XIV, as his biographer describes:

On a certain evening when he was sixteen, coming back from the bath he met his mother's personal maid, Catherine Henriette de Beauvais: not a noblewoman, but the daughter of a second-hand clothes dealer and widow of a ribbon-maker. Madame de Beauvais was prized by [Queen] Anne as a deft needle-woman and by several courtiers for quite different accomplishments. Despite a plain face she was attractive to men; and to Louis too, returning from his bath. Without fuss she initiated her King into the pleasures of *le doux savoir*. It was an incident without sequel for Madame de Beauvais was past forty, but Louis was always grateful to her. She was given a pension and a fine house in the Marais and henceforth enjoyed special prestige at Court.[6]

Not content with nurturing the boy into a man, a job well done, Mrs Wyndham, the former nursemaid, unfortunately milked the situation for all it was worth. The cherry-popper by royal appointment assumed that etiquette no longer applied and overindulged in public demonstrations of her affection for Charles. The principled Edward Hyde, the boy's social and political guardian, was dismayed at such a carry-on.

Hyde saw Mrs Wyndham as an unnecessary distraction from daily business. Charles rather thought she was the business of the day. Sure enough in her standing to fondle and kiss Charles in public, the governor's wife used her influence, according to Hyde, to see Sir Charles Berkeley and Robert Long onto the King's Council in the West. With his virginity lost and forgotten, Charles would be only too ready to sway to the whisperings of a female in favour.

Charles's first love affair, though, was a long summer romance. In 1646, the buoyant sixteen-year-old prince at the helm of the frigate *Proud Black Eagle* landed at Jersey. The island was under the staunchly royalist governership of Sir George Carteret. However, it wasn't the governor's wife who caught Charles's sexually awakened eyes this time, but rather his twenty-year-old daughter, Marguerite. It was a summer that consummated the two most powerful passions of his life: sex and the sea.

Rumours would later circulate that Charles was the father of Marguerite's son, James de la Cloche (his last name being that of Marguerite's subsequent husband, Jean de la Cloche). However, these rumours, rung out by the hapless boy himself in later life, were unfounded, disbelieved and dismissed.

In June, Charles sailed to join his mother, Queen Henrietta Maria, in France. Here he was soon infatuated with one of her maids of honour, the dark-eyed beauty, Isabelle-Angélique de Montmorency-Bouteville, Duchesse de Châtillon, affectionately (and thankfully) nicknamed Bablon. Despite the ultimate platonic nature of their relationship, Charles remained fond of her. He even granted her a licence, in 1662, to import alum (a white chalky substance used for make-up) from England, making it out to 'The Duchesse de Chastillon or Bablon'. Henrietta Maria, however, as treasurer of the increasingly diminishing royal finances, pushed her hungry son into the path of his first cousin, Anne-Marie Louise de Montpensier, the so-called grande mademoiselle, and her highly palatable fortune. Tall, blonde, blue-eyed and busty, she was almost as mouth-watering as her fortune. But as far as any romance was concerned Charles didn't even make it onto her menu. Anne-Marie knew her worth – it was Louis XIV she craved – and it certainly didn't balance with the bottom line of a penniless monarch in exile.[7]

Also, interestingly, for the confident and elegantly available Frenchwoman, the young Charles didn't cut the Dijon. He was hesitant and nervous and, for once, prone to the bouts of stammering that so afflicted his father. His mother tried to plead his cause but this backfired woefully when Anne-Marie replied that she 'did not greatly value the opinion of another relative to a man who could say nothing whatever for himself'. Neither was she amused by his table manners as he 'would not touch the ortolans [a small delicately flavoured bird] but threw himself on an enormous piece of beef and a shoulder of mutton, as though he had never been accustomed to anything else: I felt ashamed that his taste was so unrefined'. Not quite going to plan, then. Also, although in her journal, Anne-Marie described Charles as 'only sixteen or seventeen years old and quite tall for his age. He had a beautiful head, black hair, a dark complexion, and was fairly agreeable in person'. She records her annoyance at his inability to master French. *Quelle dommage.*[8]

So with little in common, spare a shared birthday and unusual height, the Montpensier millions stayed out of the Stuart store. Not conventionally handsome, Charles was, however, an attractively striking man who, at six foot two, was a commanding presence – perhaps as much as someone of about six foot eight would be today. His brother, James, would also top six foot. And this despite the fact that their parents barely averaged five foot between them. One source had Charles I at only four foot eleven – and that was with his head on.

In the summer of 1648 Charles found himself in Holland and, for the first time, in love. Unquestionably. Lucy Walter's contemporaries and fickle posterity, however, were less generous with their affection. She may have lost her footing a few times but she was no fallen angel. The diarist John Evelyn thought her 'a browne, beautiful, bold, but insipid creature' when he met her in St Germaine on 18 August 1649. His other description of her as a 'beautifull strumpet' neatly combined, for him at least, her virtue and vice. Edward Hyde thought her 'a private Welchwoman of no good Fame, but handsome.' Her notoriety as a mistress, possibly to Robert Sidney, gave rise to unfounded allegations of prostitution. Evelyn also later condemned her as the daughter of 'some very meane Creatures' although her mother, Elizabeth Protheroe, was niece to the Earl of Carbery. Lucy was born in Roche Castle, Pembrokeshire, about 1630, although she moved to London when she was about seven or eight. The family took lodgings in King Street, Westminster, a fashionable part of town where later another mistress of the king, Barbara Villiers, would live.[9]

Lucy's promiscuous parents were caught up in an unseemly legal row, lasting six years, in which her mother sued her father for desertion and refusing maintenance. Eventually in 1647 the House of Lords granted the custody and welfare of the Walter children to the father. Rather than comply, Lucy moved to Holland to live with her uncle Gosfright, a Dutch merchant. Within a year she had changed her name to Barlow (taken from a maternal uncle, John Barlow of Slebech), possibly to hide the shame of her feuding parents. It was there that Lucy met (some say again) and began a passionate affair with the Prince of Wales, heir to the throne of a kingdom at war.

And, if Lucy thought she had parental worries, King Charles I was executed on 30 January 1649. The eighteen-year-old prince was now Charles II. A king without a kingdom. But one very soon with a son. Lucy gave birth to James on 9 April 1649. The boy's legitimacy would repeatedly send tremors testing the stability of the succession for the next 36 years.

Despite rumours that James was fathered by Robert Sidney, there can be little doubting Charles's paternity. That Charles 'owned' James unfortunately in itself proves nothing, as he would later accept paternity of at least two children with Barbara Villiers who were almost certainly not his. There is, however, such a striking similarity between Charles and James that portraits of them approaching puberty and beyond are interchangeable. Also, according to Buckingham in his *Memoirs*, James 'was ever engaged in some amour'. James was a Stuart for sure. Lucy Barlow was a Stuart mother. But was she also a Stuart wife?

The first mention that James was the legitimate son of Charles is found in Pepys on 27 October 1662. Charles, clearly concerned for the child's welfare, had previously ordered him from Lucy (just as Lucy had been ordered from her mother) and he was placed in the care of Lord Crofts, whose name the young James took. A colleague, John Creed, told Pepys of the whispers at court 'that young Crofts is lawful son to the King, being married to his mother.' In 1663, Edward Hyde, Earl of Clarendon, was accused of spreading rumour to cause friction between the king and the Duke of York, the heir to the throne.[10]

Lucy, pushed aside by Charles's wandering libido, would maintain until her death in 1658 that he had married her. The story, as with Lucy herself, certainly had legs. Charles's undoubted affection for James caused surprise. He created him Duke of Monmouth in 1662. Timothy Alsop, the king's brewer, told Pepys that the king,

> loves not the Queen at all, but is rather sullen to her; and she by all reports incapable of children. He is so fond of the Duke of Monmouth that everybody admires it [in the sense that they can't believe it]; and [Alsop] says that the Duke hath said that he would be the death of any man that says the King was not married to her – though Alsopp says it was well known that she was a common whore when the King lay with her.[11]

On 22 February 1664, Pepys noted, 'The Duke of Monmouth's mother's brother [possibly Justus Walter] hath a place at Court; and being a Welchman, I think he told me, will talk very broad of the King's being married to his sister.' Later Pepys recorded how the duke

> spends his time the most viciously and idly of any man, nor will be fit for anything – yet he speaks as if it were not impossible but the King would own him for his son, and that there was a marriage between his mother and him – which God forbid should be, if it be not true; nor will the Duke of York be easily gulled in it.[12]

Charles's sister, Mary, married to the Prince of Orange, wrote letters to her brother in 1654–5, in which she referred to Lucy as his 'wife'. For example, in November 1654 she wrote, 'Your wife thanks you in her own hand and still though begs me very hard to help her.' And, in June 1654:

> Your wife desires me to present her humble duty to you which is all she can say. I tell her 'tis because she thinks of another husband, and does not follow your example of being as constant a wife as you are a husband: 'tis a frailty they say given to the sex, therefore you will pardon her I hope.

However, these references are surely jocular. There may well have been a mock ceremony – Charles indulged this fantasy with his French mistress Louise de Keroualle in October 1671: 'It was universaly reported that the faire Lady – was bedded one of these nights, and the stocking flung, after the manner of a married bride.'[13]

Despite denials, the rumours refused to lie low, and remained ripe for manipulation. Eighteen years into Charles's reign, when it was clear he would have no children with his queen, worried eyes twitched in the direction of the heir apparent, the Duke of York, a suspected Catholic. Effort was spent spinning the virtue of an assured protestant succession: and who better fitted the frame than the man who may well be the legitimate heir anyway? Charles was compelled to issue a public proclamation:

> There being a false and malicious report spread abroad by some who are neither friends to me nor to the Duke of Monmouth, as if I should have been either contracted or married to his mother; and though I am most confident that this idle story cannot have any effect in this age, yet I thought it my duty in relation to the succession of the Crown, and that future ages may not have any further pretence to give disturbance upon that score, or any other of this nature, to declare, as I do declare, in the presence of Almighty God, that I never was married nor gave contract to any woman whatsoever, but to my wife Queen Catherine, to whom I am now married. In witness whereof, I set my hand, at Whitehall, the sixth day of January, 1678. Charles R.[14]

For sure, both mother and son brought unknown joy and heartache to Charles. But the decline in affection of his son was by far the more distressing. After Monmouth had killed a London beadle in 1671, such was his fatherly indulgence that Charles signed a warrant pardoning him from 'all Murders, Homicides and Felonies whatsoever at any time before 28th of February last past committed either by himself alone or together with any other person or persons.' However, all such indulgence dried up when in 1679 Monmouth became the willing tool of the king's opponent, the Earl of Shaftesbury, and promoted himself as the Protestant champion in the race to the succession. Charles banished his son.

However, the empty-headed duke filled that particular void with notions of his own popularity. In a thunderously ill-advised display of political naïveté he returned from exile almost immediately and without permission. His 5 a.m. arrival in London in November 1679 was greeted by bells and fireworks. With such defiance there was possibly only one place Monmouth would be safe to work towards a reconciliation with his father: the home of another (possibly) Welsh royal mistress.

Nell Gwynne took Monmouth into her house at Pall Mall and agreed to do what she could to help. At first when Charles called to dine, Monmouth had to make himself scarce. In his letter to Lady Sunderland, dated 16 December 1679, Henry Sidney notes that

Monmouth 'makes great court to Nelly, and is shut up in her closet when the king comes, from which in time he expects great matters.' The French ambassador Barillon confirms the arrangement in his letter to Louis XIV in December 1679, saying that Monmouth 'every night sups with Nelly, the courtesan who has borne the king two children, and whom he visits daily.'[15]

Uncharacteristically, Nelly was unsuccessful. Charles would not see his son. A contemporary account records:

Nelly dus the Duck of Monmouth all the kindness shee can, but her interest is nothing. Nell Gwinn begg'd hard of his Majtie to see him, telling him he was grown pale, wan, lean and long-visag'd merely because he was in disfavour; but the King bid her be quiet for he wd not see him.[16]

Robert Southwell confirms Charles's refusals in a letter to the Duke of Ormond on 29 November 1679, saying that Monmouth 'supped the last night with Mrs Gwyn, who was this day at her utmost endeavours of reconciliation, but received a very flat and angry denial, and by all appearances His Majesty is incensed to a high degree'. The satires of the time also chronicled the event. Typically, they reflected Nelly's humour. She called Monmouth 'Prince Perkin', referring to the infamous Flemish-born impostor Perkin Warbeck who laid claim to the English crown of Henry VII:

> *True to ye protestant interest and cause;*
> *True to th' established government and laws;*
> *The choice delight of the whole mobile,*
> *Scarce Monmouth's self is more belov'd than she.*
> *Was this the cause that did their quarrel move*
> *That both are rivals in the people's love?*
> *No; twas her matchless loyalty alone*
> *That bid Prince Perkin pack up and be gone.*
> *Ill-bred thou art, says Prince; Nell does reply*
> *Was Mrs Barlow better bred than I?*[17]

Charles reacted to his increasingly wayward, self-deluding and feckless son's defiance by depriving him of his offices and ordered him into exile again. Once again, Monmouth defied his father and proceeded to tour the country, promoting the story of the infamous black box in which it was said existed the marriage contract between Charles and his mother. To end the rumours, Charles had Secretary of State Leoline Jenkins carry out a public enquiry. Sir Gilbert Cosins Gerard, MP for Northallerton, was reported to have seen the contract. Summoned to answer the report in April 1680, Gerard did his best to avoid answering before finally declaring on oath that he had 'never seen any such paper.' Dorothy, Lady Sunderland, wrote in 1680, 'This day will come out all the examinations about the black box, with a declaration that will not, I suppose, legitimate the Duke of Monmouth.' Her supposition was right: the black box was a red herring. The king's brother and not his first-born son would succeed him. And, in 1685, did so.[18]

Nonetheless, the exiled Monmouth continued to believe the hype. He landed near Lyme Regis that summer, declaring himself the lawful king and pronouncing his Uncle James a usurper. Monmouth had himself crowned at Taunton, raised an army of mostly peasant locals and marched on strategically important Bristol. However, when the crunch came, he crunched out and chose not to fight but instead retreated westwards, losing many recruits on the way. He was gambling on a surprise night attack at Sedgemoor. It was an awesome blunder. With the game up, he bolted leaving his poor, deluded followers to be massacred for his cause. The military mastermind was later captured in the New Forest, hiding pitifully in a ditch. Despite pleading desperately for his life, and having Catherine of Braganza speak for him, James II ordered his execution.

Monmouth was executed on 15 July 1685 on Tower Hill. He confessed to the rector of St Martin-in-the-Fields, Dr Thomas Tenison, whom he had requested to be with him at the end, that 'I dye very penitent'. He looked at the executioner, Jack Ketch, and asked, 'Is this the man to do the business? Do your work well.' Monmouth then, in a brave act of theatricality, felt the edge of the axe and said, 'I fear it is not sharp enough.' However, as 'the executioner proceeded to do his office' either Monmouth was right about the blade, or wrong to trust that Ketch would do the job well. After the third swipe Ketch threw down his axe complaining, 'I can't do it.' Compelled to try again, he attempted two more blows before deciding to finish the job with a butcher's knife, hacking Monmouth's head from his body. This was not Ketch's only inept display. He also bungled the execution of Lord Russell in Lincoln's Inn Fields after the Rye House Plot in 1683, defending himself by saying that Russell 'moved'.[19]

Back in 1650, Charles was doting on his newly born son but had less dote for the boy's mother. Another woman, Elizabeth 'Betty' Killigrew, had been catching a glance or two. Regardless of his sexual desires Charles had some unfulfilled political ones in need of attention. He had to leave his son and mistresses behind, even though Betty Killigrew, eight years Charles's senior, was also pregnant. She was married to Francis Boyle, who was later created Viscount Shannon. The future Lady Shannon gave birth to Charlotte Jemima Henrietta Maria in 1651. The child was acknowledged with the royal surname of Fitzroy. Lucy Barlow also gave birth to a daughter, Mary, in the king's absence. However, in this case, he had been absent from her bed during the conception as well. The father was most probably the Irish nobleman Theobold, Lord Taaffe, who according to the cardinal de Retz was 'Great Chamberlain, Valet de Chambre, Clerk of the Kitchen, Cup Bearer and all' to Charles in exile. Stand-in lover was clearly part of the 'and all'.[20]

In his attempt to reclaim his kingdom, Charles would spend the best part of the next two years there, culminating in his epic escape from the Battle of Worcester in 1652, part of which famously required him to hide in an oak tree in Boscobel Wood (the reason we have no shortage of pubs called the Royal Oak today). Sadly, the tree (or rather the one supposedly grown from the original, which had fallen prey to bounty and souvenir hunters) was destroyed by high winds in 2000.

In the remaining years before his restoration, Charles travelled widely in Europe. However, once he landed triumphantly in England he never left its shores again. And on his exiled travels wherever he went, dispossessed monarch or not, he could always find an understanding woman to comfort him. In Bruges it was Catherine Pegge, the beautiful daughter of a Derbyshire squire, who doubled the number of the king-in-waiting's children: Charles in 1657 and Catherine in 1658. Again, a regally recognised surname was granted; this time Fitzcharles. Their daughter died young but their son would be created the Earl of Plymouth in 1675. He was a popular figure at court, where he was known fondly as 'Don Carlos'.

In the meantime, Lucy Barlow had become an embarrassment to the king and had not only taken up with a scoundrel called Tom Howard but was shockingly living openly with him as his lover. Charles wrote to Lord Taaffe in May 1655 to 'advise her, both for her sake and mine, that she goes some place more private than The Hague for her stay here is very prejudicial to us both'. Charles's private investigator, Daniel O'Neill, sought to save Lucy from the 'publick scandall' with which her maid was threatening her. His dispatch of 8 February 1656 to Charles ran in part:

Hir mayd, whom she would have killed by thrusting a bodkin [a dagger] into hir eare ass she was asleep, would have accused hir of that, of miscarrying of two children by phissick [abortion], and of the infamous manner of hir living with Mr Howard; but I have prevented the mischiefs partly with threats, butt more with 100 gilders I am to give hir mayd.[21]

Feeling jilted, Lucy threw all sexual caution to the port winds. In 1656 she took her children James and Mary to England and promptly found herself imprisoned in the Tower of London. Although she was labelled 'wife or mistress' of Charles by the authorities, Cromwell certainly had no faith in her claimed marital status and ordered her release. Back on the continent, Charles, irritated by Lucy's behaviour, was more concerned with the welfare of young James, known then as Master Jacky. Although nearly eight, he remained largely illiterate and unable to count, and was being daily exposed to his mother's increasingly embarrassing behaviour. Charles coldly and clinically sought to settle 'the matter of the child' and directed the removal of James from his mother's care.[22]

Lucy was staying at accommodation in Brussels owned by Sir Arthur Slingsby, an agent of the king. Claiming back rent, he organised her arrest for debt. However, the arrest was an unseemly public spectacle as the officers tried to take Master Jacky from an understandably kicking and screaming mother. Neighbours and passers-by moved to Lucy and the child's defence and saw off the bullies. The city governor's secretary, Giles Mottet, wrote angrily to the Duke of Ormond:

> I am so ashamed of the proceeding of Monsieur Slingsby and all his family, against Madam Barlow and her child, that I am loath to relate the particulars thereof to your excellency... My Lord Ambassador has written to the King about it being forced thereunto by the clamour of the people who found this action most barbarous, abominable, and most unnatural; the worst of all is, that Sir Arthur doth report and say to all, that the King hath given him the order for it...[23]

Charles certainly had given the order but had also required Slingsby to proceed with discretion. Ormond replied to Mottet that the king,

> gave order to Sir Arthur Slingsby in a quiet and silent way, if it could be, to get the child out of the Mother's hands, with purposes of advantage to them both, but he never understood that it should be attempted with that noise and scandal that hath happened.[24]

Lucy repeatedly refused requests to part with her son and even foiled another kidnap plot. But then, without explanation, she handed him over to Charles. Perhaps she had been ground down by the constant pressure. Lucy Walter/Barlow would never see her son again.

Towards the end of 1658 she died 'of a disease incident to her profession'. She was about 28 years old.[25]

Charles may have reinherited his country with three surviving children and undoubtedly a string of dalliances but does this constitute the oft-depicted man of dissolution? Such was the propaganda against Charles that in a letter to Lord Taaffe he noted dryly that he would have been fortunate indeed to have had enough time to entertain only half of the women attributed to him.[26]

In the early days of his Restoration, Charles left the politics to Edward Hyde (created Earl of Clarendon in April 1661, having declined a dukedom) and directed his personal rule to pleasure. Sir John Reresby records:

> The King at this time did not soe much trouble himself with business. All things went on easily and calmly... The business was much left to the management of the Earl of Clarendon, then Lord Chancellor; and the King, as he was of an age and vigour for it, followed his pleasures. And if amongst thos love prevailed with him more then others, he was farr excusable, besides that his complexion led to it, the woemen seemd to be the aggressours, and I have since heard the King say did sometimes offer themselves to his imbraces.[27]

One woman who was certainly no such aggressor was Frances Theresa Stewart. Known as 'La Belle' Stewart, Frances had looks that put even the beautiful Barbara Villiers in her place. The king's beloved sister, Minette, described Frances as 'the prettiest girl imaginable and the most fitted to adorn a Court.' The agreement was universal. The French courtier and later ambassador in London, Marquis de Ruvigny, wrote to Louis XIV that she was 'one of the most beautiful girls and one of the most modest to be seen.' His replacement, Honore Courtin, upon taking up his position, agreed that she was the most beautiful girl at the English court. And it was, indeed, some court. The Comte de Gramont noted that 'as for the beauties, you could not look anywhere without seeing them.' The French count's roving and discerning eye marked out Frances as one of the court's two 'chief ornaments' (the other, in his view, was, unsurprisingly, his eventual wife Anne Hamilton).[28]

Pepys wrote:

> Mrs Steward in this dresse, with her hat cocked and a red plume, with her sweet eye, little Roman nose, and excellent Taille [body] is now the greatest beauty I ever saw I think in my life; and if ever woman can, doth exceed my Lady Castlemayne; at least, in this dresse.

She was elegant. But, as the French ambassador naturally observed, she had been educated in France, so *of course* she was elegant. Gramont agreed:

> she was slender, straight enough, and taller than the generality of women: she was very graceful, danced well and spoke French better than her mother tongue: she was well bred, and possessed, in perfection, that air of dress which is so much admired, and which cannot be attained, unless it be taken young, in France.[29]

Barbara Villiers had nudged Frances into centre stage. She would direct the young debutante's performance to divert the king's attention away from Barbara's own developing relationship with Henry Jermyn. She would set up scenes to tease the sensuous monarch. For the innocent Frances (Gramont commented that 'it was hardly possible for a woman to have less wit, or more beauty'), Barbara's deviousness was seen only as a game, some slapstick fun. They would sleep in bed together 'ready' for when the king arrived to see them. Gramont recalls that Barbara,

> even affected to make Mrs Stewart her favourite, and invited her to all the entertainments she made for the King; and, in confidence of her own charms, with the greatest indiscretion, she often kept her to sleep. The King, who seldom neglected to visit the Countess before she rose, seldom failed likewise to find Mrs Stewart in bed with her.[30]

Such goings-on had the added value of titillating the court gossips as well as the king: Barbara seduces Frances while the king seduces them both. A satire of that year, 'On The Ladies of the Court', reflected the rumours:

> *Strangely pleasant were their chats,*
> *When Mayne and Steward played at flats,*
> *Their marriage night so taught them;*
> *Till Charles came there*
> *And with his ware*
> *Taught how their fathers got them.*[31]

(*Mayne* – Barbara Villiers; *at flats* – refers to lesbian games. The phrase is also mentioned in 'The Ladies Complaint to Venus', c. 1691, in which Venus reprimands the ladies,

> *you are to blame*
> *And have got a new game*
> *Called flats, with a swinging clitoris.*[32])

It was widely held and believed by many that Barbara and Frances married each other in a mock wedding ceremony. Pepys certainly believed it:

Another story was how my Lady Castlemayne, a few days since, had Mrs Stuart to an entertainment, and at night began a frolique that they two must be married; and married they were, with ring and all other ceremonies of church service, and ribbands and a sack-posset [a sweet and spicy drink of hot curdled milk and wine] in bed and flinging the stocking. But in the close, it is said that my Lady Castlemayne, who was the bridegroom, rose, and the King came in and took her place with pretty Mrs Stuart. This is said to be very true.

Just over a week later Pepys hears from another source that the mock marriage was true and 'that it was in order to the King's coming to Stuart, as is believed generally'.[33]

However, a change in tactic soon backfired. Barbara stopped Frances coming to her rooms. 'There was a great row the other day among the ladies,' wrote the French ambassador Cominges to Louis XIV, continuing,

it was carried so far that the King threatened the lady at whose apartments he sups every evening that he would never set foot there again if he did not find the Demoiselle with her; and for this cause the lady is never without her.[34]

Thomas Povey told Pepys,

that the king hath taken ten times more care and pains making friends between my Lady Castlemayne and Mrs Steward when they have fallen out, than ever he did to save his kingdom...That the King is at this day every night in Hyde-park with the Duke of Monmouth or with my Lady Castlemaine.[35]

The originality and sophistication of Frances's beauty belied the simplicity that jumped for joy in her mind. She loved what Gramont called her 'childish amusements'. Seeing her hold on the king, the Duke of Buckingham realised not only the pleasure of being in the presence of beauty but the political mileage to be racked up as her confidant. So he played and amused his way into her affection. For a natural entertainer such as the Duke of Bucks, Frances would not be his toughest audience. This was child's play:

... she was childish in her behaviour and laughed at every thing, and her taste for frivolous amusements, though unaffected, was only allowable in a girl about twelve or thirteen years old. A child, however, she was, in every other respect, except playing with a doll; blind-man's buff was her most favourite amusement; she was building castles of cards, while the deepest play was going on in her apartments, where you saw her surrounded by eager courtiers, who handed her the cards, or young architects, who endeavoured to imitate her.[36]

Frances, unsurprisingly, adored Buckingham's company – often sending all over town for him. She loved to make card castles (of which the duke was the undisputed king) and delighted in his impromptu 'old women's stories'. She enjoyed music, so he wrote her songs and sang them to her in his 'agreeable voice'. Frances's love for him was complete, he surmised. But not that complete. Buckingham mistook her compliments about his wit and drollery to be directed at a more tangible, physical aspect of his being. Confidently acting upon misreceived messages, 'he met with so severe a repulse that he abandoned, at once, all his designs upon her'.[37]

Gramont himself became the hero of one of Frances's juvenile jests:

The old Lord Carlingford was at her apartment one evening, shewing her how to hold a lighted wax candle in her mouth, and the great secret consisted in keeping the burning end there a long time without its being extinguished. I have, thank God, a pretty large mouth, and, in order to out-do her teacher, I took two candles into my mouth at the same time, and walked three times round the room without their going out. Every person present adjudged me the prize of this illustrious experiment, and [Harry] Killigrew maintained that nothing but a lantern could stand in competition with me. Upon this she was like to die laughing; and thus was I admitted into the familiarity of her amusements.[38]

In a court that flirted outrageously with sexual innuendo and where the dirty deed thrust itself upon every thought, Frances retained a childlike innocence to sex. Even when recounting erotic dreams, she was unable to do so without 'reddening'.[39]

However, gossip and the known universe certainly considered the easily amused Frances to be less than innocent when it came to entertaining the king in her bedchamber. A couple of months later, Pepys on seeing the queen and her maids of honour pass through

Whitehall on their way to the park, commented, 'But above all, Mrs Stuart is a fine woman, and they say now a common mistress to the King, as my Lady Castlemayne is; which is a great pity.' In June he is pleased to hear that the queen has stopped her sulking-in-state and 'begins to be briske and play like other ladies, and is quite another woman from what she was, of which I am glad – it may be it make the King like her better and forsake his two mistresses, my Lady Castlemaine and Steward.' By the end of the month Pepys was despairing of the king's being 'greatly taken up with' the pair, of which he prays that 'God of Heaven put an end to.'[40]

However, the gossipy assumption was somewhat adrift of reality. So unsuccessful and disheartened was Charles that the Duke and Duchess of Buckingham, along with Edward Montagu, the Earl of Sandwich, and a couple of others had set up a committee 'for the getting of Mrs Stuart for the King.' Another of the committee members was the upcoming Sir Henry Bennet from Harlington, Middlesex, who was secretary of state for the southern department – a sort of home secretary for England. He was created Baron Arlington in 1665 and the Earl of Arlington in 1672.[41]

Bennet was noted for wearing a black plaster over a scar on his nose caused by a Parliamentarian sabre in the Civil War. For Bennet this symbolised his loyalty to the cause; for Buckingham it symbolised the solemn and sedate Bennet's ridiculousness. However, this indelicate procurement committee adjourned a failure. Frances proved 'a cunning slut, and is advised at Somerset-house [by the Queen-Mother] and by her mother; and so the plot is spoiled and the whole committee broke'.[42]

Charles, nonetheless, persevered gallantly, holding her attention and anything else she would permit in public. Pepys recorded on 9 November 1663,

> how the King is now besotted upon Mrs Steward, that he gets into corners and will be with her half an hour together, kissing her to the observation of all the world; and she now stays by herself and expects it, as my Lady Castlemayne did used to do...But yet it is thought that this new wench is so subtle, that she lets him not do anything more then is safe to her.[43]

Such was the king's unbridled affection for Frances that it was speculated – 'verily thought' – that, should the queen die, Charles would unhesitatingly marry her. The French ambassador Le Comte de Cominges, in a letter to Louis XIV on 1 November 1663, broadly hinted as much:

> The King seems to me deeply affected. Well! he supped none the less

yesterday with Madame de Castlemaine and had his usual talk with Mlle Stewart, of whom he is excessively fond. There is already a talk of his marrying again, and everybody gives him a new wife according to his own inclination; and there are some who do not look beyond England to find one for him.[44]

Charles wrote her love songs. One ran:

> *I pass all my hours in a shady old grove,*
> *But I live not the day when I see not my love;*
> *I survey every walk now my Phillis is gone,*
> *And sigh when I think we were there all alone.*
> *O then, 'tis O then, that I think there is no hell*
> *Like loving, like loving too well.*
>
> *While alone to myself I repeat all her charms,*
> *She I love may be locked in another man's arms,*
> *She may laugh at my cares and so false she may be*
> *To say all the kind things she before said to me.*
> *O then, 'tis O then, that I think there is no hell*
> *Like loving, like loving too well.*
>
> *But when I consider the truth of her heart,*
> *Such an innocent passion, so kind without art;*
> *I fear I have wronged her, and hope she may be*
> *So full of true love to be jealous of me:*
> *And then, 'tis I think that no joys be above*
> *The pleasures of love.*[45]

This was serious. The 'best bred man alive' was simpering after Frances like a discarded mongrel puppy seeking affection. She obsessed him not only to the exclusion of other women but of everything. On 20 January 1664, Pepys hears that,

he doth dote upon Mrs Stuart only – and that to the leaving off all business in the world – and to the open slighting of the queen. That he values not who sees him or stands by him when he dallies with her openly – and then privately in her chambers below, where the very sentries observe his going in and out – and that so commonly that the Duke or any of his nobles, when they would ask where the King is, they would ordinarily say, 'Is the King above or below?' meaning with Mrs Stuart.[46]

Perhaps because of this perceived unwholesome business, Pepys's mouth-watering attraction to Frances dries up. In April he considers her 'fatter' and 'not as fair as she was' and a month later concludes her 'endeed very pretty, but not like my Lady Castlemaine for all that.' However, he's back in touch with his libido when he spies her 'in a most lovely form with her hair all about her eares' emerging from the Chair Room, a small chamber in Whitehall Palace, where the king and about twenty others had watched her having one of her very many portraits being painted.[47]

Pepys's admiration of Frances certainly bubbled whenever she dressed up: 'a lovely creature she in this dress seemed to be,' he purrs. The picture she sat for may well have been by Jacob Huysmans (c. 1633–96) and one of a series by the Dutch artist that Pepys viewed with such pleasure – 'as good pictures I think as I ever I saw' – on 26 August 1664. Frances was depicted 'in a buff doublet like a soldier.' Nearly two years later, seeing both Barbara Villiers and Frances together, both dressed plainly, Pepys revises his previous assessment of their respective beauties, finding Barbara 'a much more ordinary woman then ever I durst have thought she was; and endeed is not so pretty as Mrs Stewart.'[48]

Later in November, he thought Frances 'the most beautifullest creature that ever I saw in my life, more than ever I thought her, as often as I have seen her – and I begin to think doth exceed my Lady Castlemayne,' adding thoughtfully, perhaps in light of previous policy statements on the matter, 'at least now'. Although not before chancing by the pair disappointingly in 'plain natural dress' in October, and declaring himself 'not pleased with either of them.'[49]

If Pepys was bumping incautiously into deliberations over the relative merits of the king's top two, Charles himself was clear who should be number one. The hunt for new flesh took precedence over that already devoured. Charles even commissioned the goldsmith Jan Roettiers to engrave Frances's features as Britannia for what was known as the Breda medal – issued in gold, silver and bronze, which Pepys saw for the first time in February 1667: 'and at my goldsmith's did observe the King's new Medall, where in little there is Mrs Stewards face, as well done as ever I saw anything in my life I think – and a pretty thing it is that he should choose her face to represent Britannia by.' In his *Numismata*, a later work after Frances had become Duchess of Richmond, John Evelyn, who although as a member of the royal society was more intrigued with technique and skill, was similarly effusive:

Monsieur Roti (Graver to his late Majesty Charles II) so accurately express'd the countenance of the Duchess of R_____ in the Head of

Britannia, in the reverse of some of our Coin, and especially in a Medal, as one may easily, and almost at first sight, know it to be her Grace: And tho' in the smallest copper, both for the Persons represented, and performance of the Artist such as may justly stand in competition with the Antient Masters.'[50]

The coins and medals that boasted Britannia basked in England's glory as sovereign of the seas. The sheer arrogance – given that Dutch ships had just recently sailed up the Medway – was not lost on satirists, such as Andrew Marvell:

> *The Court in Farthering it self does please,*
> *(And female Stewart there rules the four Seas,)*
> *But fate does still accumulate our woes,*
> *And Richmond her commands, as Ruyters those.*[51]

Nonetheless, Frances's face has graced British coins ever since. Imagine being able to select that chat-up line from your armoury: 'Go on, I'll put you on the coinage.' But even that didn't work. Seemingly, he couldn't have her for love nor money. Tumbling in the hungry turmoil of unrequited love, Charles once sighed a wish to see Frances old and willing.[52]

However, she was soon to prove *young* and willing, and with a Charles Stuart, but not the one the king had in mind. The debt-ridden, hard-drinking (Gramont, noting his particular attachment to wine, refers to him as a 'drunken sot') Charles Stuart, third Duke of Richmond and sixth Duke of Lennox, had already outlived two wives, the second of whom had died in January 1667. Prudently the two would-be lovers kept their assignations from the king. However, even the darkest secrets give up glints of light. And these were illuminating enough to one particular woman sulking in the shadows: Barbara Villiers.[53]

A seasoned pro herself at the sport of clandestine coupling, Barbara moved the whistle menacingly towards her lips. One night Frances, feigning tiredness, caused the king to depart from her apartment in a mood so ill as to bring cheer to none but the fatted calf. And Barbara. She tipped off the angry monarch and watched as he made his seething way back to Frances's apartments:

It was near midnight: the king, in his way, met his mistress's chambermaids, who respectfully opposed his entrance, and in a very low voice, whispered his majesty that Mrs Stewart had been very ill since he left her; but that, being gone to bed, she was, God be thanked, in a very fine sleep. 'That I must see,' said the king, pushing her back who had posted herself in this way. He found Mrs Stewart in bed, indeed, but far from being asleep: the Duke of Richmond was seated at her pillow and in all probability was less inclined to sleep than herself.[54]

Usurped, the normally magnanimous, laid-back, easy king was more than a tad put out by the discovery. Torrential abuse ('in such terms as he had never before used') and thunderous threats bounced off the bedchamber walls. The petrified duke, speechless, backed slowly out of the room leaving a ranting Charles and a tearfully defiant Frances alone. After being, in turn, irritated by her insolence, touched by her tears and provoked by her protestations, 'he went out abruptly, vowing never to see her more, and passed the most restless and uneasy night he had ever experienced since his restoration.' The next morning he issued orders that Richmond quit the court, but the duke had, somewhat wisely, already pre-empted such a resolution.[55]

Pepys first heard of the match from Sir William Penn on 18 March, the day Richmond 'brought in an account of his estate and debts to the King', who was, if salt were needed for his wound, the duke's nearest male heir. Pepys, who later described the duke as 'a mighty good-natured man', was 'well enough pleased' with the engagement, given Richmond's nobility since anybody of a lower rank 'would for certain have been reckoned a cuckold at first dash.'[56]

Richmond's attempts to secure the king's permission to make Frances Duchess Number Three were typically thwarted by the upstaged monarch, who was being deliberately difficult. So they married in secret on 30 March 1667 and a couple of days later eloped. Pepys heard that Richmond 'by a wilde [a ruse] did fetch her to the Beare [a tavern] at the Bridge-foot, where a coach was ready, and they are stole away into Kent without the King's leave.' The lovers absconded to Richmond's country seat, Cobham Hall, near Gravesend, Kent, from where Frances even returned all the jewellery and gifts the king had given her.[57]

Outside of the king's booth, the couple polled votes of confidence. Sir Charles Lyttleton, with the fleet at Harwich, wrote to Christopher Hatton on 21 May, asking after Frances and 'where those vacant howers are spent now that used to be passd away at her chamber.' Henry Jermyn, Earl of St Albans, in a letter to the Duke of Richmond, gave the union his blessing:

I take it for great honor in a season soe likely to take up all your thoughts that you have found leisure for the account you have bin pleased to give me of your self, and of my own concearnments. I beseeche your grace to beleeve that in order to the first I take the part that I ought to doe not onely in reference to my respects to you but the obligations of the honor I have to be related to the person you have chosen, and that I wish you both all sorts of felicity.[58]

Marriage was the mechanical means to market the production of heirs, preferably male. And by June the rumour of an instant blessing was marauding over Hadrian's Wall into Richmond's ample estates north of the border. The duke's man in Scotland, a Mr J Boreman, relayed the joy of the 'vassals' to the master:

I am afrayd the newes of her Grace's being with child will make all your Grace's vassals mad; some of them have come to me allmost 100 miles only to be informed of the certainty. It is looked upon here as no small miracle to heare soe great brutes as they be so heartily zealous for both your Graces and the young Lord Darnley...[59]

None the less, despite the mellowing effect on the duke's brutes, these hearty zealots were not to gifted a young Lord Darnley. Frances was not – nor would she ever be – pregnant.

The idyll at Cobham was, however, inevitably interrupted. On 27 June, the duke was called away on business – a small matter of defending the realm. Fearful of a Dutch invasion, Richmond, as the county's lord lieutenant, had to transport himself to Dorset to marshal resistance. While the duchess remained at her new home, she clearly wasn't idle, keeping herself abreast of news interspersed with a touch of interior decorating and, seemingly, age-old trouble with builders:

Cobham the 11 of july

My dearest Lord,

Yesterday I reseved a letter from you; it is the second since you arrived in Dorchester, and for which I give you many thankes, becasse it has easyed me of a great delle of care and trobel that I had, fearing you were not well. Oh, my dearest, if you love me, have a care for your selfe, for longer then you are in health I cannot be in rest. I will not fayle to send Mr Freeman about what you desiered. This day Captain Jonson came heyther to bring news of the Francis [the duke's yacht]. I will not give you the trobel of a dubel relation conserning her; and I beleve in this inclosed hee has don it at full. Prince Rupert has bin thisse too days in the ile of Sheppay to fortify Sheerness, which the Citty of London has undertaken to do for ten Thousand pound, and the King gives it them; so that Sir Johe Robinson [lord lieutenant of the Tower] is now thayr to see what materialls the prince will command for that purpos; ... I writ you word long since that Miller was returned, but he beeing wanting 6 days I thought he was run away: upon which I hyred the other painter you mention to paint the Bed-chamber. It is now almost done and lickwis all that apartment, but the Alcove cannot possibly be done in too months, which maid me advis you not to lett them go about it this sumer. If you did but know how hard it is to gitt workmen at this time, and how laysey thosse are which are here, I am sure you woulld be of my opinion. I have told Tempel that you have ordered hom money, but if he dos not make more hast then he has done yet I will not pay it him so sone, for in ernest he is a very iddel felow.[60]

Frances is often portrayed as somewhat dizzy and frivolous – and for the most part she slipped very cosily into that description – but, feeling increasingly isolated at Cobham, she demonstrated a shrewd touch. Unable to temper the king's animosity, she sought a positive intervention from the one person to whom the king could never close his ears: his sister Minette. She, ever the pragmatic arbiter, agreed.

However, the wound was ocean deep. Charles replied to his sister's concern on 26 August 1667:

I do assure you that I am very much troubled that I cannot in every thing give you that satisfaction I could wish, especially in this businesse of the duchesse of Richmond wherein you may think me ill natured, but if you consider how hard a thing tis to swallow an iniury done by a person I had so much tendernesse for, you will know my good nature enough to beleeve that I could not be so severe if I had not great provocation, and I assure you her carriage towards me has been as bad as breech of frindship and faith can make it, therefore I hope you will pardon me if I cannot so soon forgett an iniury which went so neare my hart.[61]

Potential disaster lurked at the end of the year as a smallpox epidemic struck London. The disease, along with plague and tuberculosis, were the most fatal of Restoration diseases. Even if you survived, pockmarks usually left a grisly memento. The wealthy diplomat Sir William Temple had spent seven years wooing the beautiful and talented Dorothy Osborne and succeeded despite their families being entrenched in the Royalist (hers) and Parliamentarian (his) divide. Unfortunately, before they finally married (in 1655) she caught smallpox, which left her face badly scarred, robbing her of her looks, but barely scratching her wit or charm.[62]

There seemed little sign that the epidemic would lessen as a new year dawned. Pepys, writing on 9 February 1668, noted 'that hardly ever was remembered such a season for smallpox as these last two months have been.' Then came the news that rattled the gossips: the latest Duchess of Richmond had caught the disease. A king couldn't conquer her body; was a disease about to claim her beauty? The worst was feared:

> my Lord Brounckner sent to Somerset-house to hear how the Duchess of Richmond doth; and word was brought him she is pretty well, but mighty full of the smallpox – by which all do conclude she will be wholly spoiled; which is the greatest instance of the uncertainty of beauty that could be in this age. But then, she hath had the benefit of it, to be first married – and to have kept it so long, under the greatest temptation in the world from a King, and yet without the least imputation.

Soon after, a letter informed Sir Ralph Verney, on 26 March, that the 'young Dutchis of Richman hathe the small pox and is very full, soe that all beleave her bewty will be spoyled which is a sad business.'[63]

The thwarted and still angry king was, nonetheless, concerned about Frances's health. 'I cannot tell,' he wrote to his sister on 4 April, 'whether the duchesse of Richmond will be much marked with the small pox, she has many, and I feare they will at least do her no good.' His mixed feelings for the duke and duchess are apparent as he adds, 'for her husband, he cannot alter from what he is, lett her never be changed!'[64]

Indeed, such was Charles's true concern for Frances, despite it all, that he forgot to write to Minette. He remedied that with an apology and a health news update on 7 May:

> I have so often asked your pardon for omitting writing to you, as I am almost ashamed to do it now, the truth is, the last weeke I absolutely forgott it till it was to late, for I was at the Duchesse of Richmond's who, you know, I have not seene this twelve monthes, and shee put it out of my head that it was post day. She is not much marked by with the smale pox, and I must confesse this last affliction made me pardon all that is past, and cannot hinder myselfe from

wishing her very well, and I hope shee will not be much changed, as soone as her eye is well, for she has a very great defluction in it, and even some danger of having a blemish in it, but now I beleeve the worst is past.'[65]

With the fear of losing her forever, he broke his self-imposed exile and visited her at Somerset House. This elegant building – the first Renaissance palace in England – was built for Edward Seymour, first Duke of Somerset (known as 'Protector Somerset' and brother to Henry VIII's third wife, Jane) between 1547 and 1750. The palace, which had been home for Charles's mother between 1625 and 1645, had a strong Stuart connection. James I gave it to his wife, Anne of Denmark, in 1603 and changed its name three years later to Denmark House in honour of Anne's brother, Christian IV of Denmark, who stayed there during a state visit. It reverted to Somerset House after Parliament took it over in 1645. Indeed, it was such a prestigious building that Oliver Cromwell lay in state there in September 1658. However, such a poor job was made of the embalming that he had to be buried rather quickly and quietly.[66]

Restored to the Stuarts, the palace was used by Queen Catherine occasionally from 1665. On 4 October 1669, the king ordered that it be 'conveyed to the Queen in like manner as formerly to the Queen-Mother.' Catherine, however, moved in permanently only after Charles's death. The original palace was demolished in 1775 and replaced with today's imposing building used, originally, as government offices. Frances had moved in towards the end of 1667.[67]

Charles's visit certainly wasn't a one-off, either. Pepys, hearing that the king 'sups every night with great pleasure with the Queene', contrasts that news with the knowledge that Charles seems

mighty hot upon the Duchess of Richmond; insomuch that upon Sunday was sennit [short for 'seven night', that is, last week], at night, after he had ordered his guards and coach to be ready to carry him to the park, he did on a sudden take a pair of oars or sculler, and all alone, or but one with him, go to Somerset-house and there, the garden-door not being open, himself clamber over the walls to make a visit to her where she is; which is a horrid shame.

Back in the fold, Frances was sworn a lady of the queen's bedchamber in July 1668.[68] She became one of the queen's two most trusted ladies. The other was the Duchess of Buckingham, with whom she might have set up a support group for wives of ridiculously devoted but sublimely unfaithful husbands. It was in the company of these two duchesses that the queen, while staying at Audley End, came up with the perfect wheeze to dress as common country folk and attend a nearby fair. However, their gait and accents soon exposed the ruse and they found themselves pursued by a curious crowd back to the king's country house.

Charles Lyttleton, while governor of Harwich and Landguard Fort, in a letter dated 8 August 1671, wrote of the terrible trio pulling rank to the distress of others:

> ...when the Queene was at Hampton Court one day rideing abroad, it raining and my Lady Marshall and Lady Gerrard being in her coach, her Majestie came into ye coach and called in the two Duchesses, Buck and Richmond, and left the other ladyes upon ye common to shift for themselves, wch you may beleeve was no small greife to them.[69]

While the duchess frolicked with the queen, the Duke of Richmond finally received a diplomatic appointment. He had already been overlooked for positions in Poland and Italy and had developed (perhaps none too misplaced) paranoia that the king's motives owed more to personal history than political ability. The paranoia thus banished, the newly appointed ambassador extraordinary to Denmark left for Copenhagen on 23 March 1672.[70]

Inevitably, the rumourmongers forged their trade with the expected gusto: of course, with the duke out of the way, the path to the duchess was gloriously clear. However, if that had been the king's motivation he would have had Richmond representing him at galas in Gdansk or masques in Milan long before. The commentators were not sitting this one out and the drolleries, such as the following, satirising Madame le Croy, the noted palmist, rose to the occasion:

> *In comes a Duke from mighty place*
> *And merit, fal'n into disgrace;*
> *She views his hand, and bids him joy,*
> *Calls him his Excellence Vice-Roy.*
> *With his high character the buble*
> *Is well content, and pays her double:*
> *Nor dreams he's banish't with his fleet*
> *A slave to Patmos or to Creet.*
> *As Richmond to the Northern Frost,*
> *And Clarendon to the Irish coast,*
> *Blinded with pride, senseless of ruin,*
> *So fools embrace their own undoing.*[71]

The French ambassador, Colbert de Croissy, also suspected a sexual coup. On 24 December 1671, he wrote that Richmond 'is getting ready to leave as ambassador extraordinary to Denmark, and the King his master has been caressing the Duchess his wife in her husband's presence, at least one can quite well see indications that she is very attractive to the King.'[72]

Although diligent, Richmond wasn't smitten with Danish life. His assistant, the dependable Henshaw, was uncompromising: 'Now in the pleasantest season of the yeare, this is one of the dullest places, that ever mortalls layd their pretious minutes in.' The duke fought off the dullness with drink. However, his liquid friend was to turn against him and before the end of the year, Charles Stuart, Duke of Richmond and Lennox, was dead.[73]

After visiting the English fleet anchored off the Danish coast on 12 December 1672, the duke went for dinner 'where severall health were drunck,' wrote the English consul Sir John Paul. He continued:

but I cannot say to any great hight of drincking as I have seen his Grace at other tymes doe, nor to my thoughts were any of the company concerned. Its trew his Grace was a littell merry but not to say much concerned. He spoke and went as well as he had never druncke nor doe I believe that he druncke 2 bottells of wine.[74]

Despite this, he became unwell in his carriage on the journey back to Elsinore. He quickly lost consciousness – something that had happened several times during his tenure – but this time he never regained it. Officially, a 'convulsion fitt' was the cause of death, although alcohol clearly pulled the strings. The body – minus the brains and bowels, which were buried at the Dutch church in Elsinore – was sent back to England in a leaden coffin. Or at least it was eventually, as Edward Clarke's letter to Secretary of State Joseph Williamson confirms:

My Lord's corpse remains at Sir John Paul's at Elsinore, and this week they finisht the leaden chest: about forming of which there was great trouble, for the people of this country never saw one made of that fashion before; yet by the care and diligence of Mr Henshaw and Dr Taylor, and by their directions it is at last well-fitted; this chest is to be put into another covered with velvet, and so the corps shall remain there untill further order from England.[75]

His body finally reached England in September 1673, being transported by a ship painted black for the task and even equipped with respectful black sails. The duke left behind a pretty, grieving widow and some pretty grievous debts. However, Charles came to his former fancy's rescue with an annual pension of £1,000 to be drawn 'by the King's special command.' The funeral ceremony at Westminster Abbey was a grand affair, although little expense seemed to have been spared for the duke's (unsurprisingly) anonymous elegy writer, who described Frances's grief as a gloomy room 'whilst her two panting breasts/like little mournful birds droop in their nests.'[76]

Frances never remarried and lived the rest of her life 'in the odour of chastity', perfectly out of kilter with the times. Her virtue, however, not only attracted scorn but a disbelief that had her holed up in hypocrisy. The satire 'Utile Dulce', dated about January 1681, certainly thought so:

> But he who undertakes this town to teach
> Does modesty to ranting Stamford preach,
> Who with more pride her tribe of fools discovers
> Than Richmond hides the number of her lovers.[77]

'A Ballad to the Tune of Cheviot Chase, part II,' 1682, echoes the thought:

> Gray-growing Richmond has just right
> To challenge here a place;
> She has maintained with all her might
> The noble whoring cause.[78]

The earlier satire 'Colin' (or 'Cullen') dated to the late summer of 1679, assesses the merits of Frances in becoming the king's replacement for *maîtresse de traite*, Louise de Keroualle, who, as part of the poet's conceit, is fleeing from the Popish Plot:

> Silence in the court being once proclaimed,
> Up stepped fair Richmond, once so famed.
> She offered much but was refused,
> And of miscarriages accused.
> They said a cunt so used to puke
> Could never bear a booby duke;
> That Mulgrave, Villiers, and Jack Howe
> For one salt duchess were enow;
> Nor would his Majesty accept her
> At thirty, who at eighteen leapt her.[79]

This excerpt reinforces the belief that Frances had been Charles's mistress in the 1660s. It also suggests that she could not give birth (although the reason cited is less than medical) since 'a booby duke' is a term applied to the sons of the king by his mistresses. In addition to her alleged affair with the king, the poet also accuses Frances of three other liaisons with John Sheffield, Earl of Mulgrave, 'Villiers' and John 'Jack' Grubham Howe.

Mulgrave had been besotted by Frances and wrote a poem elegising her and demonising her husband, into whose shoes or bed sheets he undoubtedly desired to fit. But desire for him was no reality for Frances. Mulgrave's heart, however, continued to beat loudly enough for a rumour to sound that they had married in secret in 1677. A letter to Sir Ralph Verney from his brother John ran: 'The Duchess of Richmond hath lately sold her interest in Cobham to Lord O'Brian, soe 'tis believed she will suddenly own her marriage to the Lord Mulgrave.'[80]

The reference to 'Villiers' has been thought to have referred to Francis 'Villain Frank' Villiers – a renowned bachelor and fop, but there is nothing really to link him to Frances. However, as we have seen, George Villiers, Duke of Buckingham, had a very close interest in her and was, indeed, rebuffed by her. Disbelieving that the Duke of Bucks could possibly be rejected, the poet may well have had him in mind.

John 'Libelling Jack' Howe (1657–1722) – 'a young amorous spark of the court' – was a thorn in Frances's professed virtue. Having had his advances scorned in August 1679, he took his revenge by spreading testimony that he had been in her favour and had letters and gifts to prove it. Outraged at this talk, Frances asked the king to intervene. In a letter dated 2 September, Dorothy Sidney, Countess of Sunderland, wrote of the incident:

> …I am told, but by no Privy Councillor, that the Duchess of Richmond had, notwithstanding the troubles of the time, complained to the King of the great injury How had done her, in bragging of favours and letters when she had never given him cause for either.[81]

Charles referred it to the Court of Honour and appointed the Duke of Monmouth and the Earls of Halifax, Essex and Sunderland to look into the allegations. They did, indeed, as Dorothy Sidney suspected, 'judge of the Lady's side', as Howe could produce only one letter of evidence, which was so badly forged that it resembled neither the duchess's 'hand nor style'. Jack Howe found himself vilified and banished from court (labelled in satires for 'smutty jests and downright lies'), while the victorious Frances had her virtue vindicated. And how.[82]

The accession of William III and Mary II in 1688 signalled Frances's retirement from public life and the end of her state pension (although Queen Anne reinstated it). She spent the rest of her life in the comfortable company of cards and cats. Her health deteriorated and she suffered from sciatica and violent headaches. She died on 15 October 1702 and was buried, as she wished, near her husband in the Richmond tomb at Westminster Abbey. She was 54.

It's difficult to fathom whether the scandal here is the king's open and unadulterated adulterous pursuit of Frances or whether it swims in her continued rejection of his ultimate advances. As far as Frances was concerned there was no regal right of entry.

Charles was, however, markedly more successful with other women. Apart from his main mistresses he had a number of minor affairs with, among others, the famous singer Mary Knight, Mary Killigrew, Countess of Falmouth, Elizabeth, Countess of Kildare, Jane Roberts, and the actress Mary 'Moll' Davies (or Davis), whose daughter, Mary Tudor, was another of the king's brood. Moll was subjected to a wicked trick by Nell Gwynne, who was at the time a rival for the king's attentions. Charles had given Moll a very expensive ring and Nelly (as she was popularly known) invited the proud owner to visit her and show off the present. Moll agreed. Nelly, knowing that Moll had an assignation with the king that evening, provided some sweetmeats but laced them with jalap – a potent laxative. The amorous evening did not quite go to plan for the entangled couple as a distraught Moll was unable to control her internal movements and splattered the hapless and presumably equally distraught monarch. One satire called her 'That ballocking squirter and shitten arse whore', while a two-line rhyme titled 'On the King's Chamber Door' trundled:

> *Charles, by the grace of God King of Great Britain,*
> *By little Miss Davis was all beshitten.*[83]

Not the way to impress your lover. Charles did not have far to look to recruit replacements. He was treated to countless liaisons procured for him by his page of the backstairs, William Chiffinch, and his wife, who kept a log of suitable women to keep the king's fires nourished. But, more often than not, there would be some new lady-in-waiting at court who, once she caught the eye of the king, wouldn't be waiting for much longer to be of service to the crown. One such was the featherbrained Winifred Wells.

The tall and elegant Winifred was the youngest daughter of Gilbert Wells of Twyford, Hampshire. Following the departure, in 1662, of four court women, who Gramont believed deserved their expulsion on the grounds of either their behaviour or their ugliness, the French purveyor of taste was pleased, at least, with one of the replacements as maid of honour to the queen. Winifred was clearly comfortable on the eye, although her mind was frustratingly unencumbered with thought.

She was a tall girl, exquisitely shaped: she dressed very genteel, walked like a goddess; and yet her face, though made like those that generally please the most, was unfortunately one of those that pleased the least: nature had spread over it a certain careless indolence that made her look sheepish. This gave but a bad opinion of her wit; and her wit had the bad luck to make good that opinion.[84]

However, her fresh-coloured features and her titillating inexperience marked her out as a target – albeit a practice one – for the predatory king. Her defences, if that was what they were, were briskly breached. There may have been little depth to her mind, but she proved otherwise elsewhere, if the punning swipe of the Duke of Buckingham, penned in French to mark the occasion, is to be believed. The hopelessly unreserved Bucks has the king in conversation with Sir Edward Progers, a groom of the bedchamber and sort of Mr Fixit for Charles's pleasure-seeking (basically, his pimp). One translation runs:

> *When the King felt the terrible depths of this well,*
> *'Ah Progers!' he cried, 'what's happened, and how?*
> *I sound, but can't tell;*
> *Were I seeking the centre of earth's hollow shell,*
> *I should have been there by now!*[85]

An alternative has it:

> *When the king felt the horrible death of this Well,*
> *Tell me, Progers, cried Charlie, where am I? oh tell!*
> *Had I sought the world's centre to find, I had found it,*
> *But this Well! ne'er a plummet was made that could sound it.*[86]

However, the young Mistress Wells was destined for greater infamy. A member of the Earl of Sandwich's household, Captain Robert Ferrers, told Pepys that possibly on New Year's Eve 1662 during, a Ball at Court, a child was dropped by one of the ladies in dancing; but nobody knew who, it being taken up by somebody in their handkercher. The next morning all the Ladies of Honour appeared early at Court for their vindication, so that nobody could tell whose this mischance should be. But it seems that Mrs Wells fell sick that afternoon and hath disappeared ever since, so that it is concluded it was her.[87]

The miscarriage story, apparently true, picked up momentum and inevitable embellishment. On 17 February 1663, Pepys hears that,

the story is very [true] of a child being dropped at the Ball at Court; and that the King had it in his closet a week after, and did dissect it; and making great sport of it, said that in his opinion it must have been a month and three houres old and that whatever others think, he had the greatest loss (it being a boy, as he says), that had lost a subject by the business.

The king was certainly interested in science – and anatomy in particular – and, as we know from Pepys, he had constructed a small 'elaboratory under his closet' but that he dissected the foetus sides more with rumour than fact.[88]

It wasn't the first example of a mysterious childbirth. In June 1662, just over a month after Catherine of Braganza's arrival in England, Pepys was 'told of a Portugall lady at Hampton Court, that hath dropped a child already, since the Queenes coming. But the King would not have them searched whose it is; and so it is not commonly known yet.' Another source confirms this story: 'Lisbona, the daughter of unknowne parents, accidentally found shortly after its birth in a private place of Hampton Court, but conceived to be the child of a Portugall woman, was baptised in a private chamber there, June 20, 1662.'[89]

These incidents and circumstances combined humorously at a country dance at Tunbridge Wells a few years later. Lady Muskerry, whose beauty inspired Gramont to label her as 'princess of Babylon', was 'six or seven months advanced in pregnancy'. She had the added discomfort of having the child 'fallen all on one side', causing an embarrassing and uneven shape. To remedy the problem she 'pinned a small cushion under her petticoat on the right side, to counteract the untoward appearance the little infant occasioned.' Confident in her image, Lady Muskerry,

danced with uncommon briskness... In the midst, therefore, of her capering in this indiscreet manner, her cushion came loose without her perceiving it, and fell to the ground, in the very middle of the first round. The Duke of Buckingham, who watched her, took it up instantly, wrapped it in his coat, and, mimicking the cries of a new-born infant, he went about enquiring for a nurse for the young Muskerry among the maids of honour.

This buffoonery, joined to the strange figure of the poor lady, had almost thrown Mrs [Frances] Stewart into hysterics; for the princess of Babylon, after this accident, was quite flat on one side, and immoderately protuberant on the other. All those, who had before suppressed their inclinations to laugh, now gave themselves free scope, when they saw that Mrs Stewart was ready to split her sides. The poor lady was greatly disconcerted: every person was officious to console her; but the queen, who inwardly laughed more heartily than any, pretended to disapprove of their taking such liberties.[90]

Despite the ease of the conquest, Winifred Wells seems to have secured long-standing preferred status on the king's list of minor mistresses. In February 1665, one line of gossip had the king dishing out '£1,500 or £2,000' to Winifred. It was the sort of payment, even if only a one-off, that a continuing mistress (that is one deployed beyond the one night) might expect. Some six years after her arrival at court, around early 1668, she was still being referred to as one of his lovers. Barbara Villiers, unleashing one of her hysterical outbursts during an argument with Charles, named Wells in the company of Frances Stewart and the then newly arrived Nell Gwynne, as those wheeled in to service certain of his needs. 'Floods of tears, from rage, generally attended these storms,' wrote Gramont, 'after which assuming the part of Medea [the sorceress daughter of Greek mythology who murdered her own children], the scene closed with menaces of tearing her children in pieces, and setting his palace on fire.'[91]

In June 1666 Pepys saw Winifred and another lady of honour dressed in men's riding outfits,

with coats and doublets with deep skirts, just for all the world like men, and buttoned their doublets up the breast, with perriwigs and with hats; so that, only for a long petticoat dragging under their men's coats, nobody could take them for women in any point whatever – which was an odde sight, and a sight that did not please me.

However, the sight of her on 30 May 1669 did please him rather more. More intriguingly, although Pepys was inclined to see the best in any female owner of a pretty face, his subsequent comment about the quality of her discourse undermines Gramont's description of her as a shallow *chef-d'oeuvre*. Dining at Whitehall Palace, his company was joined 'by fine Mrs Wells, who is a great beauty and there I had my full gaze upon her, to my great content, she being a woman of pretty conversation.'[92]

In 1672 Charles gave Winifred £2,150, possibly as a marriage portion, for the next year she was the wife of Thomas Wyndham, an equerry to the king. It seems at this time, for sure, Winifred left the service, so to speak, of the king, but was neatly compensated by appointment as the queen's dresser. She remained for the next twenty years or thereabouts employed by Catherine up until the dowager queen's departure in January 1692, first for France and then on to Portugal where, from 1693, she would reign as regent. However, even in the absence of her mistress, Winifred in all probability continued to receive a salary, as Catherine left £10,000 to ensure the running of a full household at Somerset House.

2

Dismal Jimmy: the Loves of the Most Unguarded Ogler of his Time

'I do not believe there are two men who love women more than you and I do, but my brother, devout as he is, loves them more.'
– Charles II to French Ambassador Henri Courtin[1]

The historian and bishop Gilbert Burnet described James Stuart (born 15 October 1633), Duke of York, and future very Catholic James II, as 'naturally candid and sincere'. Count Gramont thought him conscientious and 'a scrupulous observer of the rules of duty', but arrogant. Most of which translates literally as dull and tedious. Such was his lack of humour that Nell Gwynne labelled him 'Dismal Jimmy'. Neither was he the sharpest sword in the armoury. In comparing James with Charles, the Duke of Buckingham is reported to have said that the king could see things if he would, and the duke would see things if he could. Tipped on top of all that, James abhorred drunkenness and extravagance, and never swore, gambled or spoke irreligiously.[2]

Life in the court of his brother must have been hell. Or was it? There was one vice his dry mouth developed a taste for, as John Reresby, writing about the king's attraction to and for women, noted that the 'two dukes,* his brothers, were noe less lovers of the sex then himselfe.' Pepys was told by Thomas Povey (treasurer of the duke's household, 1660–66) that 'the Duke of York hath not got Mrs Middleton', as he had previously been led to believe,

but says that he wants not her, for he hath others and had always had, and that [Povey] hath known them brought through the Matted

---

*The other duke was Henry, Duke of Gloucester, who died of smallpox in 1660 'at the great negligence of the doctors'. (Pepys, 13 September 1660)

34

Gallery at White-hall into his closet. Nay, he hath come out of his wife's bed and gone to others laid in bed for him.[3]

James had an eye for the court ladies. Indeed, he overworked both eyes in this employment, being regarded as 'the most unguarded ogler of his time'. But, surprisingly, in a court that boasted the most beautiful women in Europe, he had his work cut out because his enchantment rose for less obvious beauties: the overweight and those with faces that even their mothers battled to lov¬. As Burnet noted, 'He was perpetually in one amour or another without being very nice in his choice: upon which the king once said, he believed his brother had his mistresses given him by his priests for penance.'[4]

One of his later mistresses, Katherine Sedley, commented on James's choice of women: 'we are none of us handsome, and if we had wit, he has not enough to discover it.' His corpulent conquests included the court ladies, Lady Muskerry, 'who had the shape of a woman big with child, without being so', Goditha Price, a maid of honour to the Duchess of York and picturesquely labelled as 'Fat Price', and Mrs Blague. The Marquis de Brisacier described Mrs Blague's eyes as marcassins. Believing this a wonderful compliment, she sought the meaning of the word. She was somewhat dismayed to find the translation meant she had the 'eyes of a pig'.[5]

As with his brother, James had already uncorked a dram of scandal while in exile. He became involved with cushioned-plumped Anne Hyde and had promised to marry her. It is most likely that they first met in 1656, when James visited his sister, Mary, the Princess of Orange, into whose service Anne had been appointed. A decision much to the chagrin of Henrietta Maria, the queen mother, who had little time for any offspring of Edward Hyde, her bitterest political enemy.

Anne was born on 14 March 1637 at Cranbourne Lodge in Windsor Park. The house at that time was in the possession of Anne's maternal grandfather, Sir Thomas Aylesbury, master of the mint and a master of requests. In 1665, while it was occupied by Sir George Carteret,* as

---

*George Carteret, born in Jersey, was granted by James, in 1664, a share in the land between the Delaware and Hudson rivers, which was named New Jersey in his honour. Of course, the naming of significant parts of the eastern seaboard did not stop with Carteret. In the summer of 1664, the Duke of York, as the Lord High Admiral and who had been granted lands by Charles II around Long Island, sent two ships to combat a Dutch stronghold which had been set up to control the beaver trade. The English, under Colonel Richard Nicholas, took the land peaceably. James stated that they surrendered 'without stricking a Strok'. The place was re-named, in honour of the duke, New York. In ending a letter to his sister Minette, dated Whitehall 24 October 1664, Charles somewhat casually informed his sister: 'You will have heard of our takeing

keeper of the lodge, Pepys stayed with him and was amused to be sleeping in the bed in which Anne was born, even though he thought her '...a plain woman, and like her mother.'[6]

She may well have resembled her mother, but this 'no perfect beauty' also unhappily inherited the physical appearance of her father – the man they called 'old fatt gutts'. Anne was solemnly considered 'one of the highest feeders in England'. Her buttocks were so big that it was suggested cruelly that her pages rode on them rather than the carriage:

> *With Chanc'lor's belly, and so large a rump,*
> *There (not behind the coach) her pages jump.*[7]

Anne's size, however, pleased some. One courtier who disapproved of the dieting trend said that her overeating was 'a pleasure to watch' and that it was 'a blessing to see her'. The betrothed couple could not be a bigger physical mismatch, for while Anne banqueted, James 'exhausted himself by inconstancy and was gradually wasting away'.[8]

Set to suffer her husband's indiscretions, Anne ate to fuel her pride. With the queen mother in best silk-from-pig's-ears form, the common Anne, who was described by Marvell as a 'buttered bun', would soon take the cake and out-duchess them all. Pepys met Ned Pickering ('And though he be a fool, and yet he keeps much company and will tell all he sees or hears, and so a man may understand what the common talk of the towne is') and their two-hour walk on 13 April 1662 was taken up with 'discourse most about the pride of the Duchesse of Yorke.' Anne 'was an extraordinary woman,' wrote Burnet. 'She had a great knowledge, and a lively sense of things. She soon understood what belonged to a princess, and took state on her rather too much.' This is borne out by Thomas Povey, who told Pepys that Anne 'doth now come like Queen Elizabeth and sits with the Duke of York's Council and sees what they do'.[9]

Of course, such inward confidence needed to be reflected externally. Povey told Pepys that 'the Duchesse is not only the proudest woman in the world but the most expenseful.' He also later suggested that Anne

---

of New Amsterdame, which lies by New England. 'Tis a place of great importance to trade, and a very good towne. It did belong to England heretofore but the Dutch by degrees drove our people out of it, and built a very good towne, but we have gott the better of it, and 'tis now called New Yorke.' If only he knew the historical importance of this throwaway aside. Nor did the naming of towns finish there either. When the British forces captured Fort Nassau they re-named it Albany – James was also Duke of Albany in the Scottish peerage. Today it is the state capital of New York. (Haswell, J, *James II*, p.151; Norrington, Ruth, *My Dearest Minette*, p.95)

kept £5,000 a year aside for her own spending while telling the duke what he should save money on. Lady Peterborough commented that Anne did 'lay up mightily Jewells'.[10]

For the humiliation caused by her husband's prowling eyes, she exacted a most scandalous revenge by being that most unheard of thing: a bossy wife. So much so that Charles, ridiculing his brother, dubbed him 'Tom Otter', after the henpecked husband in Ben Jonson's *Epicoene, or The Silent Woman.* However, Tom Killigrew drew the king's sting by enquiring whether it would be better to be a Tom Otter to your wife or mistress, making a direct reference to the king's chief mistress Barbara Villiers. Pepys said that 'the Duke of York, in all things but his amours, is led by the nose by his wife'.[11]

What's more, there was even the unthinkable suspicion that her own eyes darted gander-like through the court in search of extramarital intrigues of her own. As Marvell wrote, 'not unprovoked she tries forbidden arts.' Also, as one of her ladies, Mrs Hobart, suggested to her, 'Can a husband who disregards you both night and day, really suppose, because his wife eats and drinks heartily, as, God be thanked, your royal highness does, that she wants nothing else to sleep well too?' Her eyes thus opened and she closed in on that 'terror to husbands' and 'the hansomest youth of his time' Henry Sidney. The son of Robert, Earl of Leicester, 'Handsome' Sidney was certainly someone worth an ogle. The duchess certainly thought so, keeping 'her eyes fixed upon his personal perfections.'[12]

Anne's husband, suitably terrorised, confronted her over such flirtatious goings-on in front of his own (non-too-fidelity-focused) eyes. Anne pulled a blinder and effectively protested her innocence. Pepys picked over,

> how a great difference hath been between the Duke and Duchesse, he suspecting her to be naught with Mr Sidny – but some way or other the matter is made up; but he was banished the Court, and the Duke for many days did not speak to the Duchesse at all.

Sir John Reresby also believed what other people had told him, that Sidney was banished from court 'for another reason' rather than a dalliance with Anne. He had earlier seen the two at York together and, while the duchess was not unkind to Sidney, she was 'but very innocently'. However, later that year the rumours returned and Pepys records that 'there really was amours between the Duchesse and Sidny.'[13]

Nonetheless, despite her sparky wit and small-wins strategies, Anne ultimately led a pathetic and unhappy life. And it ended in great pain also. As Marvell noted, 'But in her soft breast love's hid cancer smarts.'[14]

By the time of her death by breast cancer at 34, she had given birth to eight children, of whom only two daughters, Mary and Anne, survived. Out of the mother's sadness came a proud legacy as both daughters would become queens of England: Mary (1685–94) as joint regent with 'The Deliverer' William of Orange (who then reigned alone until he stopped delivering in 1702) and Anne (1702–14) – 'Brandy Nan' – who despite a remarkable eighteen pregnancies did not leave any issue, thus becoming the last Stuart monarch to reign in Britain.

How far away and unreal that all seemed in early 1659, when James wrote to Anne pledging marriage. In his own turgid memoirs, written in the third person, James commented that 'Anne Hide shew'd both witt and her vertue in managing the affaire so dexterously that the Duke, overmaster'd by his passion, at last gave her a promise of marriage some time before the Restoration.' But even he realised the dangerous folly of such action and upon recovering the letter promising marriage he subsequently destroyed it. Pepys, on 7 October 1660, was told by the Earl of Sandwich,

> how the Duke of Yorke hath got my Lord Chancellors daughter with child, and that she doth lay it to him, and that for certain he did promise her marriage and had signed it with his blood, but that by stealth had got the paper out of her Cabinett.

Such is the misguided beauty of gossip. James had already married Anne by this point and the idea that a written proposal was in the duke's own blood is macabre embellishment. Sandwich, further discussing with Pepys the merits of the situation, concluded, using one of his father's sayings, 'that he that doth get a wench with child and marries her afterward it is as if a man should shit in his hat and then clap it on his head.'[15]

On the same day, Evelyn recorded:

> There dind with me a french Count, with Sir S: Tuke, who came to take leave of me, being now sent over to the Queene-Mother to breake the Marriage of the Duke with the daughter of Chancellor Hide; which the Queene would faine have undon; but it seems matters were reconcild, upon greate offers of the Chancellor to befriend the Queene, who was much indebted, & was to now have the settlement of her affaire go thro his hands.[16]

Later that year, albeit privately, James kept his word, with his own chaplain conducting the ceremony. So secret were the proceedings, it appears that the happy couple couldn't agree where it happened, although concurred on the date of 9 August. Later, in February 1661, following an inquest into the 'certainty of the marriage' they settled on the venue as being Breda, but curiously checked the date forward six weeks to 24 November 1659.[17]

Following the marriage, James sweated over the legality and wisdom of it all. His close friend Sir Charles Berkeley suggested, among other things, that as the king had not consented the marriage contract was invalid, that it was a mere jest. Who, after all, would believe a marriage between him, the heir presumptive to the English throne, and 'the daughter of an insignificant lawyer...without any noble blood'? James called a meeting of his closest allies – Richard Butler, Earl of Arran; Berkeley, who would be created Earl of Falmouth in 1664; Henry Jermyn, later Baron Dover; Richard Talbot, who would be created Earl of Tyrconnel in 1685; and Thomas Killigrew. As well as seeking their counsel, James asked them, to use a contemporary euphemism, if they had jumped the broomstick with his wife. Sensing what the duke wanted to hear, Killigrew 'boldly declared that he had the honour of being on the most intimate terms with her'. He regaled his astounded audience and confessed that the magical moment occurred 'in a certain closet built over the water, for a purpose very different from that of giving ease to the pains of love', with three or four swans as witnesses. He added that the fortunate large graceful aquatic birds 'might perhaps have been witnesses to the happiness of many others, as the lady frequently repaired to that place, and was particularly delighted with it'. The duke, rightly, was unconvinced.[18]

However, parental fury did not reside exclusively with the royal family. James's prospective father-in-law, did not so much burst with pride, as explode in anger. For Edward Hyde the marriage was, clearly unlike Anne, inconceivable. Politically, he sensibly foresaw that his enemies would use the match against him. A broadside of accusations of self-aggrandisement (his daughter, as things stood, would be the next queen of England) could sink him and his career. He was fervently opposed to the match and, it has been suggested, he demanded Anne be sent to the tower and even that her head be cut off. But she was his eldest and favourite daughter, and, as upset as he was, no such demands were made.

The episode was satire fodder for years. In 1667, 'A Ballad' ran:

> *Old fat Gutts himselfe*
> *With his tripes and his pelfe,*
> *And a purse as full as his paunch is,*
> *Will confess that his Nanny Fob-doudled our Jamy*
> *And his Kingdom came by his Haunches.*[19]

(*Old fat Gutts* – Edward Hyde, Earl of Clarendon; *tripes* – belly; *pelfe* – riches; *Nanny* – Anne Hyde, Duchess of York; *Fob-doudled* – tricked; *Jamy* – James, Duke of York.)

Hyde had been Charles's chief adviser in exile and as a reward became the restored king's first minister, his chancellor. He was on the verge of political greatness but his daughter's shenanigans left him now peering over the precipice. During this crisis, Charles supported his chancellor unequivocally and, for the short term at least, he weathered the storm. Inevitably, there was a price to pay. Hyde's standing was now severely weakened for 'he was in debt to the king, not the king to him.'[20]

The marriage was solemnised at midnight on 3 September 1660, at Worcester House, the then home of Edward Hyde. However, even this was a very quiet affair as only Lord Ossory (son of the Duke of Ormonde) and one of Anne's personal maids were in attendance. The happy couple's son was born just over seven weeks later on 22 October, but died the following year.

Evelyn entered in his diary on 21 December 1660:

The Marriage of the Chancellors Daughter being now newly owned, I went to see her... She being now at her fathers, at Worcester house in the strand, we all kissed her hand, as did also my Lord Chamberlaine (Manchester) and Countesse of Northumberland: This was a strange change, can it succeed well!

Pepys had to wait nearly five years to kiss Anne's hand. On 27 July 1665, he recorded that he saw the duchess 'whose hands I did kiss. And it was the first time I did ever or did see anybody else kiss her hand; and it was a most fine white and fat hand.'[21]

With the trauma of the indecision over his legal obligations to his wife settled in her favour, the duke decided time was ripe to carry out some disciplined extramarital duties. The object unimportant, as the need for duty was all, he alighted upon Anne Hamilton, Lady Carnegie, who had assisted a few others in performing this particular line of duty. Anne was the daughter of William, Duke of Hamilton, and was married to Robert, the styled Lord Carnegie. With the good lady's husband away, the relieved duke and his contented prey passed their time 'in frivolous amusements'. However, his father's sudden death brought Lord Carnegie's home not only sooner than expected, but also with the title Earl of Southesk. His wife detested the title but, nonetheless, took it 'more patiently than she received the news of his return.'[22]

Southesk, although tipped off about his wife's dutiful undertakings during his absence, chose only to believe what he saw for himself. James and Lady Southesk had, therefore, to conduct themselves with a suitable decorum. Thus if James called on her he was always accompanied, giving the visits a varnish of formality. On one such visit James was accompanied by Richard Talbot, who had been out of the country, and who had been inducted in the sordid enterprise, but had no idea of the identity of Lady Southesk, having known her only as Lady Carnegie.

On arrival, the duke's equipage was sent on, as the earl was reported to be at his favourite entertainment – bull and bear baiting – from which he invariably returned very late. Talbot remained in the antechamber while James and Lady Southesk conducted the business of the afternoon (continuing with their frank and earnest deliberations). However, Carnegie returned home early and was naturally surprised to see Talbot in his house. But not nearly as surprised as Talbot, who having met the then Lord Carnegie at Brussels, welcomed him warmly, and wondered what business could bring him to this house. Before Southesk could reply, Talbot clicked. Had he, Carnegie, come to visit Lady Southesk for some comfort? He continued, 'If this is your intention, my poor friend, you may go away again; for I must inform you, the Duke of York is in love with her, and I will tell you in confidence, that, at this very time, he is in her chamber.'[23]

Accompanying the shell-shocked Southesk to the door, Talbot cheerfully advised him to seek a mistress elsewhere, and with a pat on his back saw him on his way. On the duke's reappearance Talbot could not wait to acquaint his master with the episode. James, as can be imagined, did not share the storyteller's delight. Particularly so, for, if it is to be believed, Southesk feasted sweetly on a very cold revenge. As a disconcerted Pepys reveals, Southesk,

> himself went to the foulest whore he could find, that he might get the pox; and did, and did give his wife it on purpose, that she (and he persuaded and threatened her that she should) might give it to the Duke of York; which she did, and he did give it to the Duchesse; and since, all her children are sickly and infirm – which is the most pernicious and foul piece of revenge that ever I heard of.[24]

However, Gramont believed that the plan was foiled because, by the time he had contracted the pox, James's eyes were ogling another. Andrew Marvell noted the incident in 'An Historical Poem':

> *But now Yorkes Genitalls grew over hot*
> *With Denham and Coneig's infected pot.*[25]

Bishop Gilbert Burnet had heard the story but commented that 'Lord Southesk was, for some years, not ill pleased to have this believed. It looked like a particular strain of revenge, with which he seemed much delighted. But I know he has, to some of his friends, denied the whole story very solemnly.' Which is a shame.[26]

Overheating genitals notwithstanding, into the duke's ogling range came 'a beautiful young lady' called Margaret Brooke, who at 21 (or 18, dependent on the source) married the 'ancient and limping' 50-year-old (Gramont thought him to be 79) Sir John Denham at Westminster Abbey in May 1665. Within eighteen months of her marriage, Pepys heard that the 'Duke of York is wholly given up to this bitch of Denham'. Just over a week later Pepys was comparing notes of dismay with a colleague over the 'viciousness of the Court', where the duke had become 'a slave to this whore Denham – and wholly minds her.' Pepys was not only disgruntled by James's preference for 'his woman, my Lady Denham' over business, but also that he would trundle off hunting three times a week. The scent of a woman was one thing, but that of a fox clearly another.[27]

The cuckolded Denham was a tall man,

> but a little incurvetting at his shoulders, not very robust. His haire was thin and flaxen, with a moist curle. His gait was slow, and was rather a Stalking (he had long legges). His Eie was a kind of goose-gray, not big; but it had a strange Piercingness, not as to shining and glory, but (like a Momus [god of ridicule]) when he conversed with you he look't into your very thoughts.

Gramont thought him witty and entertaining and prone to 'spirited raillery'.[28]

Denham, who was succeeded by Sir Christopher Wren as Surveyor-General of the King's Works, was also a sometime dramatist and poet. His 'Cooper's Hill' (Cowper's Hill, near Runnymede), much praised by Dr Samuel Johnson, was one of the first – if not the first – poem in English to describe a local scene. He seems to have achieved little else. Evelyn thought him 'a better poet than architect', which did not bode well for English Restoration architecture. Indeed, Denham himself seemed humorously aware of his own poetic shortfalls. It was said during the Civil War that the poet George Withers, having written against the king, was in danger of his life. Denham appealed on his behalf and 'desired his Majestie not to hang him, for that whilest G.W. lived, he should not be the worst poet in England.'[29]

Denham was an addictive gambler, causing his father despair to the point of disinheritance. The son then defied all odds by experiencing a Pauline conversion, culminating in a published essay attacking the wicked and wanton world of the gamester: *The Anatomy of Play, Written by a worthy and learned gent. Dedicated to his father to show his detestation of it* (or, according to Aubrey, *Against Gameing, and to shew the Vanities and Inconveniences of it*). Restored to the will, the son later inherited between £1,500 and £2,000. And then proceeded to lose the lot at cards.

His wife's ducal affair drove Denham mad. He would ride to Hounslow Heath to demand rents on lands he long sold and even confided with the king that he (Denham) was, in fact, the Holy Ghost. However, his temporary insanity was, in a letter from Lord Lisle to Sir William Temple, credited to his 'extreme vanity'.[30]

Pepys heard how,

the Duke of York is wholly given up to his new mistress, my Lady Denham, going at noon-day, with all his gentlemen with him, to visit her in Scotland-yard – she declaring she will not be his mistress, as Mrs Price, to go up and down the privy stairs, but will be owned publicly; and so she is.

While waiting on the Duke of York, Pepys saw him and his mistress together:

Here I had the hap to see my Lady Denham; and at night went into the drawing-room and saw several fine ladies; among others Castlemayne, but chiefly Denham again, and the Duke of York taking her aside and talking to her in the sight of all the world, all alone; which was strange and what also I did not like. Here I met with good Mr Eveling [John Evelyn], who cries out against it and calls it bichering, for the Duke of York talks a little to her, and then she goes away and then he fallows her again, like a dog.[31]

Henry Brouncker (?1627–88) was behind the intrigue between James and Lady Denham. He was one of the duke's grooms of the bedchamber (1656–67) and had a short spell as MP for New Romney,

Kent. He was clearly not a man to command unbridled respect: Pepys thought him 'a pestilent rogue...that would have sold his King and country for 6d almost – so covetous and wicked a rogue he is by all men's reports.' Evelyn characterised him as 'one who was ever noted for an hard, covetous, vicious man [who] had several Bastards'. Brouncker was even ill-reputed to have run a country house 'four or five miles from London always well stocked with girls.' A poem runs:

> *Brounker, Love's squire, through all the field array'd,*
> *No troop was better clad, nor so well paid.*[32]

The near-universal dislike for the man even penetrated his family; his brother only left him £10 in his will 'for reasons I thinke not fit to mencion'. It seems that only Gramont, who also thought him disagreeable, could find anything complimentary to say about him, declaring Brouncker 'the best chess-player in England'. His career at court effectively ended when he was sacked by the Duke of York for talking out of turn against his father-in-law Clarendon, whom he said could move the king into whatever position he chose. On hearing the news, 'everybody,' sighed Pepys, 'I think is glad of it.' Check-mate.[33]

Lady Denham's scandal stock was high during her life, but it soared leading up to and after her untimely death in 1667. It sparked incredible rumours that a shockingly jealous Duchess of York had poisoned her. Pepys heard on 10 November 1666 'that my Lady Denham is exceeding sick, even to death; and that she says, and everyone else discourses, that she is poysoned.' Other suspects included her husband and the Countess of Rochester.[34]

Her sickness and its keenly speculated cause captivated the town. The next day Pepys walked in the garden by his office with his colleague John Creed,

> talking of the present ill condition of things, which is the common subject of all men's discourse and fears nowadays, and perticularly of my Lady Denham, whom everybody says is poisoned, and [Creed] tells me she hath said it to the Duke of York; but is upon the mending hand, though the town says she is dead this morning.[35]

Although the town was misinformed, she remained 'ill still' but consequently her bewitchment of the duke declined in parallel with her health. It was reported that he 'doth not haunt my Lady Denham so much'. However, their cooling off seemed fanned by political rather than physical conditions. Lady Denham, eager to develop influence as a mistress, sought to discuss matters of state with the duke. However, by siding with her uncle, George Digby, second Earl of Bristol's faction at court, which was profoundly anti-Clarendonian (and therefore anti-his-father-in-law), James lost interest in her. Her physical death did not long follow her political one.[36]

Pepys heard that Lady Denham was 'at last dead' on 7 January 1667, her ghost being given up the previous morning. The rumours of poison again circled and again targeted the duchess. James, we're told, is so 'troubled' by Lady Denham's death that he declares 'he will never have another public mistress again.' It was never a sustainable standard to set.[37]

Aubrey said that Lady Denham 'was poysoned by the hands of the Countess of Rochester, with Chocolatte'. However, he was referring to Henrietta Hyde, who was the Countess of Rochester at the time of his writing, but not at the time of the poisoning (that was Anne, wife of John Wilmot). Laurence 'Lory' Hyde married Henrietta Boyle, daughter of Richard, Earl of Burlington, in 1663. Lory was created Viscount Hyde of Kenilworth on 23 April 1681, and Earl of Rochester on 29 November 1682. Henrietta was the Duchess of York's sister-in-law.[38]

But it was at the duchess that the fat finger of suspicion pointed. To discredit the rumour-dealers, she agreed to a postmortem on Lady Denham. This uncovered no evidence of poisoning. Sir Richard Ford (a future London mayor in 1670) told Pepys that upon opening the body they had discovered 'a vessel about her matrix which had never been broke by her husband, that caused all the pains in her body, which, if true,' concluded the astute diarist, 'is excellent invention to clear both the Duchesse from poison and the Duke from lying with her.'[39] Gramont commented that the 'naturally jealous' old Denham could not do to his wife as the Earl of Chesterfield had done to his when the duke came an-ogling: he sent her out of harm's (that is the duke's) way from the court to the country seat. On 19 January 1663, Pepys records how Chesterfield,

> went and told the Duke how much he did apprehend himself wronged in his picking out his lady of the whole Court to be the subject of his dishonour – which the Duke did answer with great calmnesse, not seeming to understand the reason of complaint, and that was all past: but my Lord did presently pack his lady into the country in Derbyshire, near the peake; which is become a proverb at Court – to send a man's wife to the Devil's Arse-a-Peak when she vexes him.

The Devil's Arse-a-Peak, also known as Devil's Hole and Peak Cavern, was a cave near Castleton, Derbyshire, one of the so-called seven wonders of the Peak District.[40]

Thus having no country house to which to banish his wife, Lord Denham made her 'travel a much longer journey without stirring out of London. Merciless fate robbed her of life.' He was also assured that old Denham himself was that merciless fate: '...no person entertained any doubt of his having poisoned her.' His neighbours were all but ready to exact a 'design of tearing him to pieces' should he show his face, 'but he shut himself up to bewail her death, until their fury was appeased by a magnificent funeral, at which he distributed four times more burnt wine than had ever been drunk at any burial in England.' So that's all right, then.[41]

A rather more successful mistress of the duke's was Arabella Churchill despite her serious lack of surplus flesh. She was 'a tall creature, pale-faced and nothing but skin and bone.' The 'ugly skeleton' was maid of honour to the Duchess of York and brother to John Churchill, later the first Duke of Marlborough. It is likely that she introduced her brother into James's service as a page. If so, this was one page that would turn.[42]

James had become enamoured with Arabella after she had suffered a riding fall exposing legs and a figure that he found surprisingly agreeable. The duke's surgeon, James Pearse, told Pepys 'as a great secret that he was going to his Maister's mistress, Mrs Churchill, [with] some physic; meaning for the pox I suppose, or else that she is got with child; but I suppose the former, by his manner of speaking it.' Arabella would, however, be with child regularly, giving James four children, the second of which, James Fitzjames, would be created the Duke of Berwick. After the affair ended, Arabella married Colonel Charles Godfrey, who would become Master of the Jewel House for William III.[43]

However, James's most enduring mistress was that 'shocking creature' Katherine Sedley, daughter of the celebrated Sir Charles Sedley. Born 21 December 1657, she had so inherited her father's wit that, according to the French ambassador Barillon, even Charles II, a keen student of the subject, admired that quality in her. On 13 June 1673 Evelyn described the fifteen-year-old Katherine as 'none of the most virtuous, but a Witt &c.'[44]

By 1677 Katherine was so well known at court that the scurrilous verses had already taken flight. Sir Carr Scrope, a minor poet, described her as 'as mad as her mother and as vicious as her father.' Wise to the game of revenge, Katherine dished the dirt on Scrope and the kindly attentions he was paying to the daughter of Sir Alexander Fraser, the king's physician, suggesting that the couple may soon both be in need of Fraser's gynaecological expertise.[45]

It was as maid of honour to Marie d'Este (Mary of Modena, James's second wife) that Katherine was first caught full square in the ogler's gaze. She also caught another's attention – although this was less than affectionate. Katherine would be the contemptuous subject of lines composed by Charles Sackville. (He wrote four poems about her, casting her alternatively as 'Dorinda' and 'Sylvia'). The fact that Sackville despised affectation, particularly in the court women, probably accounts for the attention he bitingly lavishes on her. For example:

> *Dorinda's sparkling Wit, and Eyes,*
> *Uniting cast too fierce a Light,*
> *Which blazes high but quickly dyes,*
> *Pains not the Heart but hurts the Sight.*
> *Love is a calmer, gentler Joy,*
> *Smooth are his looks, and soft his pace;*
> *Her Cupid is a Black-Guard Boy*
> *That runs his Link full in your face.*[46]

(*The Black Guard* – 'idle dirty boys that lie about the Horse Guards and the Mews and Ride horses to water (commonly called the Black guard)[47]'; *Link* – A torch used for lighting people along the streets.)

Around 1677, Katherine was being linked with marriage to John Churchill, who had taken his leave of (and taken 100,000 livres* from) Barbara Villiers and had been courting Sarah Jennings, a maid of honour. However, his grasping parents were dismayed, for Sarah, for all her charm, was penniless. They urged his attentions upon Katherine Sedley, who would certainly have an inheritance to more than make up for her looks. The French ambassador Courtin wrote that Churchill was being pestered to marry an ugly rich woman. Sarah, understandably upset at being frozen out, wrote an angry letter to Churchill. Some years later she wrote on the letter: 'This letter was writ when I was angry at something his father and mother had made a disagreeable noise in the town about, when they had a mind to make him marry a shocking creature for money.' However, this seemed one time when Churchill permitted love to get the better of wealth, ambition and influence. He married his Sarah, despite his parents, in 1677.[48]

It was probably Katherine's sparky line about James and his mistresses that led to another of Charles Sackville's versified attacks, in Song:

---

*A livre was roughly the equivalent of the franc. The exchange in the 1670s was about 11 livres to the pound. This works out at over £9,000 (the modern equivalent would be £710,000)

> *Sylvia, methinks you are unfit*
> *For your great lord's embrace;*
> *For tho' we allow you wit,*
> *We can't a handsome face.*
>
> *Then where's the pleasure, where's the good,*
> *Of spending time and cost?*
> *For if your wit be n't understood,*
> *Your keeper's bliss is lost.*[49]

On 4 March 1679 Charles sent James abroad. He did, however, receive a little going-away present: Katherine had given birth to a girl, also Katherine. Letters patent conferred the title 'Lady' on the child and the surname 'Darnley'. In his diary, Peter le Neve, recorded:

> I heard that the only daughter and heir of Sir Charles Sedley baronet being reputed a Maid was brought to bed of a child and layd it to ye D. of York, before he went beyond the seas; which together with the thought of departing out of England made his Dutchess very melancholy.[50]

The satirists, not too troubling to imagine, held a fun day over the event. One such verse ran:

> *Lo thy Daughter, little Sid,*
> *She who lately slip'd her Kid,*
> *Sure a hopeful 'twill be*
> *Soaked in Pox and Popery.*[51]

A mardy and moody Mary of Modena tried in vain to emulate her rival. A letter dated 3 July 1680 runs: 'Some say the Duchess of York is with child, others that she is melancholy, not for Mrs Sedley, but greater matters. The Duke appears very thoughtful.' And another, five days later: 'The Duchess of York is not with child. She prays all day almost. She is very melancholy, the women will have it, for Mrs Sedley. She looks further than that, if she has so much wit, as she is thought by some.'[52]

The same year she was the target of Sackville, tapping into her extravagance of dress, which detracts little from a barren face:

> *Tell me, Dorinda, why so gay,*
> *Why such embroid'ry, fringe and lace?*
> *Can any dresses find a way,*
> *To stop th'approaches of decay,*
> *And mend a ruin'd face?*

Wilt thou still sparkle in the box,
Still ogle in the ring?
Canst thou forget thy age and pox?
Can all that shines on shells and rocks
Make thee a fine young Thing?

So have I seen in larder dark
Of veal a lucid loin;
Replete with many a brilliant spark,
As wise philosophers remark,
At once both stink and shine?[53]

In 1684 she gave birth to a second child, a boy this time, who took the name James Darnley. The following year the duke became king and it was all change at the station royal: duelling, swearing and drunkenness became taboo. There was a special instruction banning drunkenness in front of the queen. However, things did not begin well. James's coronation was hastily prepared to replicate the magnificence of his intended kingship. Despite being 'gay and pompous', the new king was bedevilled by irritations: the crown didn't quite fit – 'it came down too far, and covered the upper part of his face; the canopy carried over him broke.' And, after the comedy, the tragedy, as 'his son by Mrs Sedley died that day.' Buried in the Henry VII chapel, the boy's coffin plate read: 'James Darnley naturall son to King Jame ye second Departed this life the 22 April 1685 Aged about eight months.'[54]

New reign, new king. James, once again moved by the occasion, solemnly vowed his intention to change: 'He promised the Queen, and his priests too, that he would see Mrs Sedley no more, but apply to business, and live a very virtuous life. And accordingly Mrs Sedley was ordered from her lodgings in Whitehall...' However, and as ever, 'he still continued a secret connection with her.'[55]

Although publicly declaring a clean break from the licentiousness of his brother's court, James did take one quarto out of his manuscript. Charles had taken the unprecedented step of creating titles in their own right for two of his long-term mistresses, Barbara Villiers and Louise de Keroualle. Barbara, already Countess of Castlemaine through her marriage, became Baroness Nonsuch and Duchess of Cleveland. Louise, in turn, became Countess of Fareham, Baroness Petersfield and the Duchess of Portsmouth. The loser in these title bouts was the unfortunate Nelly Gwynne, for whom – even though the notion of creating her Countess of Plymouth and later Countess of Greenwich was floated – a poor background sank those rich dreams. James, amid uproar, created Katherine Baroness Darlington and Countess of Dorchester in January 1686. It was even rumoured that she was set to move into the Duchess of Portsmouth's sumptuous apartments at Whitehall, signalling that Katherine was similarly to fulfil the role of *maîtresse de titre* to her king. For the victor, the spoils: her pension was duly elevated from £4,000 a year to £5,000 (nearly £400,000 today).

Even this king realised he had to make the occasional gesture, and under pressure from an anxious James, Katherine quit court. For the queen this victory rattled with emptiness. Mistress Sedley had moved into luxurious lodgings at 21 St James's Square, the house that once belonged to Arabella Churchill. This quiet exile was deafening. Mary of Modena, unlike Catherine of Braganza, had failed to dowse her Latin spark for English forbearance, and sulked monumentally. As Evelyn recorded on 19 January 1686:

> I went to Lond: pass'd the Privie Seale amongst others, the Creation of Mrs Sidly (concubine to...) Countesse of Dorchester, which 'tis certaine the Queene tooke very grievously: so as for two dinners, standing neer her, she hardly eate one morsel, nor spake one word to the King, or to any about her...[56]

Indeed, the queen 'was alarmed at this honour, as an avowed declaration of her being his mistress. The priests complained of it heavily, as a stain to his honour, and obstruction to their best endeavours. But, to pacify them both, he promised that he would see the lady no more; that he purposed to send her into Ireland, and had only given her that title to part with her more decently.' And, obediently, Katherine popped off to Ireland.[57]

The sojourn was short-lived. She had found Dublin 'intolerable' and the Irish 'not only senceless, but a mallincolly sort of people and speak all in the tone off the cripples off London'. Once the queen and the priests thanked God for the king's sense, and James believed himself believed, he uncrossed his wily old fingers, and 'within a few months she returned again, and the old commerce continued.' Katherine returned to England on 14 November 1687. The arrival of one king's notorious mistress was sadly marked by the death of another: Nell Gwynne died that day after a long and painful debilitating illness in a neighbour's house in Pall Mall.[58]

Although the old commerce went on, the value of the trade drooped enormously. Katherine bought Ham House in Weybridge from the Duke of Norfolk to maintain a businesslike distance. The king supposedly came to visit occasionally, but his interest in her stock fell and she lost her share of influence over him. The following year, with the king, her lover, deposed, it might be imagined that Katherine would view the Revolution of 1688 as anything but Glorious. But her survival instincts shocked sympathy out of her:

> *But Sidley has some colour for his Treason*
> *A daughter Ravished without any Reason;*
> *Good natur'd man, He is most strangely blest,*
> *His Daughter's Honour is his Worship's Jest.* *
> *And she to keep her Father's honour up,*
> *Drinks to the Dutch with Orange in her Cup.*

Just over ten years later, Katherine, who remarkably remained a pensioner under William III (£5,000 was voted to her by the commons of Ireland in 1703), married a Scotsman, Sir David Colyear, in August 1696. Charles Sackville chose to mark the occasion with his usual deference.

> *Proud with the Spoils of Royal Cully,*
> *With false pretence to Wit and Parts,*
> *She swaggers like a batter'd Bully,*
> *To try the tempers of men's hearts.*
>
> *Tho' she appears as glitt'ring fine,*
> *As Gems, and Jests, and Paint can make her;*
> *She ne'er can win a Breast like mine,*
> *The Devil and Sir David take her.*[59]

Sackville wasn't the only one to shoot across her bow. This anonymous broadside was fired off in retaliation for her cutting, crude wit:

> *A wither'd Countess next, who rails aloud*
> *At the reigning Vices of the Croud,*
> *And with the product of that ill turn'd Brain,*
> *Does all her guests at Visits Entertain;*
> *Thinks it a crime for any one to be*
> *Either ill-natur'd or as lewd as she.*
> *A Sovereign Judge over her Sex does sit,*
> *Giving full Scope to her injurious Wit.*
> *Too old for Lust and proof against all Shame,*
> *Her only business now to defame;*
> *She hath done well the one the one ey'd Knight to chuse,*
> *For one, who's two wou'd ne're endure the noose.*[60]

---

*This is perhaps a reference to Sir Charles Sedley's quip that while James made his daughter a countess, he helped to make James's daughter a queen.

Colyear, about ten years Katherine's senior, was described as 'a man of honour and nice in that way' and being 'pretty well shaped, dresses clean, has but one eye', which explains the last two lines of the above lampoon. He became a baronet in 1699 and then Earl of Portmore in 1703. He died on 26 October 1717. Together they had two sons, David, Viscount Melsington (d. 1714), and Charles Colyear, who became second Earl of Portmore and died in 1785. There is an unsourced anecdote that Katherine gave her boys advice on their leaving for school: 'If any body call either of you the son of a whore, you must bear it; for you are so: but if they call you bastards, fight till you die; for you are an honest man's son.'[61]

As long as Katherine was alive so was her wit. Lady Cowper, in her diary, tells us that at the coronation of George I in 1711 when the Archbishop of Canterbury requested the consent of the people around the throne, Katherine turned to her and said, 'Does the old Fool think that Anybody here will say no to his Question, when there are so many drawn swords?' And later, when attending an assembly in the king's drawing rooms, Katherine, who found herself in the company of Charles II's mistress, Louise de Keroualle, and William III's mistress, Elizabeth Villiers, Countess of Orkney, is said to have declared, 'Who would have thought that we three whores should have met here?'[62]

Katherine was taken seriously ill in the beautiful city of Bath and died shortly after on 26 October 1717. For someone who had sparkled like spa water it was perhaps a fitting place to die.

3

Sex: an Everyday Story of Fucksters

'...to be a fine gentleman nowadays you need only gamble and tell
lies; to be a fine lady you only have to run away with your neighbour's
husband.'

– Dorothy Sidney, Lady Sunderland, 1679[1]

'...for Men are now more ashamed to be seen with [their wives] in
publick, than with a Wench.'

– William Wycherley, *The Country Wife*, 1675[2]

Unsurprisingly, with its engines chugging with vanity, Charles II's court
was reputed for its beauties, both male and female. However, not
everyone was up to flag-bearing standard. The dashingly Gallic Count
Gramont, who naturally snaffled a beauty for himself in the shapely
form of Anne Hamilton, was less than charitable in his physical
description of Lady Margaret Muskerry, 'whose husband most assuredly
never married her for her beauty'. She was, he continued, 'made like
the generality of rich heiresses, to whom just Nature seems sparing of
her gifts, in proportion as they are loaded with those of fortune...but
had good reason for limping; for, of two legs uncommonly short, one
was much shorter than the other: a face suitable to this description gave
the finishing stroke to this disagreeable figure.'[3]

For a man on the make in Restoration England, talent and ability
were often inadequate attributes on their own. The best way to get on
was to get into bed (in both senses) with someone with influence. As
women with real influence were either strictly out of bounds or lacking
in abundance, and homosexuality – although naturally practised – was
still punishable by death, the coldest but shrewdest move was to offer to
men of influence the very personal use of their wives, daughters or

sisters, or to suffer with quiet dignity when they were seduced anyway. The word 'pimp' justifiably was in common coinage. It might not be easy emotionally to be cuckolded, but you would be in good company, and, politically and financially, it had its not inconsiderable rewards.

One such pimp was Winston Churchill. He was MP for Weymouth and sat in the so-called 'Cavalier Parliament', which his fellow MP, Andrew Marvell, labelled the 'Pensionary Parliament' on account of how many owed debts of gratitude to the crown for lands and titles. He went so far as to claim that Churchill, knighted in 1664, had 'acted as a pimp to his own daughter' to forward his own career. His daughter was Arabella Churchill, who became a mistress to the Duke of York.[4]

This callous but open system of preferment has never disappeared. We're familiar with the casting couch of Hollywood producers, and the new sex – money: specifically financial donations to political parties in return for knighthoods, gongs and business procurement. Indeed, even this was a Stuart trait. James I knew titles could be won if the price was right: Sir John Roper, come on down! Ten thousand pounds later, he's Lord Teynham. Charles II even employed touts to travel the land to sell baronetcies.[5]

Naturally, not all sex was calculated or successful. Rising star and friend of Rochester, the fat, cheerful Henry (Harry) Savile was the cause of a great scandal following his 'attempt upon My lady Northumberland'. Elizabeth Wriothesley was the youngest daughter of Thomas, Earl of Southampton, and the widow of Joceline, Earl of Northumberland, who died on 23 June 1670. Her inheritance was thought to be £10,000 a year and was evidently a serious proposition for the single and engagingly unwealthy Savile.[6]

In September 1671 the unattached heiress was a guest, with Savile and others, at Althorp, Northamptonshire, the seat of Robert Spencer, second Earl of Sunderland. At one in the morning Savile sneaked his way into her ladyship's bedchamber. This resourcefulness was achieved, depending on whose account you believe, by either 'having gotten from my Lord Sunderland a master key on pretence of going into the billiard', or by 'having the day before stole a way the bolt [on her door] so there was nothing but a latch to lift.'

Having entered the room, Savile, in his shirt and nightgown, and 'there kneeling down beside told her, Madam, I am come with great confusion of face to tell you now which I durst not trust the light with, the passion which I serve and adore you'.

This outpouring of love certainly revved up the countess's heart – but with panic, not affection. She grabbed for her night bell and rang it ('with that Violence as if not only a poore lovers heart but a whole house had been on fire'), leaped out of bed and escaped through another door, which the stunned Savile, undoubtedly praying to his god to return him the last minute, was unaware. It led into a gallery 'through which she ran barefoot and knoct at the chamber door where my Lord Ashby's lady was lodged and made a shift to gett into bed to her'.

Savile, thinking desperately, went back to his chamber and began to write a note that would explain it all – that the house was haunted. But he knew the game was up. By the morning – when, still barely able to draw breath, Lady Northumberland informed the household of the night's drama, and while the outraged (male) guests bayed for 'murther and suddain death' – Savile had skedaddled. He had stolen away to the stable and ridden away with the post. The countess's brother, William Russell (who would later be beheaded for his part in the Rye House Plot) and the Earl of Sunderland gave chase to London to fight him. 'The whole Court and town abhors the insolence,' wrote Attorney-General Finch, 'and wish the Avenger of Honour may overtake him and prosper in his chastisement.' However, the king 'has notice and prevents it'. Nonetheless, the capital remained too hot for Henry, and he, 'ashamed for so ill a conduct', skipped town, although 'nobody know whither; some say beyond sea.'

In all probability he lost himself in France and was next heard of arriving at Dover on 26 April 1672, some seven months later. He may well have imposed a lengthy exile on himself, or he may have been carrying out a mission of international diplomacy – a war with Holland had been declared six weeks before – for Charles II (who was fond of Savile). Whatever, the fallout had hued and cried and Harry and his foes were at peace.

Lady Northumberland later married Ralph Montagu, the English ambassador in Paris (a post that, incidentally, Henry Savile would later fill), in August 1673. Montagu, destined to become the Duke of Montagu, would later marry Elizabeth, Duchess of Albermarle, widow of Christopher Monck, second Duke of Albermarle, the son of General Monck. Elizabeth, the daughter of William Cavendish, Duke of Newcastle, was decidedly less than sane. However, given that her mother, Margaret Lucas, although beautiful, resolute and literary, was known as Mad Madge, the poor girl had seemingly little chance. Elizabeth believed herself to be the Empress of China and as a consequence would make Montagu crawl on his hands and knees in front of her.

Pepys was partial to those who believed themselves to be someone else, though his preference was for those who did so professionally – on stage. He was particularly fond of the actress, singer and dancer at the

King's House, Elizabeth Knepp (his 'Knipp'). A keen musician – he played the viols, violin, lute, theorbo and flageolet, although he struggled to master a keyboard – he was enchanted with her voice:

> Here was the best company for Musique I ever was in my life, and wish I could live and die in it, both for music and the face of Mrs Pierce and my wife and Knipp, who is pretty enough, but the most mad-hum[ou]rd thing; and sings the noblest that ever I heard in my life . . . I spent the night in ecstasy almost.[7]

However, it wasn't just her voice that so enchanted Pepys – her breasts often took his notice and occasionally his hands: 'The company being all gone to their homes, I up with Mrs Pierce to Knipp, who was in bed; and we waked her and there I handled her breasts and did baiser la and sing a song, lying by her on the bed.'[8]

This had been a particularly good couple of days for Pepys ('my mind mightily satisfied...with one of the merriest enjoyments') as the previous day Knipp had delighted the diarist by introducing him to Nell Gwynne:

> . . . and Knipp took us all in and brought us to Nelly, a most pretty woman, who acted the great part, Celia, today very fine, and did it pretty well; I kissed her and so did my wife, and a mighty pretty soul she is . . . Knipp made us stay in a box and see the dancing preparatory to tomorrow for *The Goblin*, a play of Suckelings [Sir John Suckling] not acted these 25 years, which was pretty; and so away thence, pleased with this sight also, and especially kissing of Nell.[9]

When Pepys got a little further than just playful toying, he recorded it guiltily in his lingua franca, clearly eager to confound any prying matrimonial eyes. This doubled his security as the diaries were, with the exception of names and occasional words, written in the shorthand invented by Thomas Shelton. On 21 April 1668, after watching Dryden's *The Indian Emperor* at the King's House, he recorded:

> . . . and after that done, took Knipp out, and to Kensington and there walked in the garden and then supped and mighty merry, there being also in the House Sir Ph. Howard and some company; and had a dear reckoning but merry; and away, it being quite night, home, and dark, about 9 a-clock or more; and in my coming, had the opportunity, the first time in my life, to be bold with Knepp by putting my hand abaxo de her coats and tocar su thighs and venter – and a little of the other thing, ella but a little opposing me: su skin very douce and I mightily pleased with this.[10]

And again two days later:

Knipp and I to the Temple again and took boat, it being darkish, and to Fox-hall [Vauxhall], it being now night and a bonfire burning at Lambeth for the King's Coronacion-day. And there she and I drank; and yo did tocar her corps all over and besar sans fin her, but did not offer algo mas... [and home] and to bed, weary but pleased at the day's pleasure.'[11]

Neither was his fumbling confined to the dark or private: '...so I got into the coach where Mrs Knipp was, and got her upon my knee (the coach being full) and played with her breasts and sung; and at last set her at her house, and so good-night.'[12]

Mrs Elizabeth Pepys, not unsurprisingly, was jealous of her husband's relationship with Knepp and other women. On 9 May 1666 Pepys notes that his 'wife in mighty pain [she had a swollen cheek], and mightily vexed at my being abroad with these women – and when they were gone, called them "whores" and I know not what; which vexed me, having been so innocent with them.' His weakness for females often left her 'in ill humour' and 'slighting of them'. Indeed the diary is riddled with his wife's jealousy. Although he is rarely affectionate about her (he never calls her by her name once, preferring 'my wife') after her early death in 1669 – she had just turned 29 – he never remarried. Indeed, upon his own death in 1703, and by his direction, his body was buried next to hers in the nave at St Olave's, Hart Street, near Fenchurch Street in the city of London (a parallel street is now named Pepys Street).[13]

However, most devastating for Elizabeth was her discovery, in flagrante delicto, of his affair with Deb Willet, who had been engaged by Elizabeth as her companion on 24 September 1667. The prospect pleased Pepys: 'My wife says she is extraordinary handsome and enclines to have her, and I am glad of it – at least, that if we must have one, she should be handsome.' On meeting her three days later he is not too disappointed if somewhat prophetic:

though she seems not altogether so great a beauty as had before told me, yet endeed she is mighty pretty; and so pretty, that I find I shall be too much pleased with it, and therefore could be contented as to my judgment, though not to my passion, that she might not come, lest I may be found too much minding her, to the discontent of my wife.

His affection towards her did very soon discontent his wife. On 12

October he was aware that Elizabeth is 'already a little jealous of my being fond of Willett, but I will avoid giving her any cause to continue in that mind, as much as possible.'[14]

However, Pepys's policy of crisis avoidance crashed with the inevitable policy U-turn: 'and thither came to me Willet with an errand from her mistress, and this time I first did give her a little kiss, she being a very pretty-humoured girl, and so one that I do love mightily'. On 31 March 1668, as she undressed him for bed, he would need his faithless hybrid language again: 'and yo did take her, the first time in my life, sobra mi genu and did poner mi mano sub her jupes and toca su thigh, which did hazer me great pleasure.' Frequent caresses and clinches are recorded, including one night when he was masturbated by Deb: 'This night yo did hazer Deb tocar mi thing with her hand after yo was in lecto – with great pleasure.'[15]

Pepys's pleasure was soon his torment as Elizabeth walked in on the lovers:

> ...and after supper, to have my head combed by Deb, which occasioned the greatest sorrow to me that ever I knew in this world; for my wife, coming up suddenly, did find me imbracing the girl con my hand sub su coats; and endeed, I was with my main in her cunny.[16]

The initial silence, shock and embarrassment at the discovery was short-lived:

> I was at a wonderful loss upon it, and the girl also; and I endeavoured to put it off, but my wife was struck mute and grew angry, and as her voice came to her, grew quite out of order; and I do say little, but to bed.[17]

The cagey adulterer, unclear exactly what his wife saw, played a quiet game, casting the Restoration version of the 'I never meant to hurt you' line with aplomb:

> But after her much crying and reproaching me with inconstancy and preferring a sorry girl before her, I did give her no provocations but did promise all fair usage to her, and love, and foreswore any hurt that I did with her – till at last she seemed to be at ease again.[18]

With such complications and provocations, loveless sex, so to speak, came into its own. In his self-described 'book about dirty books', Roger Thompson stretches for the Restoration top shelf and shows that even without photographs the words painted a pretty explicit picture. The serial *The Wandering Whore* combined fictional characters with the increasingly obvious reality. Part Five, published in 1661, lists what amounts to a whores' *Who's Who*. This London directory depicted 138 bawds, 269 common whores, and sundry male foylers (violaters), kidnappers, decoys, pimps and hectors. Another book estimated a prostitute population of 1,500 in 1660.[19]

They plied their unlicensed trade in notorious areas: around Covent Garden, Drury Lane, Whetstone's Park (an alley north of Lincoln's Inn Fields), Moorfields, Holborn and Tower Hill. The notion of the itinerant whore was nothing novel. During the civil war, women would follow the troops: some were wives and mistresses with hearts to fill; others were less attached – the 'leaguer-bitches' and 'camp sluts' – with purses to fill.

The Wandering Whore mud-wrestles its joyous way through unbridled description. Exciting the customer was all part of the portfolio of your average sexual-commerce entrepreneur:

> They kiss with their mouths open, and put their tongues in his mouth and suck it. Their left hand is in his Cod-piece, their right in his pocket; they commend his Trap stick, and pluck their coats above their thighs, their smocks above their knees, bidding him thrust his hand into the best Cunt in christendom, tickling the knobs thereof till they burst out laughing, as W____ the Butchers son in Stocks did Honor Brooks, the rammish Scotch whore at D____ between her legs, not forgetting that Ursula had 2/6d for shewing her twit-twat there and 2/6d for stroking the marrow out of mans gristle.[20]

Inevitably, despite such top-notch customer service, not every blade was up to scratch:

> *With whores and pox, there forty years worn out,*
> *He sweats and stinks for one poor single Bout,*
> *'Till wench half stifl'd cry'd, my Lord, I'le Frig:*
> *Your Prick's too short, your Belly is too big.*

Frig – to masturbate

An anecdote in *The Wandering Whore* relates to Mall Savory, who picked a gentleman client's watch and hid it in her 'commodity' for safekeeping, only to be – somewhat embarrassingly – found out once the alarm went off. Every age has its euphemisms. A woman's 'commodity' could also be her cunny or coney, her perfum'd cabinet, her hairy manor or her twit-twat. A man's 'yard' could also be his tarse, his pintle, his trap-stick, his bauble or his Squire Pego. The merging of the two could have them riding the ring, swiving or jumping the broomstick.[21]

The word 'whore' also needs clarifying. Sure, it meant prostitute, but it was a term equally (and perhaps more so) applicable to adulteresses and kept women. It was for this reason, for example, that Nell Gwynne cheerfully referred to herself as a whore. Most famously, she had taken loan of Louise de Keroualle's carriage and travelled to Oxford in 1681. On her way to meet with the king some citizens noticed the initials of the carriage's owner and assumed that Louise was inside. A small crowd hurled insults and began to push the carriage of the hated French Catholic. Nelly pulled back the curtain, stuck her head out to the protesters and cried, 'Pray, good people, be civil: I'm the protestant whore!'

However, it was the growth of the more professional strain that was the subject of violent demonstrations by the apprentice boys amid the holiday fervour in Easter 1668. Pepys recorded that the court was abuzz with 'great talk of the tumult at the other end of town about Moorefields among the prentices, taking the liberty of these holidays to pull down the bawdy houses'. Such was the concern that these riots were more politically motivated that 'the order was given for all the soldiers, horse and foot, to be in armes.' Intrigued, our intrepid correspondent made his way to Lincoln Inn Fields to catch sight of the spectacle, only to find the 'fields full of soldiers all in a body, and my Lord Craven commanding of them, and riding up and down to give orders like a madman'. Pepys overheard bystanders bemoaning the military presence preventing the apprentices from their noble work, suggesting that the assault on the bawdy houses was morally inspired rather than politically loaded. Nonetheless, with slogans such as LIBERTY OF CONSCIENCE! and REFORMATION AND REDUCEMENT! ringing through the streets, the three-day riots clearly did have ulterior political motives.[22]

Any serious talk in Whitehall Palace – for some the largest bawdy houses to remain unscathed from the wrath of apprentices – about republican undertones of the disorder was in a general perception of mirth. The Duke of York, as Lord High Admiral, for one was 'mighty merry' that the seaman's brothel run by Damaris Page – 'the most Famous Bawd in Towne' – was pulled down. And he directed mock outrage at the apprentices for pulling down two properties from which he received £15 a year in wine licences.[23]

Confronted with evidence that bawdy houses were a grievance of the nation, the king replied 'Why, why do they go to them, then?' Pepys thought this 'a very poor, cold, insipid answer'. Nonetheless, despite the apparent flippancy, no chances were apparently taken since Pepys heard on 5 April 'that eight of the ringleaders in the late tumults of the prentices at Easter are condemned to die'. In all, fifteen were arrested and tried for high treason (the riots being perceived legally as a war on the crown), four being condemned and executed on 9 May 1668 with the rest acquitted.[24]

The lighter mood in Whitehall was captured by the efficiently written and published (it being received on 25 March) plea entitled 'The Poor Whores' Petition'. It was addressed to the most famous 'whore' in England, Barbara Villiers – 'the most Splendid, Illustrious, and Eminent Lady of Pleasure, the Countess of Castlemayne'. It requested 'protection against the company of London apprentices, through whom they have sustained the loss of habitations, trades and employments, and for a guard of "French, Irish, and English Hectors", who are their approved friends'. The petitioners also promised to contribute financially to Barbara 'as their sisters at Rome and Venice do the Pope'.[25]

The petition opened:

We being moved by the imminent danger now impending, and the great sense of our present suffering, do implore your Honour to improve your Interest, which (all know) is great, That some speedy Relief may be afforded us, to prevent Our Utter Ruine and Undoing. And that such a sure course may be taken with the Ringleaders and Abetters of these evil-disposed persons, that a stop may be put unto them before they come to Your Honours Pallace, and bring contempt upon your worshipping of Venus, the great Goddess whom we all adore . . . And we shall endeavour, as our bounden duty, the promoting of your Great Name, and the preservation of your Honour, Safety, and Interest, with the hazzard of our Lives, Fortunes and Honesty.

And it concluded:

And your petitioners shall (as by custom bound) Evermore Play &c. Signed by Us, Madam Cresswell and Damaris Page, in the behalf of our Sisters and Fellow Sufferers (in this time of our Calamity) in Dog and Bitch Yard, Lukeners Lane, Saffron Hill, Moor-fields, Chiswell-street, Rosemary-Lane, Nightingale-Lane, Ratcliffe-High-way, Well Close, Church-Lane, East Smithfield, &c, this present 25th day of March, 1668.[26]

The petition, published for a hoot, was probably the work of a suitably anonymous courtier, and certainly not that of the named authors. Madam Cresswell would be convicted on 22 November 1681 'after above thirty years practice of bawdry.' She reputedly left a bequest of £10 in return for a funeral sermon in 'which nothing but what was well should be said of her.' The preacher obliged, pronouncing that 'she was born well, lived well and died well.' And then delivered the qualification: 'She was born with the name of Cresswell, she lived in Clerkenwell and died in Bridewell.'[27]

Another notable madam on the roll call, in addition to the Misses Page and Cresswell, was the triumphant Pris Fotheringham, who ran the Six Windmills tavern (formerly the Jack-a-Newbery) in Upper Moorfields. As with a windmill, the fragrant Fotheringham's special turn was somewhat against the grain. Her party piece – as lucrative as it was novel – saw her, as she herself explained, 'stand upon my head with a naked Breech, bare Belly, spread Legs, with the orifice of my Rima Magna open whilst several Cully-Rumpers chuck in sixteen half-crowns into it for their pleasure and my profit.' A fully paid-up member of the suffering sisterhood 'responsible' for the poor whores' petition, no doubt.[28]

Pepys, who owned a copy of the petition, was less than impressed, declaring it as 'not very witty; but devilish severe against [Lady Castlemaine] and the King'. The insult stung sharply for Barbara, who was 'horribly vexed' by the whole incident. A triumph, no less.[29]

Spurred on by the reaction, it did not take long for 'a reply' to be skipping its merry way into circulation. The sequel entitled 'The Gracious Answer of the most Illustrious Lady of Pleasure the Countess of Castlem[aime] . . .' was dated 'Given at our Closett in King Street, Westminster, die Verneris April 24 1668'. It began:

Right Trusty and Well-beloved Madam Cresswell and Damaris Page, with the rest of the suffering Sisterhood, We greet you well, in giving you to understand our Noble Mind, by returning us our Titles of Honour, which are but our Due. For on Shrove-Tuesday last, Splendidly did we appear upon the Theatre at W.H. [Whitehall] being to amazement wonderfully deck'd with Jewels and Diamonds, which (abhorr'd and to be undone) Subjects of the Kingdom have payed for. We have seen also Serene and Illustrious ever since the Day that Mars was so instrumental to restore our Goddess Venus to her Temple and Worship; where by special grant we quickly became a famous Lady: And as a Reward of our Devotions soon created Right Honourable, the Countess of Castlemain.[30]

Indeed, Barbara was wonderfully decked in jewels and diamonds:

This Evening I saw the Trajedie of Horace (written by the virtuous Mrs. Philips) acted before their Majesties: 'twixt each act a Masque & Antique: daunced: The excessive galantry of the Ladies was infinite, Those especialy on that... Castlemaine esteemed at 40000 pounds & more: & far out shining the Queene &c:[31]

Forty thousand pounds' worth of jewellery translates today as being over £3.15 million. That is some serious decking.

Other whores' petitions included a couple to the 'London Prentices' themselves: one arguing that lust – the whores' stock in trade – was small beer compared with the stealing notoriously associated with apprentice boys; a second, in 1672, begging the boys for custom, as trade had dropped off owing to the war. Another, albeit a peacetime petition, was addressed to the king, expressing gratitude for the abundant working opportunities granted them courtesy of his majesty's shining example to the people.

Indeed, satires and libels fastened on to the idea that it was not the king but his too easily aroused member that ruled the nation. John Oldham's 'Sardanapulus' holds little back in condemning the 'cunt-struck' king who, as a so-called 'fuckster', wasted wantonly his time, energy, money and seed:

> *Cunt was the Star that rul'd thy Fate,*
> *Cunt thy sole Bus'ness and Affair of State,*
> *And Cunt the only Field to make thee Great...*
> *Som Saucy Pedants and Historians idly Rail*
> *And thee Effeminate unjustly call.*[32]

Sir Frances Fane's elegy 'Iter Occidentale' echoes the same sentiment and the sense of waste and loss:

> *Prick, Natures Pump, Cunts Pioneer,*
> *Love under Sail, Lifes Harbinger...*
> *The Virgins Bait, the Womans Hook:*
> *To Save the Trouble to Create,*
> *The worlds great Axis on whose Poles*
> *Turn Kingdoms, Churches, Bodyes, Souls,*
> *How Great a Soveraign would'st thou be*
> *If Poor Cunt did not Master Thee.*[33]

John Wilmot, Earl of Rochester was predictably no less scathing:

Poor Prince! thy prick, like the buffoons at Court,
Will govern thee because it makes thee sport.
'Tis sure the sauciest prick that e'er did swive,
The proudest, peremptoriest prick alive.
Though safety, law, religion, life lay on 't,
'Twould break through all to make its way to cunt.[34]

The licentiousness of the court also made it a breeding ground for sexual experimentation. Sodomy was outlawed but for the courtiers this illegality was as effective as it was for duelling. The Duke of Buckingham had been decried twice for buggery. The second time, he was charged with misusing a woman called Sarah Harwood, whom he was alleged to have sent abroad and ordered her assassination to cover up his sins. However, it was vindictive nonsense and Bucks easily proved his innocence, winning £30,000 damages into the bargain under *scandalum magnatum* – literally 'a scandal of magnates' – a Restoration version of criminal libel. This law prevented the 'utterance or publication of a malicious report against any person holding a position of dignity'.[35]

More provable was the fashionable rise of homosexuality. A baffled Pepys recorded a conversation between him, Sir John Mennes (or Minnes), comptroller of the navy, and William Batten, surveyor of the navy, on 1 July 1663:

> ...both say that buggery is now almost grown as common among our gallants as in Italy...But blessed be God, I do not know to this day what is the meaning of this sin, nor which is the agent nor which the patient.[36]

It does appear that gentlemen and men of quality practised this new-fangled art on their pages, as suggested by Rochester in his 'Song', which begins 'Love a woman? You're an ass!' Pages were generally young, unpaid male servants who worked for food and shelter and the opportunity for advancement within the household. It seems that being buggered by the master was a duty commensurate within the grading of the post. Pepys noted, however, that 'the very pages of the town begin to complain of their masters for it.' They'll be wanting to unionise next.[37]

In July 1683, 'Satire on both Whigs and Tories', seemingly inspired by the Rye House plot, an assassination attempt on Charles II, took time out to comment on the penchant of Jack Howe and probably the younger George Porter ('Nobs') for sodomy:

How oft has Howe (by Rochester undone,
Who soothed him first into opinion
Of being a wit) been told that he was none?
But found that art the surest way to glide
Not into's heart but his well-shaped backside.
Not Nobs's bum more adoration found,
Though oft 'twas sung, his was more white and round.[38]

It has even been credibly suggested that the rakish toying with homoeroticism was 'a sign not of effeminacy, but of super-masculinity'. Indeed, the fops – all dandified and false – who laboured solely after women were considered effeminate. As (probably) Rochester described in 'Sodom': 'For none but easy ffops to Cunt will bow.'[39]

It was the foppish heterosexual who developed into the effeminate homosexual:

In three generations between 1660 and 1750, public attitudes toward the fop changed dramatically by generation. Between 1660 and 1690 the fop was firmly rejected in favour of the rake. After 1690, however, the rake himself fell to the power of romantic marriage on the stage, and the fop's domesticated interests came to be more highly valued. But between 1720 and 1750 the fop's effeminacy came under a new type of criticism... After 1720 the fop's effeminacy, in real life and on the stage, came to be identified with the then emerging role of exclusive adult male sodomite – known in the ordinary language of his day as a molly, and later on as a queen.[40]

Such was the growth of all-male sex following the Restoration that by 1698 it was being asserted that 'Nothing is more ordinary in England than this unnatural vice', and London boasted its own Sodomite Club.[41]

Nonetheless, its illegality kept it underground and it inevitably crossed over with other clandestine activists – namely Catholics. It was the interwoven status of Catholic and sodomite that proved such a deep well for 'Dr' Titus Oates, the grotesque psychopath and patent-holder of the hysterical Popish Plot. Oates and his accomplice Israel Tonge had, they declared, uncovered a dastardly plot of Jesuit assassins and French-aided uprisings in the three kingdoms to overthrow the king in favour of his Catholic brother James. Despite the absurdity of it all, tension was in the air, and it was exploited brilliantly by Oates and Tonge and the leader of the anticourt faction, the Earl of Shaftesbury.

With the monarchy replacing a republic that had replaced a monarchy, disaffection was never more than a drumbeat away. Plots and counterplots, real and imagined, punctured society. The Duke of Buckingham's play *The Rehearsal*, first produced in 1671, included the memorable line: 'the plot thickens upon us.' In 1680, Sir Roger L'Estrange was right on the money:

> There are Plots of Passion, and Plots of Interest; Plots General and Particular; Publick and Private: Foreign and Domestique; Ecclesiasticall and Civill: There are Plots to undermine Governments and Plots to Support them; Plots Simple and Counter Plots; Plots to make Plots; and Plots to spoil Plots; Plots to give Credit to Sham Plots; and Plots again to Baffle, and Discountenance Real Ones: Plots Jesuiticall and Phanatique; Plots Great and Small; High and Low; In short, there is not anything under the sun that may serve us either Pleasure or Convenience, but we have a Plot upon't...[42]

Oates, an active homosexual, was propelled to hero status as 'the saviour of the nation'. His dubious means justified his ends. His sexual preferences had caused his dismissal from schools and his job as a chaplain on the frigate *Adventure*. It was his errant past that gave him a pass into those Catholic circles ringed with secrecy: how else would an Anglican clergyman be so admitted? Oates kept company with the Catholic actor, Matthew Medburne, who 'had picked him up in the Earl of Suffolk's cellar at Whitehall'. Together they became regulars at a 'low club' in Fullers' Rents, Holborn, which attracted religious and sexual dissidents. It was to prove a costly relationship for Medburne, who would become one of 35 people executed as a result of the plot before it was exposed as a fraud.[43]

The association of homosexuality and Catholicism is alluded to in Rochester's 'A Ramble in St James's Park':

> *But cowards shall forget to rant,*
> *Schoolboys to frig, old whores to paint;*
> *The Jesuits' fraternity*
> *Shall leave the use of buggery;*
> *Crab-louse, inspired with grace divine,*
> *From earthly cod to heaven shall climb;*
> *Physicians shall believe in Jesus,*
> *And disobedience cease to please us,*
> *Ere I desist with all my power*
> *To plague this woman and undo her.*[44]

With the enormous difficulties inherent in (whatever form of) intercourse, it's little wonder that people took sexual satisfaction into – for the most part – their own hands. Masturbation (or 'frigging') was as prevalent as ever. However, a more enlightened approach lessened the intrinsic evil of such an act, particularly for women, and new opportunities were to present themselves for consideration. Enter the dildo.

'Signior Dildo' was primarily written as an attack on Mary of Modena, the new Italian Catholic wife of the Duke of York. They were married here by proxy on 30 September 1673. Her arrival in England was delayed by illness until 21 November. There was little celebration offered for the arrival of 'the eldest daughter of the pope' as she was called. The Earl of Rochester (and very probably a few other hands) penned 'Signior Dildo' to mark the occasion. The first of its 24 stanzas runs:

> *You ladies all of merry England*
> *Who have been to kiss the Duchess's hand,*
> *Pray, did you lately observe in the show*
> *A noble Italian called Signior Dildo?*[45]

The satire also suggests that items used in the past cannot compete with our conquering hero:

> *The signior is sound, safe, ready and dumb*
> *As ever was candle, carrot or thumb;*
> *Then away with these nasty devices, and show*
> *How you rate the just merits of Signior Dildo.*[46]

Another typically unsubtle stanza called upon the singer and minor mistress of Charles II, Mary Knight, to advocate the adaptability of the device to fill all openings:

> *He civilly came to the Cockpit one night,*
> *And proffered his service to fair Madam Knight.*
> *Quoth she, 'I intrigue with Captain Cazzo;*
> *Your nose in mine arse, good Signior Dildo!'*[47]

(*Cazzo* – a vulgar Italian word for 'penis')

Of course, not all talk of sex and its organs necessarily had to be crude or comical. Some of it strove to be instructive. 'The Clitoris is a sinewy hard body,' instructed Mrs Jane Sharp (practitioner in the Art of Midwifery above thirty years),

full of spongy and black matter within it, as it is in the side ligaments of a mans Yard, and this Clitoris will stand and fall as the Yard doth,

& makes women lustfull and take delight in copulation, and were it not for this they would have no desire nor delight, nor would they ever conceive.[48]

The delight must have been brain-blowing for Anne Montagu, who had married Sir Daniel Harvey, the ambassador to Turkey (1668–72). For the scheming Lady Harvey reputedly had some prodigious sexual apparatus: a protracted clitoris. Lady Harvey was active in the Country Party (opposing the court) and often sought to influence the king through the introduction of rival mistresses. One such attempt was made to dislodge rock-solid Nell Gwynne with Jenny Middleton, the young daughter of the court beauty Jane Middleton, who herself was once touted as a rival to Barbara Villiers in 1665. Jane's undoubted physical attraction ('one of the handsomest women in town' – Gramont; 'that famous & indeede incomparable beautifull lady' – Evelyn) was somewhat offset by her less than perfumed body odour, which given the culture of poor personal hygiene, must have been quite shocking to be worthy of note:

> Middleton, where'ver she goes
> Confirms the scandal of her toes.
> Quelled by the fair one's funky hose,
> Even Lory's forced to hold his nose.[49]

(*Funky* – stinking; *hose* – stockings; *Lory* – Laurence Hyde, later Earl of Rochester.)

Pepys, catching up on gossip, is told that 'the fine Mrs Middleton is noted for carrying about her a continued soure base Smell that is very offensive, especially if she be a hot.' Her daughter, Jenny, just to add some incestuous spice, was thought to have been fathered by the equally scheming Ralph Montagu, Lady Harvey's brother.[50]

And it was in the satire 'Cullen with his Flock of Misses', 1679 (also known as 'Colin'), that all this comes together:

> Next Midleton appear'd in view,
> Who strait was told of Montagu,
> Of baits from Hyde, of clothes from France,
> Of Armpits, Toes of Nauseance:
> At which the Court set up a Laughter,
> She never pleads but for her Daughter;
> A buxom Lass fit for the place,
> Were her father not in disgrace:
> Besides some strange, incestuous Stories
> Of Harvey and her long Clitories.[51]

As part of Lady Harvey's plan she first ingratiated herself with Nelly – a tactic observed by Henry Savile, who felt compelled to warn a mutual friend.

I will venture att one small piece of intelligence, because one who is allways your friend and sometimes (espeacially now) mine, has a part in it that makes her now laughed att and may one day turne to her infinite disadvantage. The case stands thus if I am rightly informed:- My Lady Hervey who allwayes loves one civil plott more, is working body and soule to bring Mrs Jenny Middleton into play. How dangerous a new one is to all old ones I need not tell you, but her Ladyship, having little opportunity of seeing Charlemayne upon her owne account, wheadles poor Mrs Nelly into supping twice or thrice a week at W C's and carryeing her with her; soe that in good earnest this poor creature is betrayed by her Ladyship to pimp against herselfe, for there her Ladyship whispers and contrives all matters to her owne ends, as the other might easily perceive if shee were not too giddy to mistrust a false friend. This I thought it good for you to know, for though your Lordship and I have different friends at court, yet the friendship betwixt us ought to make mee have an observing eye upon any accident that wound any friend of yours as this may in the end possibly doe her, who is so much your friend and who speakes obliging and charitable things of mee in my present disgrace. When all this is done I doe not see in my present condition how you can make her sensible of this, for to write to her were vain; but I fancy my Lady Southaske has soe much witt and cunning that you might give her some directions in this matter that might prevent any future ill accident. I leave all to your Lordship to whom alone of all men living I would write with this freedome, where prudence would have advised silence, but my zeale for your service and my trust in your secrecy overcome all other thoughts or considerations.'[52]

(*Charlemayne* – Charles II; *W C* – William Chiffinch, the king's groom of the backstairs, his trusted private secretary; *Lady Southaske* – Anne Hamilton, wife of Robert Carnegie, Earl of Southesk.)

That Nelly was being duped (too innocent and trusting, or 'giddy' in Savile's phrase) by Lady Harvey is also evident from a letter written for her to Laurence Hyde, in 1678, saying 'We are goeing to supe with the King at whithall & my lady Harvie'. Nelly, who may well have been illiterate, never wrote her own letters (or at least none of the ones that survive), which may explain Savile's point 'that to write to her were vain'.

In June 1678, Rochester replied with advice on how to love a king:

But to confess the Truth, my Advice to the Lady you wot of, has ever been this, Take your measures just contrary to your Rivals, live in peace with All the World, and easily with the King: Never be so Ill-natur'd to stir up his Anger against others, but let him forget the use of a Passion, which is never to do you good: Cherish his Love where-ever it inclines, and be assur'd you can't commit greater Folly than pretending to be jealous; but, on the contrary, with Hand, Body, Head and Heart and all the Faculties you have, contribute to his Pleasure all you can, and comply with his Desires throughout: Make Sport when you can, at other times help it. Thus, I have giv'n you an account how unfit I am to give you the Advice you propos'd: Besides this, you may judge, whether I was a good Pimp, or no.[53]

On matters, for the most part, more regular than love, midwife Sharp had some blunt words. Menstruation, she argued, was no problem for 'Lusty and Men-like women,' who could 'send them forth in three days, but idle persons and such as are always feeding will be seven or eight days about it'. A woman's 'month' was scarily taboo. But that didn't stop the fearless Rochester. The target of his 'On Mrs Willis' was Sue Willis, a (relatively speaking) high-class prostitute who serviced the outer court and ran a bawdy house in Lincoln's Inn Fields. She became involved with Lord Colepeper of Thoresby and gave him a daughter, Susan. The affair was chronicled in the satires:

> *Thence in a playhouse, where a goatish peer*
> *Feeling her cunt liked it, but not her.*[54]

But she obviously found rude acceptance among the glitterati. The playwright Sir George Etherege, while ambassador in Ratisbon, asked in a letter to 'make the kindest compliment you can for me to Mrs Willis, and let me know how she and her little family does.'[55]

She was also notorious enough to be the subject of a spitting Rochester squib on Willis, which included a shocking reference to 'the flowers' – or menstrual discharge:

> *Against the charms our ballocks have*
> *How weak all human skill is,*
> *Since they can make a man a slave*
> *To such a bitch as Willis!*
>
> *Whom that I may describe throughout,*
> *Assist me, bawdy powers;*
> *I'll write upon a double clout,*
> *And dip my pen in flowers.*

Her look's demurely impudent,
Ungainly beautiful;
Her modesty is insolent,
Her wit both pert and dull.

A prostitute to all the town,
And yet with no man friends,
She rails and scolds when she lies down,
And curses when she spends.

Bawdy in thoughts, precise in words,
Ill-natured though a whore,
Her belly is a bag of turds,
And her cunt a common shore.[56]

(*Shore* – sewer.)

It was the sexual revolution (or revulsion) of the Restoration that peeked at a pornographic prosperity. And it is no sop to coincidence that perhaps the most popular creative pastime – the theatre – should provide the most explicit proof of all. Unsurprisingly, the play *Sodom, or The Quintessence of Debauchery* – an everyday story of fucksters – was never given a public airing, but was restrained, steaming and sweating on the private page. Stage directions and dialogue that call for incest, bestiality, group sex, the insertion of a dildo in her queen by a lady of the court while the maids of honour do likewise to themselves, and a male chorus to play their harps with their penises, all dish up an indication that the Lord Chamberlain might not look too favourably upon a licence application.

This explicit sexual parody of the court of Charles II has been credited to the Earl of Rochester, although this has been doubted, vociferously so by some. One contemporary confirms suspicion of his involvement:

The Reader is to know also that a most wretched and obscene and scandalously infamous Play, not wholly compleated, passed some hands privately in MS, under the name of *Sodom*, and fathered upon the Earl (as most of this kind were, right or wrong, which came out at any time, after he once obtained the name of an excellent smooth, but withall a most lewd Poet) as the true author of it.[57]

Suffice to say that – as with 'Signior Dildo' – it is highly probable that he wrote it, but – spurred on by the graphic freedom of the piece – others contributed, possibly including Christopher Fishbourne. A surviving prologue spells out the pornographic purpose of the piece:

> *I do presume there are no women here,*
> *'Tis too much debauch'd for their fair sex I fear,*
> *Sure they will not in petticoats appear.*
> *And yet I am informed here's many a lass*
> *Come for to ease the itching of her arse,*
> *Damn'd pocky jades, whose cunts are as hot as fire,*
> *Yet they must see this play to increase desire,*
> *Before three acts are done of this our farce,*
> *They'll scrape acquaintance with a standing tarse,*
> *And impudently move it to their arse.*[58]

Sodom was never going to be a defining moment in theatrical history, but neither is it perhaps 'an obscene farce of no value'. The king of Sodom, Bolloxinian, (who opens the play with: 'Thus in the zenith of my Lust I Reigne/I drink to swive, and Swive to drink again') and his barren queen, Cuntigratia, are openly based on Charles II and Catherine of Braganza. Bolloxinian craves the love of his people, not their fear, and in so doing rules with not so much a rod of iron but his rod of flesh.[59]

This king's declaration of indulgence concerns not religious freedom, as with Charles II, but sexual licence, as he expresses his own boredom for the usual sexual conventions:

> *Let Conscience have its force of Liberty.*
> *I do proclaim that Buggery may be us'd*
> *O're all the Land, so Cunt be not abus'd.*[60]

General Buggeranthus, who is also the queen's lover, reports the soldiers' satisfaction with sodomy, who demonstrate it by buggering each other (upon pain of forfeiting two weeks' wages). We're treated to incest as Princess Swivea seduces her younger brother Prince Prickett, only to be interrupted by their mother, Cuntigratia, who then fights with the daughter over who should arouse the spent prince for a second session. And so on.

However, it's all not all-out 'shock, horror!' stuff. There are moments of tenderness and humour (the inevitable parody of Dryden's heroic verse). In the incest scene, Princess Swivea tempts her brother with sight of her vagina and, despite the matter-of-fact sexual brutality of the context, gently describes it as:

> *... the workhouse of the world's great trade;*
> *On this soft anvil all mankind was made.*[61]

The comic reality of their coupling (and the rhyming couplet) seek to undermine the grim immorality of it all:

PRICKETT: I'm in. I vow it is as soft as wool.
SWIVEA: Then thrust and move it up and down, you fool.[62]

Inevitably, there's a price to pay, tax included. The nation crumbles under such rule and the play ends in a cloud of smoke of fire and brimstone. An ending – and indeed a warning – about as subtle as what went before.

Similarly over the top, but dealing devilishly in exaggerated wit, is Rochester's 'A Ramble in St James's Park'. It begins,

> *Much wine had passed, with grave discourse*
> *Of who fucks who, and who does worse.*[63]

Then our poet takes the titled trip to cool his head and fire his heart. St James's Park was the equivalent of a modern-day lovers' lane of 'parked' cars and alfresco assignations: truly, the cruising fields where class, sex, age, religion and race matter not in an equality of pleasure. The images of the park, a Sodom of the night, do not bode sweetness:

> *Poor pensive lover, in this place*
> *Would frig upon his mother's face;*
> *Whence rows of mandrakes tall did rise*
> *Whose lewd tops fucked the very skies.*
> ...
> *And nightly now beneath their shade*
> *Are buggeries, rapes, and incests made.*
> *Unto this all-sin-sheltering grove*
> *Whores of the bulk and the alcove,*
> *Great ladies, chambermaids, and drudges,*
> *The ragpicker, and heiress trudges.*
> *Carmen, divines, great lords, and tailors,*
> *Prentices, poets, pimps, and jailers,*
> *Footmen, fine fops do here arrive,*
> *And here promiscuously they swive.*[64]

4

Barbara Villiers: a Lively and Demanding Woman

O Barbara, thy execrable name
Is sure embalmed with everlasting shame.[1]
– Charles Sackville, Lord Buckhurst, 'A Faithful Catalogue of
Our Most Famous Ninnies', 1683

That pattern of virtue, Her Grace of Cleveland,
Has swallowed more pricks than the ocean has sand.[2]
– John Wilmot, Earl of Rochester, 'Signior Dildo', c. December 1673

Her temper, greed, influence and promiscuity may have been questioned or pilloried, but nobody doubted that the auburn-haired and blue-eyed Barbara Villiers* was anything but beautiful. Pepys glutted his eyes on her and thought her a 'great beauty', so much so that while he disapproved of the king's sexual shenanigans, he secretly hoped that Charles would continue his affair with Barbara, just so he could get to see her more. He even dreamed about her:

> ... something put my last night's dream into my head, which I think is the best that ever was dreamed – which was, that I had my Lady Castlemayne in my armes and was admitted to use all the dalliance I desired with her, and then dreamed that this could not be awake but that it was only a dream. But that since it was a dream and that I took so much real pleasure in it, what a happy thing it would be, if when we are in our graves (as Shakespeere resembles it), we could dream, and dream but such dreams as this...[3]

---

* Barbara was referred to throughout her life by four different names; her birth name, Villiers (the one chosen for this short study); her married name, Palmer; her first fitted name, Castlemaine; and, finally, her fitted name in her own right, Cleveland.

He also proved mightily satisfied at her undergarments, which he happily happened upon in the privy garden at Whitehall. There he saw 'the finest smocks and linen petticoats of my Lady Castlemaynes, laced with rich lace at the bottomes, that ever I saw; and did me good to look upon them.'[4]

Sir John Reresby thought her 'the finest woeman of her age.' Although unable to speak her name (referring to her only as 'the lady'), even her sworn enemy, Edward Hyde, Earl of Clarendon, conceded her looks, calling Barbara 'a lady of youth and beauty.'[5]

Barbara Villiers was christened in St Margaret's Church, Westminster, on 27 November 1640, the daughter of Viscount Grandison and Mary Bayning. Edward Hyde thought Grandison a man of 'rare piety' and 'faultless'. Not the characteristics he would consider that the honourable man's daughter had inherited.[6]

Barbara's first love was Philip Stanhope, the dashingly arrogant Earl of Chesterfield, whose moral spire, in his youthful days at least, appeared somewhat crooked. At the ripe old age of sixteen (in Paris) he discovered the thrill of duelling, wounding his opponent. 'He had,' according to Gramont, 'a very agreeable face, a fine head of hair, an indifferent shape, and a worse air; he was, however, deficient in wit.' At seventeen, back in England, he married Lady Anne Percy – eldest daughter of the Earl of Northumberland – whose death from smallpox after childbirth, released (after an appropriate period of mourning, naturally) the errant earl to seek the scent again in Europe.[7]

So much so, that Lady Essex – 'sister to my first wife' – felt compelled to castigate him:

> ...though I live here where I know very little of what is done in the world, yet I hear so much of your exceeding wildness that I am confident I am more censible of it than any friend you have; you treat all the mad drinking lords, you sweare, you game, and commit all extravagances that are insident to untamed youths, to such a degree that you make yourself the talke of all places, and the wonder of those who thought otherwise of you and of all sober people, and the worst of all is I heare there is a handsom young lady (to both your shames) with child by you.[8]

Chesterfield's defence was succinct: 'Your ladyship knowes that the world is strangely given to lying.' He would maintain that Cromwell offered him a tempting package including one of the Lord Protector's own daughters – Frances – in addition to £20,000 and the command of his choice. However, Frances refused to be her father's political pawn and married the man she loved – one Robert Rich. In 1656, the earl almost married Mary Fairfax, daughter of Lord Fairfax. The banns were read three times at St Martin-in-the-Fields. Saved from a potentially loveless marriage, Mary promptly leaped out of her frying pan into the fire stoked by George Villiers, second Duke of Buckingham. Evidently, some women are magnetically drawn to misery.[9]

By 1657, Chesterfield had enchanted the young Barbara Villiers, who, despite her teenage love-crush, demonstrated the sexual teasing that would so guide her life. A letter from 'the Lady Anne Hambleton [Hamilton] and Mrs Villars' read invitingly:

My friend and I are just now abed together a contriving how to have your company this afternoune, if you deserve this favour, you will come and seek us at Ludgate hill a bout three o clock at Butlers Shop, where wee will expect you, but least we shall give you so much satisfaction at once, we will say no more, expect the rest when you see.[10]

Seemingly a man of means, while servicing Barbara and Anne, Chesterfield was also tinkering with Elizabeth Howard (the playwrighting Howard boys' sister, who would eventually marry John Dryden). Barbara also had another man in her life and somewhat emphasised the point by marrying him. Roger Palmer was born on 3 September 1634 at Dorney Court, near Windsor. He was educated at Eton and King's College, Cambridge, becoming a law student at Inner Temple in October 1656. His father, for one, feared for his happiness. An observer wrote that Sir James Palmer,

having strong surmises of the misfortunes that would attend this match, used all the arguments that paternal affection could suggest to dissuade his son from prosecuting his suit in that way, adding that if he was resolved to marry her he foresaw he should be one of the most miserable men in the world.[11]

Despite his father's astonishingly acute foresight, the couple were married on 14 April 1659 at the Church of St Gregory by St Paul's. Palmer was 24, Barbara 18. However, even with Palmer's ring around her finger, it was Chesterfield who still danced rings around her heart. But her husband was wise to it (and indeed would have to get used to it). She wrote to her lover in 1659:

My Lord

Since I saw you I have been at home, and I find the mounser in a very ill humer, for he says that he is resolved never to bring mee to Towne againe, and that nobody shall see mee when I am in the country, I would not have you come to day for that will displease him more, but send mee word presently what you would advise mee to doe, for I am ready and willing to gow all over the world with you, and I will obey your commands that am whilst I live, yours[12]

The teenage love-soused letters continued:

My dearest life

When I consider how seldom I have your company, it brings a melancholy upon mee that I cannot overcome. Pray when you wright to mee, send mee a long letter and tell me what you doe all day, Tell me how you divert your self, tell mee what you think, nay tell me what you dreame...but above all tell mee truly how I am in your thoughts[13]

Having caught smallpox, a besotted Barbara thought she would die and composed a letter she may well have considered to be her last:

My Dear Life

I have been this day extreamly ill, and the not hearing from you hath made mee much worse than otherwayes I should have been. The doctor doth believe mee in a desperat condition, and I must confess that the unwillingness I have to leave you makes mee not intertaine thoughts of deathe so willingly as otherwais I should. For there is nothing besides yourselfe that could make me desire to live a day; and, if I am never so happy as to see you more, yet the last words I will say shall be a praire for your happyness. And so I will live and dey loving you above all other things, who am,

My Lord,

Yours, &c.[14]

Barbara recovered from her smallpox with, importantly for her future fortune, her face unscarred. She would never err on the soppy side of romanticism again. Love was a business with sex as the dividend – and this woman was a major shareholder. With her private turmoil over, a nation's very *public* turmoil took her attention, as did the nation's king in exile. Roger Palmer had been 'promoting the royal cause at the utmost hazard of life and great loss of fortune' and had donated £1,000 to the king's cause, which he could ill afford, specially given he now had a 'gay wife' to keep.[15]

Roger had become a member of the Sealed Knot, a secret Royalist organisation set up around 1653 to coordinate conspiracy in England, believing that an effective restoration must be seen to come from within the realm: English hands must crown the king, not foreign money. Looking for a suitable messenger, eyes fell on the young wife of the reliable Palmer. It would be a task that would change her life beyond her wildest dreams.

Chesterfield, meanwhile, had been imprisoned for his part in a hugely incompetent Royalist uprising in August 1659. Having bought his way out of trouble, he immediately reacquainted himself with it, this time through duelling. Three months earlier, Chesterfield had bought a mare for 18 shillings from one Francis Wolley, son of a Hammersmith doctor. He had decided that he no longer wanted the beast and by chance passed Wolley in the street and demanded his money back. Unsurprisingly, the former owner refused and Chesterfield thus insisted on satisfaction. The duel was fought on 17 January 1660 at dawn 'on the backside of Mr Colby's house at Kensington'. Having cut Wolley's hand, Chesterfield then ran him through the heart. Such an outcome simply forced another return to the continent. Pepys commented on his way to Twickenham that 'at Kinsington, we understood how that my Lord Chesterfield had killed another gentleman about half an hour before and was fled.'[16]

Chesterfield would return to England aboard the *Naseby* with Charles II and land at Dover on 26 May 1660, once again a married man. Elizabeth Butler, daughter of the Duke of Ormond, exacted a feminine revenge on her sexually cavalier husband. It seems she treated him as shabbily as he had his previous lovers. Gramont tells us that Elizabeth was,

> one of the most agreeable women in the world: she had a most exquisite shape, though she was not very tall: her complexion was extremely fair, with all the expressive charms of a brunette: she had large blue eyes, very tempting and alluring: her manners were engaging: her wit lively and amusing; but her heart ever open to tender sentiments, was neither scrupulous in point of constancy nor nice in point of sincerity.[17]

When the inconstant Elizabeth died in July 1665 there were rumours that she had been poisoned by her jealous husband, who had tampered with the wine used for the sacrament. Chesterfield denied the rumours, claiming she died of the 'spotted feaver'.[18]

There has been speculation that the king spent the first night of his Restoration with his new mistress. Certainly, Barbara's first child was born almost nine months to the day (on 25 February 1661). Roger Palmer bravely asserted fatherhood and the child was known as Anne Palmer. However, she was said to have rather resembled the Earl of Chesterfield – whom Barbara didn't sack as her lover until 1661. In that year, he wrote to her, 'After so many years of service, fidelty and respect, to be banished for the first offence is very hard, espetially after my asking so many pardons.'

However, this shrewd businesswoman knew which side this piece of bread needed buttering. Charles did acknowledge Anne as his daughter but not until her marriage to Thomas Lennard, Lord Dacre and newly created Earl of Sussex, in 1674.

So, did Charles spend his first night in the soft embrace of Barbara? Certainly, as has been argued, it would have been in character (of both of them) to do so. However, on 13 July 1660, some six weeks after Charles's return, a late-working Pepys records his distraction by 'great doings of Musique' from the house next door where the King and the Duke of York were entertaining 'Madam Palmer, a pretty woman that they have a fancy to make her husband a cuckold.' Clearly, as far as he was aware, the king had not yet dallied with Barbara. Others were more suspicious:

> *But in his thirtieth year began to reign.*
> *In a slashed doublet then he came to shore,*
> *And dubbed poor Palmer's wife his Royal Whore.*[19]

Nonetheless, a man more reliable than gossip and 'bitcherings', Edward Hyde, said that Charles 'had lived in great and notorious familiarity from the time of his coming into England', which suggests that he was having a relationship with her at the time of the Restoration. It's feasible that she was having physical relationships with the three men. Regardless of who the true father was, Barbara knew who ultimately should own her daughter.[20]

Now she was established as the king's mistress, all that was missing was a title to honour her position. On 11 December 1661, the patent to create Roger Palmer Earl of Castlemaine and Baron Limerick was sealed. Although made nominally to Mr Palmer (perhaps as a reward for not being near his wife when the king was), the openness of Barbara's relationship with the king meant that nobody was fooled. The title could only pass on to the sons of Barbara (now, of course, the countess of Castlemaine herself); 'the reason,' commented Pepys, 'whereof everybody knows.' The titles actually became extinct with the death of Roger in 1705; Barbara's male heirs were destined to spin in ducal circles.[21]

The young mother and her erstwhile, hapless and hopeless husband had a house on King Street, Westminster. It was formerly owned by the regicide Major-General Edward Whalley, who had, in astute fear of his life, exiled himself to the New World. The house now belonged to Sir Edward Montagu. With Chesterfield banished, it wasn't long before her marriage was also effectively exiled, as Pepys informs us on 16 July 1662:

> This day I was told that my Lady Castlemayne (being quite fallen out with her husband) did yesterday go away from him with all her plate, Jewells and other best things; and is gone to Richmond to a brother of hers [it was actually her uncle, Colonel Edward Villiers, who lived in Richmond Palace]; which I am apt to think was a design to get out of town, that the King might come at her the better. But strange it is, how for her beauty I am willing to conster all this to the best and to pity her wherein it is to her hurt, though I know well enough she is a whore.[22]

The clearing out of valuables coupled with a dramatic storming out were tactics that Barbara would warm to. Pepys again, ten days later:

> Since that, she left her Lord, carrying away everything in the house; so much as every dish and cloth and servant but the porter. He is gone into discontent into France, they say, to enter a Monastery. [He travelled to France and Italy and in 1664 served in the Venetian navy] And now she is coming back to her house in Kingstreete.[23]

However, perhaps the split was more amicable, as they were witnessed together a month later on 'Whitehall bridge' – the public pier for Whitehall palace – to watch the scene as the queen came to town from Hampton Court. It also shows a rather different picture of Barbara, just being a mother.

> But that which pleased me best was that of my Lady Castlemayne stood against us upon a piece of White-hall – where I glutted myself with looking at her. But methought it was strange to see her Lord and her upon the same place, walking up and down without taking notice one of another; only, at first entry, he put off his hat and she made him a very civil salute – but afterwards took no notice one of another. But both of them now and then would take their child, which the nurse held in her armes, and dandle it.[24]

Indeed, it was a simple affection shared by Charles. 'But it seems,' wrote Pepys, '...that the King is mighty kind to these bastard children and at this day will at midnight to my Lady Castlemaynes nurses and take the child and dance it in his arms.'[25]

However, with his crown and country restored, England awaited the arrival of a legitimate heir. The king needed a queen, and Clarendon had arranged the match. A royal wedding was imminent, but amid the celebrations there was a whiff of trouble down King Street. Barbara was pleasure, Catherine of Braganza was politics, but could the two coexist? The nation celebrated Catherine's arrival with bonfires. Barbara, pregnant again, chose not to. Perhaps she knew that she and the queen were set to create a firework display of their own.

On 21 May 1662 Pepys recorded Lord Sandwich's housekeeper Sarah telling him:

> how the King dined at my Lady Castlemayne and supped every day and night the last week. And that the night that the bonefires were made for the joy of the Queenes arrivall, the King was there; but there was no fire at her door, though at all the rest of the doors almost in the street; which was much observed. And that the King did send for a pair of scales and weighed one another; and she, being with child, was said to be the heavyest. But she is now a most disconsolate creature, and comes not out of doors – since the King's going.[26]

Nonetheless, Barbara wouldn't be disconsolate for long. By the end of the year, the king's 'dalliance with my Lady Castlemayne being public everyday' showed which woman ruled the king. Barbara had even begun to threaten to have her second child at Hampton Court – where the king and queen were to spend their honeymoon. How far she now appeared from that sweet, love-struck, naïve teenager. Despite her threat, Barbara gave birth to Charles Palmer, afterwards Fitzroy (created Duke of Southampton in 1675), in her house at King Street. He was christened on 18 June in St Margaret's Church, Westminster (as was his mother 22 years before), attended by the king and Barbara's aunt, the Countess of Suffolk. This soothed the panic of a few days before, when the estranged Roger had had the boy christened a Catholic.[27]

The two women in the king's life would make the summer of 1662 a hot and scandalous one, resulting in the so-called Bedchamber Crisis. Charles seemed, on the political surface at least, contented with his new bride. He wrote to Clarendon on his wedding day (21 May 1662): 'If I have any skill in visiognomy, which I think I have, she must be as good a woman as ever was borne.' Four days later he confirmed his initial happiness: 'I cannot easily tell you how happy I think myselfe; and I must be the worst man living (which I hope I am not) if I be not a good husband. I am confident never two humours were better fitted together than ours are.'[28]

However, she was no match for Barbara. Catherine was described by the poet Edmund Waller as 'the best of queens' while the republican Andrew Marvell thought her an 'Ill natured little goblin'. Sir John Reresby noted that Catherine 'had nothing visible about her capable to make the King forget his inclinations to the Countess of Castlemaine.' Lord Dartmouth also reckoned that the king told Colonel William Legge (Dartmouth's father) that on seeing his bride for the first time 'thought they had brought him a bat instead of a woman'.[29]

Catherine's female entourage were 'for the most part old and ugly and proud, incapable of any conversation with persons of quality and a liberal education.' Evelyn thought the 'Portugueze Ladys' with their olive complexions to be 'sufficiently unagreable'. Typically, Gramont labelled them as 'six frights who called themselves maids of honour, and a duenna [a chief lady in waiting], another monster, who took the title of governess to those extraordinary beauties'. Amid such competition it is unsurprising that the queen was reckoned 'the handsomest Countenance of all the rest, & tho low of stature pretily shaped, languishing & excellent Eyes, her teeth wronging her mouth by stiking a little too far out: for the rest sweete & lovely enough.'[30]

Catherine also brought over 'six chaplains, four bakers, a Jew perfumer, and a certain officer, probably without an office, who called himself her highness's barber'. Catherine's 'Ladys' counselled her to adopt a fierce Catholic Portuguese countenance that would serve as a model for English women to follow. They discouraged her from speaking in English or wearing English fashions. Indeed, the English tailor sent to her in Portugal was unceremoniously stitched up by his unwelcoming hosts. He wasn't even permitted an audience with the queen-to-be, let alone an opportunity to measure her. Catherine and her attendant ladies all wore farthingales (hooped petticoats), which even the sombre Evelyn thought 'monstrous'.[31]

Catherine's mother had warned her about Barbara and she arrived in England resolved 'never [to] suffer the lady who was so much spoken of to be in her presence'. However, Charles had other ideas and a horse-drawn resolve of his own. At a reception held for the new queen, Charles led in his mistress and presented her to Catherine. Initially unawares, Catherine 'received her with the grace as she had done the rest'. However, the instant she realised who this woman was 'her colour changed, and tears gushed out of her eyes, and her nose bled, and she fainted.' Some reaction. The marital lines were quickly and obstinately drawn. For Catherine it was a matter of principle; for Charles it was a matter of how he was viewed at court: governor or governed. Both, they thought, would have their way, but only one could win. Charles's fancy French heels only dug in the deeper as the Portuguese failed to deliver Catherine's dowry in full. The promised cash payment of £40,000 (nearly £28 million in today's money) was replaced with an offer of 'sugars and other commoditys and bills of exchange'.[32]

Charles then upped the ante. Not only should his queen treat his mistress with respect, but she must also appoint Barbara one of her ladies of the bedchamber. Catherine was having none of it. As Pepys observed:

> I hear that the Queene is prick her out of the list presented her by the King, desiring that she might have that favour done her or that he would send her from whence she came; and that the King was angry and the Queene discontented a whole day and night upon it; but that the King hath promised to have nothing to do with her hereafter. But I cannot believe that the King can fling her off so, he loving her too well.[33]

Barbara's elevation to countess, in itself, argued Charles, meant that she was eligible for higher preferment and he would see it done. Or rather he would see that Catherine saw it done, because such an appointment would be in the gift of the queen. Charles tried numerous lines of attack on Catherine's intransigence: ignoring her, wooing and caressing her, and using 'threats and menaces, which he never intended to put into execution.' He even went as far to claim to Catherine 'that he had not had the least familiarity with [Barbara] since her majesty's arrival, nor would ever after be guilty of it again, but would live always with her majesty in all fidelity for conscience sake.' And this during which time Barbara had moved into lodgings at the palace and was paraded in the presence of the queen with 'the king in continual conference with her.' Catherine found that such promises – if she believed them – only antagonised a fury out of her, which in turn, met with an equally furious entrenchment.[34]

Ignoring his queen, Charles 'sought ease and refreshment in that jolly company, to which in the evenings he grew every day more indulgent, and in which there were some who desired rather to inflame than pacify his discontent.' The king's companions paraded memories of his own maternal grandfather, Henri IV of France, who brought his mistresses to court and 'obliged his own wife the queen to treat them with grace and favour; gave the highest titles of honour, to draw reverence and application to them from all the court and all the kingdom.'[35]

Henriette-Anne, his 'Minette', who exercised great sibling influence, wrote to Charles from Paris on 22 July 1662, commenting on the much talk of Catherine's distress and, unusually, sides against her brother: '...to speak frankly I think she has only too good reason for her grief.' Charles tried a new route to satisfaction. He ordered his chancellor, Clarendon, whom the queen seemingly had regard for, to advise her of the error of her ways. Despite Clarendon's stoic opposition, Charles argued that all this was his own doing: he, the king, was the architect of Barbara's shame and the cause of her husband's leaving her. Therefore, her appointment to an office of honour would redress the balance. He also added, menacingly, that if the appointment was not made he would involve himself with many mistresses to spite Catherine further.[36]

Clarendon, with a heart as heavy as his stomach, undertook the king's bidding. He despaired of Charles's increasing debauchery and he certainly harboured no affection or respect for Barbara, who, in a return with knobs on, hated Clarendon 'mortally'. The awkwardness of the 'delicate' situation increased as Clarendon's first conciliatory effort succeeded only in causing 'such a torrent of tears'. It was amid tears the next day that Catherine said 'she did not think that she should have found the king engaged in his affection to another lady.'[37]

Clarendon, believing headway was at last being made, saw it dashed following the king-and-queen of all public shouting matches that shocked the court, providing a healthy carcass for the gossip vultures. Charles's demeanour also worried Clarendon. The king had been troubled by 'the conflict' at first and ached with sadness, but was now more carefree, full of good humour and 'without any clouds in his face'. However, there was little humour in the king that then rounded on Clarendon. In a fierce letter to him, Charles reminded his chancellor: 'You know how true a friende I have been to you', referring no doubt to his support of the vulnerable Clarendon following the secret marriage of his daughter to James, Duke of York. It was unequivocally payback time. The letter barely seeks to veil the threat: if you want to keep your public office then bring Catherine into line:

> ...whosoever I find use any endeavour to hinder this resolution of myne (excepte it be only to myselfe), I will be his enimy to the last moment of my life. You know how true a friende I have been to you.

If you will oblige me eternally, make this businesse as easy as you can, of what opinion soever you are of; for I am resolved to go through with this matter, lett what will come on it; which againe I solemnly sweare before Almighty God. Therefore, if you desire to have the continuance of my friendship, meddle no more with this businesse, except it be to beare down all false and scandalous reports, and to facilitate what I am sure my honour is so much concerned in: and whosoever I finde to be my Lady Castlemaine's enimy in this matter, I do promise, upon my word, to be his enimy as long as I live...[38]

However, any more painful soul-searching was averted by an unexpected and complete change of heart. Catherine 'on a sudden let herself fall first to conversation and then to familiarity, and even in the same instant to a confidence with the lady; was merry with her in public, talked kindly of her, and in private used nobody more friendly.' Catherine's immaculate conversion was astonishing. Perhaps she realised this was to be her lot and she had better make the best of it. Life would certainly be more tolerable and pleasant if she succumbed to the king's whims and wishes rather than confront them.[39]

Catherine, so long the Portuguese square, squeezed herself into the court circle. She ditched the farthingales (preferred because they kept men at a distance) for more comely English fashions – to the extent of even wearing a dress that exposed her breasts. Her dignified reticence at receiving the king was retired in favour of running up to him and embracing him. She became hooked on cards and gambling. Save for chalking up a string of lovers, the transformation was complete.

With the queen embracing England, the country returned the affection. Thus, Barbara's status as *maîtresse de titre* made her increasingly unpopular. In St James's Park, accompanied only by a maid and a little page, Barbara was confronted by,

three noblemen (so at least they seemed from their garments) who wore masks and addressed to her the harshest and bitterest reprimand that can well be imagined. They even went so far as to remind her that the mistress of Edward IV [Jane Shore] died on a dunghill, scorned and abandoned by everybody. You can well imagine that the time seemed long to her, for the park extends over a large space from Regnard's to the Pavilion. As soon as she was in her bedroom she fainted. The King being informed of this ran to her, caused all the gates to be shut and all the people found in the park to be arrested. Seven or eight persons who happened thus to be caught were brought in, but could not be identified. They have told the tale; it was wished to hush up the affair, but I believe the secret will not easily be kept.[40]

With such physical threats, Barbara sought some comfort for her soul. In December 1663 Barbara, for once following her estranged husband, became a Catholic. Upset at her conversion, 'the King has been asked by the relations of the lady to interfere and prevent her; but he answered that, as for the soul of ladies, he did not meddle with that.'[41]

Charles concerned himself with the flesh that housed the soul. As did Barbara. And together they were rumoured to be salaciously adventurous. Pepys was told that,

> my Lady Castlemayne rules him, who hath all the tricks of Aretin that are practised to give pleasure – in which he is too able, hav[ing] a large prick; but that which is the unhappiness is that, as the Italian proverb says, *Cazzo dritto non vuolt consiglio.* If any of the Sober counsellors give him good advice and move him to anything that is to his good and honour, the other part, which are his counsellors of pleasure, take him when he is with my Lady Castlemayne and in humour of delight and then persuade him that he ought not to hear or listen to the advice of those old dotards . . . [42]

(*Aretin* – Pietro Aretino (1492–1556), who wrote *Postures,* a series of obscene sonnets accompanying pornographic illustrations by the Italian painter Giulio Romano; *Cazzo dritto non vuolt consiglio* – 'a man with an erection needs no advice'.)

Indeed, between them (if not always together) they proved fabulously productive. Charles would eventually acknowledge the first five of Barbara's six children: Anne, born 25 February 1661; Charles Fitzroy, baptised 18 June 1662; Henry Fitzroy, born 20 September 1663; Charlotte Fitzroy, born 5 September 1664; and George Fitzroy, born 28 December 1665. Barbara's sixth child, also Barbara and born 23 August 1670, was thought to be the daughter of John Churchill. All the acknowledged males were granted titles: Charles became the Duke of Southampton; Henry, the Duke of Grafton; and George, the Duke of Northumberland.

As the decade progressed, so Barbara's influence waned, but she more than kept pace with the king in the chase for infidelity. Charles declared that George would be the last child he would acknowledge. In July 1667, with the great lady cavorting none too discreetly with young

Henry Jermyn and seemingly pregnant again, John Fenn, paymaster to the navy treasury, told Pepys,

> that the King and my Lady Castlemayne are quite broke off and she is gone away, and is with child and swears the King shall own it; and she will have it christened in the Chapel at White-hall as, and owned for the King's as other Kings have done; or she will bring it into White-hall gallery and dash the brains of it out before the King's face.[43]

The scandal kept the diarist busy the next day also. Barbara, he writes, 'is with child, and the King says he did not get it; with that she made a slighting "puh!" with her mouth and went out of the house' to stay with Sir Daniel Harvey (whose wife was said to be mistress to the Duke of York) at his house in Covent Garden. There she would remain until the king visited her 'to pray her' return to court. Characteristically refusing to back down, Barbara 'told the King that whoever did get [her child], he should own it'. Pepys tried to make sense of it all: 'the bottom of the quarrel is this: she is fallen in love with young Jermin, who hath of late lain with her oftener then the King and is now going to marry my Lady Falmouth [he didn't]. The King, he is mad at her entertaining Jermin, and she is mad at Jermin's going to marry from her, so they are all mad; and,' Pepys adds wearily, 'thus the kingdom is governed.'[44]

The next day the story is confirmed by a slightly inebriated Mr Cooling, secretary to the Lord Chamberlain, 'in the plainest words in the world.' Cooling reports that 'the King hath declared that he did not get the child of which she is conceived at this time, he having not as he says lain with her this half year,' adding that 'for a good while the King's greatest pleasure hath been with his fingers, being able to do no more.' Nonetheless, Barbara told Charles: '"God damn me! but you shall own it." It seems he is jealous of Jermin and she loves him...and he, it seems, hath lain with her from time to time continually, for a good while.'[45]

Henry Jermyn was but the beginning. Barbara's lovers would include the actor Charles Hart, John Churchill (the future Duke of Marlborough), the playwright William Wycherley, the English ambassador in France, Ralph Montagu, and, for a bit of rough, the rope dancer Jacob Hall.

In addition, it was rumoured that Barbara's third child and second son, Henry Fitzroy, was fathered by the handsome Captain James Hamilton, a groom of the bedchamber:

Own to the world her brat's not thine at all,
For father Hamilton shines through him all,
His impudence, his falsehood, and ill nature,
Each inward vice and each outward feature;
True Hamilton in every act and look,
Yet to record thy blindness made a duke.[46]

Others believed that it was Charles Berkeley (1630–65), created
Viscount Fitzhardinge in 1663 and Earl of Falmouth in 1664. He was, it was
said, to have been made a duke but died in action at the Battle of
Lowestoft. Pepys was told by Captain Robert Ferrer(s) and Mr Howe that
they had 'often seen through my Lady Castlemayne's windows, seen her go
to bed and Sir Ch. Berkeley in the chamber all the while with her.' The
diarist, on 20 January 1664, is also kept abreast of the rumours circling
Barbara's increasing promiscuity: 'That the King doth not openly disown
my Lady Castlemaine, but that she comes to Court; but that my Lord Fitz-
harding and the Hambletons [James, George and Anthony Hamilton],
and sometimes my Lord Sandwich they say have their snaps at her.'[47]
A keen patron of the theatre, Barbara, upset at Charles's
relationships with the actresses Moll Davies and Nelly Gwynne, sought
revenge by bedding the actor Charles Hart – who had previously been
Nelly's lover. The satirists were not slow to comment:

Then there's Castlemaine,
That prerogative Queane:
If I had such a bitch, I would spay her:
Shee swives, like a stoate,
Goes to 't hand and foote,
Level-Coyle with a prince and a player.[48]

(*Spay* – to remove the ovaries and destroy the reproductive power; *swives* – has sexual
intercourse.)

Of all the sexually charged targets for satirists Barbara became the
wide-open bull's-eye. One attack, devilishly titled 'Lampoon', dates
from March 1676 and almost serves as a résumé. It opens:

Cleveland was doubtless to blame
On such a he-whore to dote,
Who, wanting both wit and shame,
Betrayed her with a laced coat.

(*Laced coat* – a uniform coat with lace and gold braid.)

The he-whore – John Churchill (1650–1722) – became Barbara's lover in about 1670, after she had been created the Duchess of Cleveland, as a sort of long-service award. The impression handed down has been that of the ageing has-been (Barbara) seducing the young innocent (Churchill). And yet Barbara was about thirty (and unlike her fortune, well preserved) and Churchill out of his teens and an accomplished – if tanned and handsome – operator. She treated him lavishly. And he performed slavishly. One classic and credible story relates how the Duke of Buckingham, knowing that the mistress and her sex pet were mid-liaison, impressed upon the king the need to visit Barbara. On his arrival, the panic-stricken young ensign not only leaped out of Barbara's bed but the bedchamber window also and made his rapid way to freedom, only to hear the comically cynical king call from the open window, 'I forgive you, for you only do it for your bread!'[49]

Barbara gave him £5,000 for clothes but the financially canny Churchill instead used the money to buy himself a £500 annuity from Lord Halifax – a deal that was regarded as 'the foundation of his subsequent fortune.' Indeed, Churchill, for whom money so easily came, did not so easily let it go. He could, according to the Earl of Chesterfield, 'refuse more gracefully than other people could grant'. On being mistaken for Churchill (who by then had been created Duke of Marlborough), Lord Peterborough is said to have replied, 'I can convince by two reasons that I am not the Duke. In the first place, I have only five guineas in my pocket, and in the second, they are heartily at your service.'[50]

Churchill's meanness and overgrown ingratitude combined one evening to snub and humiliate his bankrolling lover. High gambling was infectious at court (although the king had little taste for it himself) and card games drew the classiest packs of players. The French game basset (in which players gamble on the identity of the next card) was top dog. One night, Barbara, no stranger to losing heavily, in a game with, several people,

> lost all her money & begged the favour of [Churchill], in a very civil manner, to lend her twenty pieces; which he absolutely refused, though he had a thousand on the table before him, and told her coldly, the bank never lent any money. Not a person in the place blamed him but in their hearts: as to the Duchess's part, her resentment burst out into a bleeding at her nose, and breaking of her lace; without which aid, it is believed, her vexation killed her upon the spot.[51]

The means by which Barbara came by the money to give to Churchill the £5,000 snack has long been considered unsavoury. It is said that Sir

Edward Hungerford, dissolute, rakish, wealthy and seventy years old, wanted a slice of the infamously juicy Cleveland pie. He was offered it on a plate, but at a cost. Ten thousand pounds' cost, in fact. Cash. Upfront. Which was how Barbara was when she told the doddering fool that he had been tricked and that the fumbling assignation in a darkened room was not with her after all. But, remarkably, once again she offered the service as originally agreed, but only for a further £10,000. The two stories are married by Alexander Pope in 'Sermon Against Adultery' *or* 'Sober Advice from Horace':

> *Who of ten thousand gulled her Knight,*
> *Then asked ten thousand for another night;*
> *The gallant too, to whom she paid it down,*
> *Lived to refuse the mistress half-a-crown.*[52]

As well as poaching the theatre for one of its finest actors, Charles Hart, Barbara also bagged herself one of the finest playwrights – William Wycherley, as 'The Lampoon' commemorates:

> *But lechery so oversways her,*
> *She had no discretion at all;*
> *The cunt that first raised her*
> *Was now the cause of her fall.*
>
> *Churchill's delicate shape*
> *Her dazzling eyes had struck,*
> *But her wider cunt did gape*
> *For a more substantial fuck.*
>
> *Which made her in pattens, they say,*
> *To the Temple so often to trudge,*
> *Where brawny Wycherley lay,*
> *Who performed the part of a drudge.*
>
> *'Twas bad in such as did know it*
> *To go about to betray her.*
> *Why might she not fuck with a poet,*
> *When his Majesty fucks with a player?*

(*Pattens* – clogs, worn to keep shoes off wet ground; *the Temple* – Wycherley lived in Inner Temple: William Oldys in a manuscript note to Gerard Langbaine's *Account of the English Dramatick Poets*, 1691, comments that Barbara 'used to visit Wycherley at his chambers in the Temple, dressed like a country maid in a straw hat, with pattens on, a basket or box in her hand, etc.'; *drudge* – to toil at distasteful work; *player* – Nell Gwynne.)

Wycherley's first play, *Love in a Wood, or, St James's Park* had opened around March 1671. In the first act, he makes solid use of Mary Knepp's excellent voice as her character, My Lady Flippant ('an affected Widow in distress for a Husband, though still declaiming against marriage'), sings Mr Ranger (played by Charles Hart) a new song against marriage:

> *A spouse I do hate,*
> *For either she's false or she's jealous;*
> *But give us a Mate,*
> *Who nothing will ask us, or tell us.*
>
> *She stands on no terms,*
> *Nor chaffers by way of Indenture,*
> *Her love for your Farms;*
> *But takes her kind man at a venture*
>
> *If all prove not right,*
> *Without an Act, Process or Warning,*
> *From wife for a night,*
> *You may be divorc'd in the morning.*
>
> *When Parents are Slaves,*
> *There Bratts cannot be any other;*
> *Great Wits, and great Braves,*
> *Have always a Punk to their Mother.*[53]

It was this song that proved the catalyst in Barbara and Wycherley's relationship, if an entry in John Dennis's *Original Letters*, published in 1721, is to be believed.

As Mr Wycherley was going thro' Pall-mall toward St James's in his Chariot, he met [Barbara] in hers, who thrusting half her Body out of the Chariot, cry'd out aloud to him, 'You, Wycherley, you are a Son of a Whore', at the same time laughing aloud and heartily.[54]

Barbara was referring to the last verse above, although it took a surprised Wycherley a short time to make sense of the reference. When he did so, he asked 'his Coachman to drive back and over take the Lady. As soon as he got over-against her' the following exchange took place:

– Madam, you have been pleased to bestow a Title on me which generally belongs to the Fortunate. Will your Ladyship be at the Play to Night?

– Well, what if I am there?

– Why then I will be there to wait on your Ladyship, tho' I disappoint a very fine Woman who has made me an Assignation.

– So, you are sure to disappoint a Woman who has favour'd you for one who has not.

– Yes, if she who has not favour'd me is the finer Woman of the two. But he who will not be constant to your Ladyship, till he can find a finer Woman, is sure to die your Captive.

And then, apparently, she blushed (some achievement or some embellishment, you figure) and bade her coachman to drive off. 'In short,' continues Dennis, 'she was that Night in the first row of...the King's Box in Drury Lane, and Mr Wycherley in the Pit under her, where he entertained her during the whole Play. And this...was the beginning of the Correspondence between these two Persons, which afterwards made a great Noise in the Town.'[55]

In the printed version of the play, Wycherley dedicated it 'To Her Grace The Dutchess of Cleavland' and followed it with the usual flattering epistle, which, comparatively speaking, was almost reserved. He offers,

> ...your Grace my humble acknowledgements for the favours I have receiv'd from you: This, I say, is the Poets Gratitude, which in plain English, is only Pride and Ambition; and that the world might know your Grace did me the honour to see my Play twice together; yet perhaps the Enviers of your Favour will suggest it 'twas in Lent, and therefore for your Mortification; then, as a jealous Author, I am concern'd not to have your Graces Favours lessen'd, or rather, my reputation; and to let them know, you were pleas'd, after that, to command a Copy from me of this Play; the way without Beauty and Wit, to win a poor Poets heart.[56]

Another anecdote is captured neatly by the sometime poet Sir Frances Fane:

> The King being jealous of the Duchess of Cleveland, and having intelligence by her maid that she and Mr Wycherley lay at Mrs Knight's, the famous singer, in Pall Mall that night, early the next morning went thither and found him muffled in his cloak upon the stair head, and then went into the chamber where he found the duchess in bed, whom he asked what she made there, who replied it was the beginning of Lent and she retired hither to perform her devotions. The King replied, Very likely, and that was your confessor I met on the stairs.[57]

It was all very well mixing it with the choicest ingredients from the arts world, but sometimes Barbara just wanted a basic meat and two veg. And they weren't served up much better than the supple rope dancer Jacob Hall. As 'The Lampoon' notes:

> *Jermyn should not be forgot,*
> *Who used to fuck her before;*
> *From good King Charles the Second*
> *To honest Jacob Hall.*

> *But now she must travel abroad*
> *And be forced to frig with the nuns*
> *For giving our sovereign lord*
> *So many good buttered buns.*

(*Travel abroad* – Barbara moved to France on account of her sons' education and was widely thought to be entering a nunnery; however, she really moved to live in the greater splendour her money could buy; her most religious experience probably came when she apparently bedded François de Harley de Chapvalon, the Archbishop of Paris; *frig* – masturbate; *buttered buns* – well-occupied prostitutes.)

Tightrope performers were all the rage at Restoration fairs, and 'Jacob Hall', said Gramont,

> was at that time in vogue in London; his strength and agility charmed in public, even to a wish to know what he was in private; for he appeared, in his tumbling dress, to be quite of a different make, and to have limbs very different from the fortunate Jermyn. The tumbler did not deceive Lady Castlemaine's expectations, if report may be believed; and as intimated in many a song, much more to the honour of the rope-dancer than of the countess; but she despised all these rumours, and only appeared still more handsome.[58]

Indeed, Charles, possibly irritated at her dalliance with the awkward Henry Jermyn, once suggested to Barbara that she,

> bestow her favours upon Jacob Hall, the rope-dancer, who was able to return them, than lavish money upon Jermyn to no purpose, since it would be more honourable to pass for the mistress of the first than for the very humble servant of the second.

She did not take this advice well:

The impetuosity [commented Gramont] of her temper broke forth like lightning. She told him, 'that it very ill became him to throw out such reproaches against one, who, of all the women in England, deserved them the least; that he had never ceased quarrelling thus unjustly with her, ever since he had betrayed his own mean low inclinations; that to gratify such a depraved taste as his, he only wanted such silly things as Stewart, Wells, and that pitiful strolling actress [Nell Gwynne], whom he had lately introduced into society'.[59]

However, it appears that Hall was more than a one-trick pony (professionally, at least). According to his poster, he also performed a 'variety of rare feats of activity and agility of body' such as 'doing of somersets and flipflaps, flying over thirty rapiers and over several men's heads, and also flying through several hoops'. A Restoration Evel Knievel, no less. Pepys was certainly impressed with him, considering his show 'mighty worth seeing' and Hall himself 'a mighty strong man'. Barbara, suitably impressed, put Hall on the payroll: it was money for the old rope dancer.[60]

At around the same time, so the story goes, Barbara had treated a young civil servant, correspondent and future undersecretary of state, John Ellis, 'to be where Charles had been before.' Unfortunately, he took it upon himself to boast manfully of his conquest, and Barbara in turn (and in vengeance) took it upon herself to hire thugs to leave Ellis somewhat less than manful. The castration was uncut from Pope's 'Advice Against Adultery' *or* 'Sober Advice from Horace':

> *What pushed poor Ellis on th' imperial whore?*
> *'Twas but to be where Charles had been before.*
> *The fatal steel unjustly was apply'd,*
> *When not his lust offended, but his pride:*
> *Too hard a penance for defeated sin,*
> *Himself shut out, and Jacob Hall let in.*[61]

Thankfully, Barbara's frantic appetite did not diminish over time. Bishop Gilbert Burnet, no friend, noted that he 'never heard any commend her but for her beauty, which was very extraordinary and has been now of long continuance.' In 1684, she was in her 43rd year. Age, the old warhorse, was having a rare old battle to wither her. In Restoration England, if you made it to thirty you were very likely to be tumbling helplessly over the hill; but, with Barbara's beauty, age had a mountain to climb. Stubbornly handsome, she retained all her other well-known characteristics, the calendar quenching nothing of her thirst for sexual and financial extravagance.[62]

A friend to the theatre and a patron (knowing wink to the audience) to its players, she produced one more act of defiance that soon played as a remarkably mellow piece. A bedroom farce that became a quiet night in. And it ran and ran. In a theatrical world that bludgeoned its characters with names that overemphasised their personalities (Dapperwit, Flippant, *et al.*) the actor Cardell Goodman could not have misappropriated – and, boy, did he know about that – a more inappropriate name. Cardell was no good man. But Barbara was no good woman, either. Could this be dream casting?

Goodman's background was a touch gentlemanly for a player. His father, also Cardell Goodman, a parson, died a few months after Cardell Jr's birth in late 1653. He appeared to be a bright child and at thirteen was admitted to his father's old college, St John's, Cambridge. But the young scholar yearned for adventure not to be found in dusty libraries, and around November 1672 left the comfort of Cambridge for the magic of the metropolis. By the following spring, the name of Cardell Goodman was added to the list of the king's company of comedians.*

The stage was set – metaphorically, at least, as a fire had destroyed the King's House (today's Theatre Royal, Drury Lane) in Brydges Street in January 1672. In attempts to contain the fire, houses nearby were blown up – a policy that resulted in the death of the young actor, Richard Bell. A letter dated 25 January 1672 related the events:

> 'A fire at the King's play-house between 7–8 on Thursday evening last, which half burned down the house and all their scenes and wardrobe; and all the houses from the Rose Tavern on Russell Street on that side of the way to Drury Lane are burned and blown up, with many in Vinegar Yard; £20,000 damage. The fire began under the stairs where Orange Moll keeps her fruit. Bell the Player was blown up.'[63]

The homeless company moved to the rival Duke's Company's old haunt, the Lincoln's Inn Fields theatre, which had reverted to its former life as a tennis court. The company opened there on 26 February 1672 – with a revival of the popular Beaumont and Fletcher's *Wit without Money* – and would stay for two years. The Brydges Street theatre, designed by Sir Christopher Wren, would not reopen until 26 March 1674.

However, it would be three years before Goodman, the new hireling and spear carrier, would take lead roles. He had to supplement his very

---

*'Comedians' in Restoration England was a general term for actors

meagre income but had chosen to do so by taking to highway robbery. Fortunately, as the king's servants, the players more often than not received their master's pardon. A warrant dated 18 April 1681 was issued as a 'Pardon unto Cardell Goodman of all Felonies, Robberies upon the Highways or elsewhere, Burglaries, Assaults, Batteries and Woundings, whatsoever by him committed before the 16th day of this instant April and of all Indictments, Prosecution, Convictions, Outlawries, Paines, penalties and forfeitures incurred by reason thereof.'[64]

By the time Barbara fell into bed with him, the two rival theatre companies had amalgamated and moved into the King's House. Goodman might have been Barbara's idea of a leading man, but he remained steadfastly B-list, although he did excel in the lead for *Othello* and, in particular, as Alexander, in Nathaniel Lee's *The Rival Queens, or The Death of Alexander the Great.* Ironically, it was a role first premiered by Barbara's other actor-lover, Charles Hart, on 17 March 1677. A contemporary described how Hart performed Alexander 'with such Grandeur and Agreeable Majesty, That one of the Court was pleas'd to Honour him with this Commendation; That Hart might teach any King on Earth how to Comport himself.' And yet it would be Goodman who would be 'known' as Alexander the Great in tribute to his later interpretation.[65]

Indeed, Thomas Betterton, 'the greatest figure of the Restoration stage' commented on Goodman's 'agreeable smoothness' in speaking voice:

> I remember, among many, an Instance in the Madness of Alexander the Great, in Lee's Play. Mr Goodman always went through it with all the Force the Part requir'd, and yet made not half the Noise as some who succeeded him; who were sure to bellow it out in such a manner that their Voice would fail them the End, and lead them to such a languid and ennervate Hoarseness...[66]

Although he was only 31 when he fell under Barbara's direction, his acting career had petered out. He would perform occasionally and, as the story goes, did so once free of charge for the benefit of the theatre's hirelings, whose daily plight he knew only too well. He agreed, naturally, to resurrect his greatest role. And a special lady was to be guest of honour. The dowager Queen Catherine had arrived and settled down to enjoy the performance. However, there was a delay. She was not the special guest Goodman had in mind. Agitated at this disrespect, Catherine sent a message for the play to begin immediately. 'Damme,' said the leading man, 'I care not if the playhouse be filled with queens from top to bottom. I will not tread the stage until my duchess comes.'

With timing decidedly more immaculate than her reputation, Barbara entered the auditorium and saved a tricky situation.[67]

Given Barbara's propensity for handsome or rich or well-equipped or fashionable or influential men (or any combination thereof), it is surprising that she had it bad for Goodman. The only criterion he could have fulfilled would have been handsome. And yet some of the satires make play of his rank ugliness. One ran:

> *Pardon me, Bab, if I mistake his Race,*
> *Which was Infernal sure, for tho' he has*
> *No cloven foot, he has a cloven face.*[68]

While another observed:

> *Goodman the Thief Swears 'tis all Womens Lots*
> *To dote upon his Ugliness and Pox.*[69]

It was standard practice for actresses to strut the stage to attract the attentions of the beaux and fops in hope of capturing hearts (with money, if not marriage, to follow). It was less usual for actors to find themselves kept men. But Goodman now counted himself a member of that exclusive club. Barbara 'appointed' her personal stallion Gentleman of the Horse. He attended the duchess on her travels, commanded her staff of grooms and footmen, and in addition to all board and lodgings received an annual salary: 'Goodman had a good Allowance to live upon from the Dutchess.'[70]

It was clearly an attempt to instil a sniff of respectability into the proceedings. But it just put people's noses out of joint. The anonymous author of 'The Dutchess of Cleveland's Memorial' smelled a rancid rodent:

> *Poor Rowley being dead and gone*
> *I howl'd and had Remorse Sir,*
> *To comfort me scum Goodman came*
> *Whom I made Master Horser.*[71]

Satires instinctively label their subjects. Goodman is often referred to as a 'rake-hell', 'ugly', a 'pock-fret' and so on. However, only once is he referred to as 'scum Goodman'. Nonetheless, once was clearly widespread enough for Thomas Macaulay, in his *History of England*, to conclude safely that the rich lady's plaything was 'popularly called Scum Goodman'. Thus is Historical damnation guaranteed. In this respect

he, at least, has a dead soul-mate in Barbara, who in the following
'Tunbridge Satyr' is depicted as Aurelia:

> *There with contempt and scorn behold*
> *The proud Aurelia now grown old*
> *The quondam great Sultana of the land.*
> *So mean her spirits are now grown*
> *Stoop to a dunghill from a Throne*
> *Now walk with Rakehell Goodman hand in hand.*
> *Beside so Ugly he would be*
> *Ador'd in China for a Diety.*
> *Unbridled lust in this Example View*
> *What will it not provoke some Women to do.*[72]

A kept man, he found life good. Cardell was at last dealt a fine hand.
He must have felt untouchable. But in high places this low life was an
unwelcome chancer. They wanted him disgraced and dismissed and
sought suitably damning information. In 1681, a grand Italian canary
was ready to sing. Alexander Amadei, 'a Hebrew by the grace of God
turned Christian', made the astounding claim that Goodman had
attempted to recruit him to poison two of Barbara's (and thus the
king's) sons – the Dukes of Grafton and Northumberland. The
principal secretary of state, Robert Spencer, Earl of Sunderland,
instructed Lord Chief Justice Jeffreys to 'examine this whole matter'.[73]

On 23 October 1681, Goodman faced Jeffreys in court. An observer
commented that the defendant was very well dressed (noting that 'it is
reported that the D. of Cleveland keeps him') and 'talked boldly, but
the Lord Chief Justice was sharp upon him, and told him he must not
huff the court'. Goodman pleaded 'not guilty' but was sent for trial all
the same. On 7 November, he was charged with 'being a Person of a
Wicked Mind, and of an Ungodly Disposition, and Conversation...did
solicite, perswade, and endeavour & procure two Flasks of Florence
Wine, to be mix'd with deadly Poison for the poisoning of the Right
Noble Henry, Duke of Grafton, and George, Duke of
Northumberland'.[74]

Despite the court's failure to question what Goodman's motivation
could be to kill his mistress's children, he was found guilty of a high
misdemeanour and sentenced to pay a thousand-pound fine. Unable
to pay the fine, and Barbara strapped by her everyday extravagance,
Goodman was sent to the Marshalsea Prison. However, Barbara must
have returned to her demanding best, as, two months later, with no
fine paid, her lover was at liberty, courtesy of his majesty's command.

Goodman proved a comfort for Barbara following the death of Charles II in February 1685. The dying monarch asked his brother to take care of his three main mistresses: 'He spake to the Duke to be kind to his Concubines, the DD: of Cleveland, & especialy Portsmouth, & that Nelly might not sterve.' The new king provided Barbara with more comfort by continuing her pension. In April 1686, Peregrine Bertie wrote that Barbara 'is brought to bed of a son which the towne has christned Goodman Cleveland.' However, there is no other reference to the birth – not something, even in her faded glory, that Barbara could keep secret, can be assumed to be misplaced gossip.[75]

The removal of James II in favour of his son-in-law and daughter, William and Mary, was not so comfortable for our lovers. Goodman was a Jacobite – as the followers of the deposed king were known. And as a result he would become embroiled in conspiracy and plots and end up an informant and political refugee with a £1,000 price on his head. Barbara's discomfort was not political, religious or moral, but financial: the Dutch king of England closed down her account. In February 1696, Goodman was arrested after a plot to kill the king was betrayed. Barbara may well have sympathised but she was no fool. She sacked the ex-actor from her service. Without recourse to easy money Barbara spent the very best part of the next ten years living quietly outside of the public gaze or interest.

And then, on 21 July 1705, her sad and estranged husband, Roger Palmer, died. The 64-year-old widow was single again. But only for four months. By 25 November she was Mrs Robert Feilding. Her second marriage would prove as farcical as the first was harmlessly shambolic. Popularly known as 'Handsome' or 'Beau' Feilding, the new husband was a sharper with a pretty eye for a profit. The previous two wealthy Mrs Feildings (the Honourable Mary Swift, daughter of Viscount Carlingford, and Viscountess Muskerry) had sadly left this earth but happily left him in financial heaven. He was now looking for the hat-trick. And an ageing duchess with a £5,000 annual pension out of the post office proved irresistible. Thing was, so did Mrs Ann Delau, a widow with a strapping fortune reputedly worth £60,000. Having checked the validity of her will in the Doctors Commons he set about launching a brisk courtship.

He enlisted the aid of one Mrs Streights, who recommended Ann Delau's hairdresser, Charlotte Henrietta Villars, as a point of introduction. Villars, who was to get £500 for brokering the deal, delivered the prize and Feilding, relying not only on his sparkling looks and handsome wit, presented himself falsely as 'the earl of Glascow' and Viscount Tunbridge. But then his prey was not Ann

Delau, either. Convinced she could not sway the real heiress to meet Feilding, but fancying the rewards, Villars recruited an acquaintance, Mary Wadsworth, 'who was somewhat like the widow', to pose as Ann Delau, and 'she readily embraced the idea.' So swimmingly did the courtship go that, on Friday 9 November when she was visiting him, Feilding locked her 'in his apartment, drove in a hackney-coach directly to Count Gallas's, the Emperor's envoy, in Leicester Fields, and returned with one Don Francisco Drian, a Popish priest, styled The Father in Red, on account of a red habit he wore. On his arrival the marriage took place.'[76]

As the wedding was in secret – the less-than-blushing bride explaining that her father must not know, because he had influence over the estate – Feilding filled in his spare time with a certain other acquaintance. And then it dawned on him: marry Barbara as well. Sixteen days after his marriage to 'Ann Delau' he 'married' the Duchess of Cleveland. This ceremony, although privately celebrated at Barbara's house in Bond Street, was not so secret. One contemporary letter from Lady Wentworth to her son reported the 'old Boe Feelding is maryed to the Dutchis of Cleevland.' The old Boe moved into Barbara's house, while keeping his own home in Pall Mall for his assignations with his other wife.[77]

However, our handsome beau was not a pretty sight behind closed doors – the man with two wives beat them both. Lady Wentworth wrote from Twickenham on 29 July 1706:

> Just as I came down hear I hard that the Dutchis of Cleevland's Feeldin was dead, and she in great greef for him; but it was no such thing, for instead of that she has gott him sent to Newgate for thretning to kill her twoe sons for taking her part, when he beet her and broack open his closset doar and toock fower hundred pd. out. Thear is a paper put out about it. He beat her sadly and she cryed out murder in the streete out of the windoe, and he shot a blunderbus at the people.[78]

Barbara was not alone in feeling the force of the Beau's ugly side. Even before he discovered Mary Wadsworth's true identity he 'did beat and abuse her in a most barbarous and cruel way.' Upon discovery of the truth, he summoned her to his lodge in Whitehall Gate. A witness at the trial takes up the story:

> Mr Feilding came...in a chariot, he lit out of it. There was a hackney-coach brought two women; one of these women got out of

the coach and came up to Mr Feilding. Mr Feilding called her 'Bitch'. The lady called him 'Rogue' and said she was his lawful wife. At that, Mr Feilding having a stick, he punched it at her; it happened upon her mouth and made her teeth bleed.[79]

It was this outrage that caused Mrs Wadsworth to visit the Duke of Grafton and inform him that his grandmother's husband was a bigamist. Barbara was devastated. We hear that she 'was given over by her physitians'.[80]

Barbara wanted her very public revenge – she not only sued Feilding in Doctors Commons for divorce, but also had him arraigned for felony. The trial began on Wednesday, 4 December 1706, at the Sessions House in the Old Bailey. The trial papers show that in May, when Barbara found out that Feilding was already married, he also discovered the true identity of his false bride: 'Then finding how he had been served, that instead of marrying a fortune of £60,000 he had been imposed upon and married one not worth so many farthings, he discarded her with great wrath.' He attempted to defend himself by charging that Mrs Wadsworth was in fact Mrs Bradby, and married, which if proved would delegitimise their marriage and thus legitimise his marriage to Barbara. However, the jury, after much deliberation, found Feilding guilty of felony as charged. By craving the benefit of clergy,* Feilding saw his sentence reduce to branding of his hand. However, he was also pardoned this, Queen Anne assuming, no doubt, that publicity was punishment enough.[81]

The court judgment turned Barbara's petition for divorce into a formality. On 23 May 1707, it was declared that Feilding, lacking the fear of God before his eyes, had contracted a pretended marriage with the Duchess of Cleveland and she 'was and is free from any bond of marriage with the said Robert Feilding, and had and hath the liberty and freedom of marrying with any other person'. False husband dispatched, Barbara never saw him again. Bountyless, he struggled and ended up in debtors' prison. He died on 12 May 1712, by which time he had patched things up with Mary Wadsworth. In his will, he refers to her as 'my dear and loving wife Mary Feilding.' However, not everyone was reconciled to the Beau. One 'epitaph' ran:

---

*benefit of clergy – originally the privilege allowed to clergymen of exemption from trial by a secular court; modified and extended later to everyone who could read. Abolished in 1827.

> *If Feilding is Dead*
> *And lies under this Stone,*
> *That he is not alive,*
> *You may bet two to one;*
> *But if he's alive,*
> *And do's not lie here,*
> *Let him live till he's hang'd,*
> *For no man do's care.*[82]

Barbara might have been a free agent again, but she was a 66-year-old free agent. She retired from the fray and moved to Chiswick, then a sleepy village. Age had finally rid her of scandal. She died as she had never lived – quietly. She was reported as

> having lived about two years after [the Feilding case], at length fell ill of a dropsie, which swelled her gradually to a monstrous bulk and in about three months' time put a period to her life, at her house at Cheswick, in the county of Middlesex, in the 69th year of her age.[83]

Barbara died on Sunday, 9 October 1709. She had little to bequeath, but made her loyal grandson, the Duke of Grafton, residuary legatee. The remains of her scavenging of the old palace of Nonsuch went to her eldest son, Charles Fitzroy, who also inherited the title of Cleveland. She was buried in Chiswick parish church four days later 'in a manner privately'. Her resting place was unmarked.

Barbara has had a bad press. She may well, in Sedley's words, be the sort of woman to 'wed a coffin were the hinges gold' or even deserve Burnet's characterisation that, 'in short, she was a woman of pleasure, and stuck at nothing that would either serve her appetites or her passions; she was vastly expensive, and by consequence very covetous.' Her motto was *Et decus et pretium recti* – 'Decency and the price of virtue'. You could, indeed, argue that she certainly knew the virtue of getting a decent price for everything. But, for all the greed, there was a kinder, softer side. As a mother, she gave no quarter in ensuring her children got their respective halves. Pepys recorded a rarely conceded moment of humanity showing that the sweetness was not just in the wrapping. On 23 August 1662, while the crowds awaited the arrival on the Thames of the new queen, the diarist had eyes only for another great lady:

> One more thing; there happened a scaffold below to fall, and we feared some hurt but there was none; but she, of all the great ladies only, run down among the common rabble to see what hurt was

done, and did take care of a child that received some little hurt; which methought so noble.[84]

But more grasping than her greed was her need for sex. The satires plundered her perceived sordidness:

> *When shee has jaded quite*
> *Her allmost boundless Appetite*
> *Cloy'd with the choicest Banquetts of delight,*
> *She'l still drudge on in Tasteless vice*
> *As if she sinn'd for Exercise*
> *Disabling stoutest Stallions ev'ry hour,*
> *And when they can perform no more*
> *She'l rail at 'em out of door.*[85]

The poor woman enjoyed sex. No doubt had she been a man, history (or at least the man-made or less puritan variety) would celebrate her as redoubtable rake, a rogue, a self-made man amusingly in love with his creation, a terror to husbands. But women must be viewed as prey and not predator. So she is reviled and dismissed. She mixed sex into a casserole of greed and influence, and spiced it with wit, fun and deviousness. She simmered and boiled over a lot. Unquestionably, she was as Burnet described 'a lively and demanding woman.' Barbara was, indeed, a banquet of delight.

5

Confident Young Men:
Sir Charles Sedley and
John Wilmot, Earl of Rochester

...the king spent most of his time with confident young men, who abhorred all discourse that was serious, and, in the liberty they assumed in drollery and raillery, preserved no reverence to God or man, but laughed at all sober men, and even at religion itself.
– The Duke of Ormond to the Earl of Clarendon, 1661

...A Wit is like a running Horse, good for no earthly thing beside; when did you ever know any of 'em well with a great man, or so much as taken down to a Lord's house a Buck-hunting? They can drink, some of 'em; but then they talk of Philosophy, History, Poetry, as if they came into company to study: this stuff the Devil would not hear.[1]
– Thomas Shadwell, from *A True Widow*, Act III, 1678

The London that welcomed back the king was largely divided into the old and the new: to the east, 'the city', the walled environs of trade and craft; and to the west, 'the town', the open and expanding area of inherited wealth and nobility. And in the middle (politically if not exactly geographically) was the court. It was here that real power lived. The court drove laws, fashion, the arts, science and policy.

As with all monarchs and leaders, Charles II relied on advisers. He appointed men with ranging skills, experience and knowledge. He needed to be stimulated by them, but not to inspire him on fiscal policy. Charles disliked business. He needed people about him to entertain him, keep him from boredom or falling asleep. He wanted to amuse and be amused. Not for him solid, dependable, hard-working bureaucrats. He wanted the quickest minds, the sharpest tongues, the happiest faces. He might suffer the presence of Clarendon's unfaltering addiction to the drudgery of governance, but he preferred the company of the so-called court wits. He would take them with him wherever he went – he liked to keep his wits about him.

However, the specification of a wit wasn't watertight. Wit, in any conventional sense, sometimes played no part. Your drinking ability, self-estimation or your family name could outrank any writing skill or poetic capacity. But normally you needed to have impressed your peers (in both senses of the noun) with some literary achievement or dextrous verbal ability, and sprinkled in some posturing intellectualism. As Rochester declared in his 'An Allusion to Horace', it is only the views of those you know and respect that matter:

> *Or when the poor-fed poets of the town,*
> *For scraps and coach room, cry my verses down?*
> *I loathe the rabble; 'tis enough for me*
> *If Sedley, Shadwell, Shepherd, Wycherley,*
> *Goldolphin, Butler, Buckhurst, Buckingham,*
> *And some few more, whom I omit to name,*
> *Approve my sense: I count their censure fame.*[2]

Also as the anonymous poem ran:

> *Sidley indeed and Rochester might write*
> *For their own credit and their friends delight,*
> *Showing how farr they cou'd ye rest outdoe*
> *As in their fortunes, so their writings too.*[3]

Sedley, Rochester and most of the wits didn't write for money (they didn't need to, although Rochester was never financially flushed) and therefore didn't really have their works published – copies would circulate and be copied – and so the authors retained their noble gentleman-amateur status. Others, such as Dryden and Shadwell, however, made their living from writing and could never be part of the in-crowd, no matter how famous, popular or good.

It has been suggested that only fourteen men qualified as 'members of the charmed inner-circle', and indeed, more or less, their names provide this book with its spine. The fourteen cited, naturally in order of rank, are: George Villiers, Duke of Buckingham; Charles Sackville, Lord Buckhurst, Earl of Dorset and Middlesex; John Sheffield, Earl of Mulgrave; John Wilmot, Earl of Rochester; 'Lord' John Vaughn, later Earl of Carbery; Sir Charles Sedley; Sir Carr Scroope; Sir George Etherege; Sir Henry Savile; William Wycherley; Henry Bulkeley; Harry Killigrew; Fleetwood Shepherd; and Henry Guy.[4]

Whatever their capabilities, they enjoyed life and were sure to scandalise. A typical example could be the minor poet, Fleetwood Shepherd, who, according to a contemporary commentator, 'after his majesty's Restoration he retir'd to London, hang'd on the court, became a debauchee and atheist.' Around this circle of wits were the dapper-wits, woodcocks (a fool, simpleton or dupe) tattlers (idle talkers) and fops. It must surely have been representatives of the court wits that Jonathan Swift (1667–1745) had in mind in an allegorical sequence in *A Tale of a Tub*, when three sons of one birth go to town (again in both senses):

They writ, and rallied, and rhymed, and sung, and said, and said nothing. They drank, and fought, and whored, and slept, and swore, and took snuff. They went to new Plays on the first Night, haunted the Chocolate Houses, beat the Watch, lay on Bulks and got claps. They bilked Hackney Coachmen, ran in debt with shopkeepers, and lay with their wives. They killed bailiffs, kicked fiddlers down stairs, ate at Locket's, loitered at Will's.[5]

(*Bulks* – stalls in front of shops; *bilked* – didn't pay, did runners; *Locket's* – a large fashionable ordinary on Charing Cross run by Adam Lockett; *Will's* – a coffee house named after its owner William Unwin, where Swift himself was a regular.)

The debauched life of a wit or courtier could be seen as an antidote to the repressive and religious regime of the commonwealth. Suddenly it was all piety in the sky. Wine and women both needed to be drunk plentifully and young. It was these two delights and ultimate curses that perpetuated the day. As Rochester wrote in 'Upon His Drinking a Bowl':

> *Cupid and Bacchus my saints are;*
> *May drink and love still reign:*
> *With wine I wash away my cares,*
> *And then to cunt again.*[6]

The most celebrated poetical description of this lifestyle, 'The Debauchee', has also been attributed to Rochester, but may well be the work of Charles Sackville:

> *I rise at eleven, I dine about two,*
> *I get drunk before seven, and the next thing I do,*
> *I send for my whore, when for fear of a clap,*
> *I dally about her, and spew in her lap;*

There we quarrel and scold till I fall asleep,
When the jilt growing bold, to my pocket does creep;
Then slyly she leaves me, and to revenge the affront,
At once both my lass and my money I want.
If by chance then I wake, hot-headed and drunk,
What a coyl do I make for the loss of my punk?
I storm and I roar, and I fall in a rage,
And missing my lass, I fall on my page:
Then crop-sick, all morning I rail at my men,
And in bed I lie yawning till eleven again.[7]

(*Jilt* – one who capriciously spurns advances after much encouragement; *crop-sick* – stomach disorder from excessive eating and drinking; *coyl* (coyle) – to beat or to thrash; *punk* – a strumpet.

The company of wits was much in demand, particularly at mealtimes, by those who sauntered outside of the elite but thought themselves tastily compatible. As Sparkish declares in Wycherley's *The Country Wife* (I, i): 'I think wit as necessary at dinner as a glass of good wine ...'[8]

Written in 1674, Rochester's 'Timon' (although Buckingham may have a hand also) is an entertaining poem about how the titled character – probably the earl himself – is cajoled into eating with 'a dull dining sot' on the pretext that they would be joined by Sedley, Buckhurst and Savile, only to find the actual guests are the everyman wannabe wits, Halfwit, Huff, Kickum and Dingboy. It illuminates sharply, but sweetly, the perfunctory pseudo-intellectual table talk of Restoration London. The host (to whom Timon, in a neat satirical wink, wearily listens as he babbles on about how he lost his estate fighting for the Royalists in the civil war) and his guests perform verbally to Timon in jousting for critical acknowledgement and agreement. As the wine pours, they pore over poetry, plays and politics ('... of several things we prate/some regulate the stage, and some the state'), each championing his own over the other, with it ending horribly and inevitably with flying plates and swords drawn, until:

Their rage once over, they begin to treat,
And six fresh bottles must the peace complete.[9]

Two of the most confident young men in Restoration England were Charles Sedley and Rochester: when on song, they were unquestionably top of the fops. They were debauchery on wheels. Or at least that's how popular history has treated them. Certainly they had their moments of unbridled scandal but their reputations have been largely overblown. Time to let some air out

SIR CHARLES SEDLEY – A HAPPY TALENT

For songs and verses mannerly obscene,
That can stir nature up by springs unseen,
And without forcing blushes, warm the Queen –
Sedley has that prevailing gentle art,
That can with a resistless charm impart
The loosest wishes to the chastest heart;
Raise such a conflict, kindle such a fire,
Betwixt declining virtue and desire,
Till the poor vanquished maid dissolves away
In dreams all night, in sighs and tears all day.[10]

> – John Wilmot, Earl of Rochester, 'An
> An Allusion to Horace', c. 1675/6

There go divers[e] with him, but especially the Lord Buckhurst and Sir Ch. Sidly, who will lead the muses and graces such a dance as may instruct and civilise fair France.[11]

> – Mr Henshaw to Sir R Paston, 16 July 1670

The Charles Sedley of legend is undoubtedly Restoration Man. He 'lived mostly in the great city, became a debauchee, set up for satyrical wit, a comedian, poet, and courtier of ladies and I know not what.' So said Anthony à Wood in his *Athenae Oxonienses*. The king, with no mean a short list from which to select, 'singl'd him out for the best Genius of the Age, and frequently told his Familiars, that Sedley's Stile, either in Writing, or Discourse, would be the Standard of the *English* Tongue.' It was, his original biographer gushed, by Sedley's 'Judgment [that] every Performance was approved, or condemned, which made the King jest with him, and tell him, Nature had given him a Patent to be *Apollo's* Viceroy'.[12]

The anonymous 'eminent hand' that wrote Sedley's life in 1722 recalled a quotation that was originally dedicated to 'pretty, witty' Nelly Gwynne: 'but as was written under the Picture of a late eminent Lady of Sublime Parts, must be said of his with far more Justice:

> *The Painter's Art is done, the features hit*
> *Of Sedley's Face – No Art can shew his Wit*[13]

And there was plenty to show. Pepys went to see *The General* by Roger

Boyle, Lord Orrery, which, first produced in 1661, was one of the first heroic dramas much loved by the age. Although Pepys found it 'so dull and ill acted' his day was saved by having Sedley sit next to him,

> who I find a very witty man, and did at every line take notice of the dullness of the poet and badness of the action, and that most pertinently; which I was mightily taken with – and among others, where by Altemira's command Clarimont the Genrall is commanded to rescue his Rivall whom she loved, Lucidor, he after a great deal of demurre breaks out – 'Well – Ile save my Rivall and make her confess. That I deserve, while he doth possesse.' 'Why, what! Pox!' says Sir Ch. Sydly, 'would he have him have more, or what is there more to be had of a woman then the possessing her?'[14]

His presence at the playhouse also raised the competitive stakes of those around him. On 18 February 1667, Pepys attended *The Maid's Tragedy*, another stock tragicomedy by those Restoration favourites Beaumont and Fletcher, but was,

> vexed all the while with two talking ladies and Sir Ch. Sidly, yet pleased to hear their discourse, he being a stranger; and one of the ladies would, and did, sit with her mask on all the play; and being exceeding witty as I ever heard woman, did talk most pleasantly with him; but was, I believe, a virtuous woman and of quality. He would fain know who she was, but she would not tell. Yet did give him many pleasant hints of her knowledge of him, by that means setting his brains at work to find out who she was; and did give him leave to use all means to find out who she was but pulling off her mask. He was mighty witty; and she also making sport with him very inoffensively, that a more pleasant recontre I never heard. But by that means lost the pleasure of the play wholly, to which now and then Sir Ch. Sidlys exceptions against both words and pronouncing was very pretty.[15]

More guarded praise came from the 'confident but tactless' historian, Bishop Gilbert Burnet, who considered that Sedley 'had a more sudden and copious wit, which furnished a perpetual run of discourse; but he was not so correct as Lord Dorset, nor so sparkling as Lord Rochester'. It was in such company that Sedley was continually cast.[16]

It seems certain that Sir Charles's last name was pronounced 'Sidley', which would account for the virtual consistency of contemporary spellings of his name in this way. However, family deeds, mortgages and autographed letters show that the family and Sir Charles used 'Sedley'.

However spelled, it was a name so notorious as to serve as a benchmark for scandal. Pepys recorded a conversation with an old colleague, John Gregory, on the plight of Clarendon. He described John Vaughan (styled Lord Vaughan and later third Earl of Carberry), who championed the chancellor's impeachment for treason, as 'one of the lewdest fellows of the age, worse than Sir Ch. Sidly.' We get a further measure of Vaughan from Clarendon himself, who proclaimed him 'a person of as ill a face as fame.'[17]

Sedley's name also struck horror at the heart of the sober and pious. In 1667, Charles Sackville, Lord Buckhurst, had retired to Epsom for the summer with his latest mistress, the stage's star of comedy, Nell Gwynne. The regularity with which the court delighted in taking the waters meant that spa towns sparkled. Bath, Tunbridge Wells and Epsom were great favourites. Water had many uses in London, but drinking was never one of them. Epsom was a serious resort. Thomas Shadwell in his comedy *The Virtuoso* would later write that 'Your glass coach will to Hyde Park for air; the suburb fools trudge to Lambs Conduit or Tottenham; your sprucer sort of citizens gallop to Epsom.' The resort was also the inspiration for the same author's *Epsom Wells*. Pepys, a huge fan of the actress, had been informed of Nelly's retirement to Epsom on 13 July 1667. He was such a fan that the very next day he made his way there himself. Leaving at just past five o'clock in the morning (a little annoyed that his wife had taken so long to get ready) and armed with 'wine and beer and cold fowl', Pepys arrived in Epsom with his coach and four about three hours later. After drinking four pints of water at the well, he went to the King's Head in the town to 'hear that my Lord Buckhurst and Nelly are lodged at the next house, and Sir Charles Sedley is with them: and they keep a merry house. Poor girl! I pity her; but more the loss of her at the King's House.'[18]

The 'merry house' had two little bay-windowed rooms overlooking the street, and came complete with a secret exit door (a structural extra that has become almost a traditional requirement of any house, inn or tavern claiming that little Nelly ever lived, stayed or supped there). During his stay Sedley took his leave of Nelly and Buckhurst and travelled about a mile away to Durdans, the country seat of George, ninth Baron Berkeley of Berkeley, who would be created Earl Berkeley in 1676. Another of the guests was the virtuous Mary Rich, Countess of Warwick who was a mite apprehensive about sharing a table with the outrageously virtue-free Sedley, but, as her diary entry for 5 August 1667 showed, the boy was on his best behaviour:

Went with Lady Robartes and her lord to Durdans to see my lord who was there. At dinner that day dined Sir Henry [sic] Sedley, which was much trouble for me to see him lest he be profane. But it pleased God to restrain him; yet the knowledge I had how profane a person he is much troubled me to be in his company.[19]

Unfortunately, the pious Mary would undoubtedly have also disapproved of the shenanigans of my Lord Berkeley's clan. His fourth daughter Mary married Lord Grey, who subsequently eloped with his wife's younger sister Henrietta in August 1682. He was brought before the King's Bench the following November to answer charges of abduction, but, despite a fight during the trial, Grey managed to get off.

Sedley's first imprint on the pages of history come by way of tradition. It is said that he burned down Harefield House (owned by his sister-in-law, Lady Chandos) while 'amusing himself by reading in bed.' History, however, has been rather unkind to his own writings. Pope thought him 'a very insipid writer; except in some few of his little love verses.' His anonymous biographer thought his poems, unlike his morals, 'mannerly and modest' causing no virgin to 'blush to read them'. However, some of the incidents in his life, or rather one in particular in his youth, would guarantee a pink, rosy glow swamping the face of the most riotous rake-hell. And it all went off at the embarrassingly aptly named Cock Tavern.[20]

The Cock Tavern was in the heart of Bow Street, at the end of Suffolk Street in Covent Garden. It was an 'ordinary' a tavern that served fixed-price meals; a sort of Restoration Harvester. Pepys tells us that the Cock was 'mightily cried-up' and 'famous for good meat, and perticularly pease-porridge' – a thick pea soup dish that was a great favourite of the diarist. More popularly known as Oxford Kate's in reverence to its wonderfully disreputable owner, the tavern featured in Shadwell's *The Sullen Lovers* and was a regular in contemporary writings. For example:

> *Farewell good places old and new,*
> *And Oxford Kates once more adieu;*
> *But it goes unto our very hearts,*
> *To leave the Cheese-cakes and the Tarts.*[21]

However, no matter how well deserved its reputation for food it would always be remembered for 'that notorious business in the balcony in the Strand at London'. Oxford Kate hosted a riotous dinner for Sir Charles Sedley, Sir Thomas Ogle and Charles Sackville, Lord Buckhurst, on or about 16 June 1663. It was reported that Withyam Church, Suffolk, host to the Sackville family tomb, 'burnt ('tis not knowne how) on that day when Sir Ch. Sedley and lord Buckhurst played their freaks in a balcony.' The parish records show that the church 'burnt down by a tempest of thunder and lightning' on 'June ye 16, 1663'. Pepys records gossip on 1 July of the trial 'the other day'. It may or may not have been the same day, but such a coincidence exhibiting God's infernal disfavour could not be disregarded.[22]

Sedley and Co. 'had six dishes of meat brought in by six naked women.' After feasting their eyes on the women and their bellies on the meat, 'they went forth in their shirts into the Balcony'. Anthony à Wood recorded that our three lions,

> were at the cook's house at the signe of the Cock in Bow-street nearer Covent-Garden within the libertie of Westminster; and being all inflam'd with strong liquors, they went into the balcony joyning to their chamber-window, and putting down their breeches, they excrementized in the street. Which being done, Sedley stripped himself naked ... [23]

It's unclear whether only Sedley disrobed or all three did so. Such expressions of freedom were fairly common recreational pursuits for the upper classes. Indeed, Burnet wrote that the Earl of Rochester and his friends '... in their Frolicks they would have chosen sometimes to go naked if they had not feared the people.' Interestingly, Wood later changed his commentary to 'They all (I am sure Sedley) ... stripped themselves naked.'[24]

However, Sir William Batten, surveyor of the navy, told Pepys about the 'late triall of Sir Charles Sydly the other day, before my Lord Chief Justice Foster and the whole Bench – for his debauchery a little while since at Oxford Kate's; coming in open day into the Balcone and showed his nakedness – acting all the postures of lust and buggery that could be imagined'.[25]

Following this opening crowd-grabbing sequence, Sedley then 'with eloquence preached blasphemy to the people.' He then, according to Pepys, began,

> abusing of scripture and, as it were, from thence preaching a Mountebanke sermon from that pulpitt, saying that there he hath to sell such a pouder as should make all the cunts in town run after him – a thousand people standing underneath to hear him.
>
> And that being done, he took a glass of wine and washed his prick in it and then drank it off; and then took another and drank the King's health.[26]

Charles II (b 1630, r 1660-85). As all flowed from the king, Pepys could 'hope for no good to the State from having a prince so devoted to his pleasure'.

James, Duke of York (1633-1701). 'The most unguarded ogler of his time.'

Barbara Villiers, Duchess of Cleveland (1641-1709). 'O Barbara, thy execrable name / Is sure embalmed with everlasting shame'.

John Wilmot, Earl of Rochester (1647-80). 'See my credentials written in my face'.

'Colonel' Thomas Blood (1618 - 80). 'That Impudent Bold Fellow'.

George Villiers, Duke of Buckingham (1628-87). 'He was both the father and the mother of scandal'.

Frances Stewart, Duchess of Richmond (1647-1702). 'The prettiest girl imaginable and the most fitted to adorn a Court.'

Samuel Pepys (1633-1703).
'Blessed be God, at the end of the
last year I was in very good health...'
And so began, on 1 January 1660,
possibly the most famous diary in
the world.

John Dryden (1631-1700).
The poet and playwright tried
without success to become one of
the court wits: '...Aukwardly was
Lewd / Drunk 'gainst my Stomack,
'gainst my Conscience Swore'.

Louise de Keroualle,
Duchess of Portsmouth
(1649-1734). The king's
French mistress, although
generally unpopular, was
thought '...the most dear of
all his dears'.

Andrew Marvell (1621-78).
The poet and politician considered
Rochester to be 'the only man in
England that had the true veine of
satyre'.

Peter Lely (1618-1680). Court painter, who 'on animated canvas stole / the sleepy eye that spoke the melting soul'.

Anne Hyde, Duchess of York (1637-71). A 'plain, ordinary woman' who 'took state on her rather too much'.

The Breda medal. Charles II commissioned goldsmith Jan Roettiers to engrave Frances Stewart's features as Britannia. In February 1667, Pepys 'did observe the King's new Medall, where in little there is Mrs Stewards face ... and a pretty thing it is that he should choose her face to represent Britannia by'.

Wood continues:

Whereupon a riot being raised, the people became very clamorous, and would have forced the dore, next to the street, open; but being hindred, the preacher and his company were pelted into their rome or chamber, and the windows belonging thereunto were broken.[27]

The thousand-strong crowd were so outraged that they could not leave. Their mounting fury took the shape of stones and rocks, which they hurled at the balcony. The under-fire threesome, before retreating inside, replied with a volley of wine bottles 'pist in'. Thus, not only were they taking it, but throwing it back as well. It may have begun as an attempt to court scandal but it ended up the scandal of court. The king's friends were charged with breaking his peace. The trial was no less society-shocking owing to the continued irreverence of Sedley.

This frolick being soon spread abroad, especially by the fanatical party, who aggravated it to the utmost, by making it the most scandalous thing in nature, and nothing more reproachful to religion than that; the said company were summoned to the court of justice in Westminster hall, where being indicted of a riot before Sir Robert Hyde [it was actually Sir Robert Foster; Hyde succeeded him in October 1663], Lord Chief Justice of the Common Pleas, were all fined, and Sir Charles Sedley being fined *500li* he made answer, that he thought he was the first man that paid for shiting. Sir Robert [Foster] asked him if he ever read the book, called '*The Compleat Gentleman*' &c [by Henry Peachman] to which Sir Charles made answer that, 'Set aside his lordship, he had read more books than himself,' &c.[28]

Pepys added:

It seems my Lord and the rest of the Judges did all of them round give him a most high reproofe – my Lord Chief Justice saying that it was for him and such wicked wretches as he was that God's anger and judgments hung over us – calling him 'Sirrah' [a title used contemptuously] many times. It's said they have bound him to his good behaviour (there being no law against him for it) in 5000l. It being told that my Lord Buckhurst was there, my Lord asked that whether it was that Buckhurst that was lately tried for robbery; and when answered 'Yes,' he asked whether he had so soon forgot his deliverance at that time, and that it would have more become him to have been at his prayers, begging God's forgiveness, then now running into such courses again.[29]

The Buckhurst trial concerned Charles and his brother, Edward Sackville, who, in February 1662, were two of five men who had attacked and killed a suspected robber around Stoke Newington. At the time of the Restoration, highwaymen were such a scourge that the king placed a £10 bounty on every capture. Unfortunately, the suspected highwayman, John Hoppy, was no such thing: he was a tanner. It was thought that these 'five persons of quality' may have been hanged within a week had the had king not intervened. In the end, on 10 April 1662, they were convicted of manslaughter, only to be pardoned by the king one week later.

The Rev. Philip Henry, shaking his head, lamented of Sackville that 'evil men wax worse and worse.' Such fortune in luck, if not hard cash, certainly funded Sackville's extravagances. Indeed, it was surely these escapades that the Earl of Rochester was recalling in his quote to the king referred to by the poet Matthew Prior (1664–1721) in his dedication to *Poems on Several Occasions,* 1709, that 'he did not know how it was, but my Lord Dorset [Sackville became the sixth earl of Dorset in 1677] might do anything, yet was never to blame.'

Bishop Burnet wrote that Sackville,

was a generous, good-natured man, and a very merry companion when once a little wine had got the better of his phlegm. Never was there so much ill-nature in any pen as in his, joined with so much good nature as was in himself. He was bountiful, even to run himself into difficulties; and so charitable that he commonly gave away all he had about him when he met with a moving object of compassion; but he was lazy and indolent, and though courted to be a favourite, would not give himself the trouble of being one.'[30]

The third of the three at the Cock Tavern escapade was Sir Thomas Ogle of Pinchbeck, Lincolnshire. He would become the first governor of the Royal Hospital, Chelsea, appointed only after the original choice, Sir Thomas Daniell, had died before taking office. Ogle, knighted at the Restoration for his loyal support, became governor on 1 November 1685 and remained so until his death in 1702. His seventeen-year tenure was marked by its unswerving ineffectiveness. He never involved himself in the management of the hospital, never became a commissioner, and presided serenely and unsuspectingly over the embezzlement and abuse of public funds by the paymaster-general,

Richard, Earl of Ranelagh (after whom the hospital's magnificent gardens are tactlessly named). Ogle was buried in the hospital grounds on 23 November. Curiously, his tomb was not donated by his fellow officers, the hospital or his family, but rather by the fifty-year-old Utricia Ashley, who by 1705 became the hospital's appointed housekeeper. The mysterious Utricia died 44 years later and was buried in Ogle's grave.

Unlike Sedley, neither Ogle nor Sackville were fined, apparently because they were 'not able to pay such a sum'. We know that Sedley was fined; however, the amount has been less clear. As seen above, Wood (£500) and Pepys (£5,000) fail to agree their figures. And they are by no means all. Joseph Keble, in his reports in the Court of the King's Bench at Westminster, says Sedley 'for shewing himself naked on a Balcony, and throwing down Bottles (pist in) *vi et armis* among the people in *Covent* Garden contra pacem and to the Scandal of the Government' was fined 2,000 marks (£1,333). The Rev. Phillip Henry thought it a rather unholy £4,000.[31] Thomas Siderfin reported that '...as he was of a very ancient Family of the County of Kent, and as his Estate was encumbered (since the Court did not intend his ruin but reform), he should be fined 2,000 marks, imprisoned for a week without Bail and bound over for good behaviour for three years.' Keble says Sedley was bound over for one year.[32]

Sedley, for his part, whatever the amount was, sought to have it reduced, quashed or regally covered:

The day of payment being appointed, Sir Charles desired Mr Henry Killigrew and another gent. to apply themselves to his majestie to get it off, but instead of that, they beg'd the said sum of his majestie, and would not abate Sir Charles two pence of the money.[33]

Nonetheless, a letter from Henry Bennet (later Earl of Arlington), keeper of the privy purse, states that Sedley was fined 'ye sum of 1000 markes' for 'severall offences and misdemeanours' and authorised a crown payment to cover it. Thus, with a mark valued at two-thirds of a pound (or 13s. 4d.), Sedley's actual fine was £667 (about £50,000 today). However, with the crown paying it, he could, 'prick out the debt'.[34]

Sedley managed to embroil himself in scandal at will – some high-spirited and some decidedly mean-spirited. On 23 October, Pepys recorded:

This day Pierce doth tell me, among other news, the late frolic and Debauchery of Sir Ch. Sidly and Buckhurst, running up and down all night with their arses bare through the streets, and at last fighting and being beat by the watch and clapped up all night; and how the King takes their parts and my Lord Chief Justice Keeling hath laid the constable by the heels to answer it next sessions – which is a horrid shame.[35]

A similar story emerges from the House of Commons Journals. Sedley was stopped, possibly on a warrant from a creditor, in his coach by a constable called Daniel (or Samuell) Axton (or Ackson) near the Old Exchange. He was forced to surrender the carriage and horses to 'the Greene Yard' – a sort of creditors' compound. He then found himself impounded with his coachman and footmen at the Compter – a debtors' prison in Southwark. Having obtained his release – probably with a knowing smile and a much more knowing bag of coins – he complained of his arrest in the House on 8 February 1672. His fellow MPs ordered the sergeant-at-arms to arrest the constable for such a blatant breach of parliamentary privilege. Fifteen days later the unfortunate Axton was pleading extenuating circumstances to the House. His release from prison was ordered on 7 March but not before Sedley had the pleasure of watching him kneeling at the bar of the house being rebuked by the Speaker of the House for such audacious behaviour towards an MP.[36]

Being an MP clearly had its added-value benefits. So, too, did being mates with the king. In the autumn of 1668 Charles had been on a royal progress to eastern England and brought Sedley and co. along with him, ostensibly to break the boredom of business – why break what you can shatter? While at Thetford, Norfolk, the king's company made the fiddlers 'sing them all the bawdy songs they could think of.' On 6 October, Charles visited the home of William, Lord Crofts, in Little Saxham, near Bury St Edmonds, Suffolk. Seemingly, the wine flowed as sweetly as the wit, for Pepys wrote that 'the King was drunk at Saxam with Sidly, Buckhurst, &c. the night that my Lord Arlington [Sir Henry Bennet, secretary of state] came thither, and would not give him an audience, or could not – which is true, for it was that night that I was there and saw the King go up to his chamber, and was told that the King had been drinking.' The next day, Arlington wrote from Bury St Edmonds to Sir Joseph Williamson, his undersecretary of state, on 7 October with the news that the king was unable to see him 'by reason of the uncertainty of his motions.' Presumably, the Restoration equivalent of phoning in sick.[37]

The king's hangover was not the only fallout from the night. Pepys was also told that, the Duke of York did the next day chide Bab. May for his occasioning the King's giving himself up to these gentlemen, to the neglect of my Lord Arlington; to which he answered merrily, that, by God, there was no man in England that had heads to lose, durst do what they do everyday with the King; and asked the Duke of York's pardon – which is a sign of a mad world. God bless us out of it.[38]

Sometimes, even for a wit such as Sedley, words were not enough. With reputations on the line, action was required. And that usually meant one thing: violence. It mattered not that the recipient was a small, meek, effeminate actor. Edward 'Ned' Kynaston had to be dealt with.

Pepys arrived at the King's House expecting to see *The Heiress* but found the play cancelled: 'Kinaston, that did act a part therein in abuse to Sir Charles Sidly, being last night exceedingly dry-beaten with sticks by two or three that assaulted him – so as he is mightily bruised and forced to keep his bed.' He was out for a week.[39]

There appears no record of the play *The Heiress* and it may therefore be lost to us. Pepys was unsure of the author but heard that it was 'by my Lord Newcastle.' However, no play of that name has been credited to William Cavendish, Duke of Newcastle. A letter by John Evelyn's wife, dated 10 February 1669, noted a play 'of my Lord of Newcastle's, for which printed apologies are scattered in the assembly by Briden's order, either for himself who had some hand in it, or for the author most; I think both had the right to them.' It has been suggested that it might have been *The Triumphant Widow or The Heir* by Thomas May, first performed in 1620.[40]

Kynaston, a ringer for Sedley, and proudly so, had taken it upon himself to also dress like him during this production. For a mere player to imitate a gentleman was a serious affront to the peculiar Restoration interpretation of honour. Thugs, in the pay of Sedley, tracked Kynaston to St James's Park, where he was taking the air while dressed up cutely as the aggrieved knight. The attackers made it clear to the hapless actor that they believed him to be Sedley and were exacting physical revenge for a slight he had made upon them.

It certainly aped a scene in Sedley's play *The Mulberry Garden*, where the character Sir Samuel Forecast is caned after being mistaken for Sir John Everyoung owing to his fine clothes. 'It was,' suggested Genest, 'perhaps meant by Sidley as a hint to Kynaston. Kynaston was, however, far from taking the hint and he seems to have proceeded to greater liberties with Sir Charles.' However, the show must go on. Unfortunately, it seemed the practice of understudy was underdeveloped as Kynaston's part was – literally – read by one Beeston 'out of a book all the while, and thereby spoils the part.' Kynaston made his reappearance post-assualt on 9 February playing the King of Tidore in *The Island Princess* (a tragicomedy by John Fletcher), being 'well enough to act again, which he doth very well, after his beating by Sir Ch. Sidly's appointment'.[41]

It was a method of business that proved attractive. A month later Pepys met with Sir William Coventry, MP, one time secretary to the Lord High Admiral (the Duke of York), who had just been sacked from the Privy Council. Coventry spoke scathingly about a planned play – *The Country Gentleman* – in which he (as Sir Cautious Trouble-all) and Sir George Carteret (as Sir Gravity Empty) were to be lampooned. The production was to make great play of Coventry's desk-cum-filing cabinet – a large desk with a hole in the middle in which he sat on a swivel-stool and spun around to attend each next piece of business. He told Pepys that if the play went ahead, he had warned the theatre manager, Thomas Killigrew, that, should an actor impersonate him, he wouldn't complain to the Lord Chamberlain, who was seen as too weak, or resort to a beating 'as Sir Ch. Sidly is said to do', but would rather ensure that the actor's nose was cut.[42]

One of the authors of *The Country Gentleman*, along with Sir Robert Howard, was the ubiquitous Duke of Buckingham, who, it was said, greatly admired Sir Charles's effect on women, calling it 'Sedley's Witchcraft'. And yet for someone so patently a debaucher there is surprisingly little evidence of Sedley's sexual activities. Four possible mistresses, the last of whom he spent his final thirty or so faithful years with, is not the stuff of rakish legend. However, any story of the Sedley women must begin with his wife.

The Anglican Sedley married the Catholic Katherine Savage in St Giles-in-the-Fields on 9 February 1657. Their daughter, also Katherine, was born the following year. Perhaps it was a doomed business from the start, but the new Lady Sedley was undeniably unstable. Sedley's antics and notoriety may not have aided and abetted her sanity, but her growing eccentricities developed into full-blown madness. After a few years Katherine 'lost her reason and had to be placed under the care of a Catholic Physician skilled in this kind of malady'. Naturally, being 'skilled in this kind of malady' in the 1660s meant simply being only mostly clueless. Her sad, lonely and painful existence virtually imprisoned in the family house in Great Queen Street presented a sobering antidote to that of her carefree socialite husband. Their home address also proved prophetically ironic. Katherine would later believe herself to be a queen, dressing herself in all the pomp imaginable and insisting on being addressed as 'your majesty'.[43]

With a life hauntingly framed by a picture of such pathetic domesticity, the dutiful husband did what was naturally expected of his class and standing: he packed her off to a convent. This took place sometime during 1665–72, when the Carmelite friar Father Bede of St Simon Stock (whose lay name was Walter Joseph Travers) was vicar provincial of a Roman Catholic mission in London. He described Lady Sedley as 'the wife of a most eccentric English nobleman with a revenue of twenty thousand scudi.' Given that a scudo – a silver Italian coin – was usually worth about four shillings (20 pence), the venerable Bede estimated Sedley's income at a rather comfortable £4,000 a year (over £315,000 today).[44]

Father Bede takes up the story:

> Though I had not known her, I was requested to pay her a visit, as she greatly disliked being where she was. After giving me a most kind welcome, she complained of being constrained by force to take certain medicines that would impair her health; for excessive vanity was one of her delusions. I did my best to console her, expressing a hope that the rigorous treatment applied in her case would not wholly undermine her constitution, for I well knew that she had been far from an exemplary Catholic, and the chief object of my visit was to induce her to make a general confession.[45]

It so happened that at that time Dame Mary Knatchbull, the lady abbess of a society of English Benedictine nuns at Ghent, was in England fundraising to offset debts accrued by building work at the nunnery. It seemed heaven was arranging another of its marriages. The good father made an offer they couldn't refuse. Casting aside her initial doubts about leaving England, Katherine agreed to go to Ghent. Sedley was said to have been 'well pleased'.[46]

Katherine would be escorted there by Father Bede – her husband declining to do so. He did, however, agree to pay a pension of £400 a year (10 per cent of his estimated annual income) for Katherine's upkeep. He also had one last request:

> On the day of our departure, her husband told me that his wife wore jewels to the value of four thousand scudi (£800), and requested me to obtain them if possible. At first it seemed unlikely that the lady would ever part with them, but when we came near the sea she asked me to take care of them, and I gave half to the husband, restoring half to the lady later on. They consisted of a gold watch studded with diamonds, and several other articles. Nothing whatever remained in my hands.[47]

Katherine's sanity might have matched that of a march hare or wet hen but her memory could challenge an elephant, as Father Bede found out:

Having some business in Flanders the following year, I did not omit to call on the lady. Her first question was about the jewels. I said that her husband kept them for 'Her Majesty,' because she insisted on being addressed in that style. She answered in dreadful excitement: 'I shall have the gates of the town closed, and you will go to prison,' and left the room. After a while I received a message that I was to stay, and presently she returned herself, very much calmed down, and said, quite cheerfully: 'Sir, the cause for which I came hither no longer exists, and I am quite willing to return to England.' I had to politely decline the honour of accompanying Her Majesty, and left Ghent quietly.[48]

The Flemish air had done little for her peace of mind: Bede recorded that 'many other incidents occurred in regard of that case' but he tactfully withholds the detail. However, the air seemingly did wonders for Katherine's physical health: she did, at least, outlive her errant husband, and died at the nunnery on 1 July 1705.

Thus, with a wife mostly out of the way, a man of Sedley's wit, wealth and reputation should find the comfort of females not through the chase so much as a leisurely stroll. Reputation is one thing, record another. Pepys's cousin Roger told him,

a thing certain, that the Archbishop of Canterbury [the unmarried Gilbert Sheldon] that is now doth keep a wench, and that he is as very a wencher as can be. And tells us it is a thing publicly known, that Sir Ch. Sidly hath had got away one of the Archbishop's wenches from him, and the Archbishop sent to him to let him know that she was his kinswoman, and did wonder that he would offer any dishonour to one related to him. To which Sir Ch. Sidly is said to answer, A pox take his Grace! Pray tell his Grace that I believe he finds himself too old, and is afeared that I should outdo him among his girls and spoil his trade.[49]

The poet Andrew Marvell, well, marvelled at the scandal. In his 'Last Instructions', he accused Sheldon of having affairs with Katherine Boynton and Jane Middleton. He also commented in 'The loyall Scot':

> 'Tis necessary Lambeth never wed,
> Indifferent to have a wench in bed.

Katherine Boynton was, from 1660, maid of honour to the queen. In 1669 she would marry Richard Talbot, later Earl of Tyrconnel. On 26 October 1664, the queen and her maids arrived at Woolwich to attend the launch of the *Great Catherine*, a second-rate ship built by Christopher Pett, which the king declared the best ship ever built. However, the river had been rough that day, poor Katherine Boynton (along with the Duchess of Buckingham) was publicly seasick. Rather than demonstrate sympathy or concern, the king and his group made fun of the ill women. Thus Katherine's only entry in the greatest diary ever written describes her throwing up.

It is sorry state of affairs for a rake-hell when the Archbishop of Canterbury is outscoring you in the bedchamber. Pepys offers some hope while calling at the King's House (after seeing *The Man's the Master* at the rival Duke's House) to meet his friend the actress Mary Knepp: 'Here I did see the pretty woman newly come, called Pegg, that was Sir Ch. Sidly's mistress – a mighty pretty woman, and seems, but is not, modest.' It has been suggested that this 'Pegg' was the actress Margaret 'Peg' Hughes, but this is unlikely. It has also been suggested that it might be Catherine Pegge (later Lady Green), mother of one (if not two) of the king's children. Again unlikely. However, it is possible that Sedley's dating of a King's Theatre actress was the reason his long awaited playwrighting debut, *The Mulberry Garden*, opened at that venue.[50]

It has also been suggested that Mary Knepp, who was given the female lead in Sedley's *The Mulberry Garden*, surrendered to the author's carnal manoeuvres. One of his poems, 'To Celia' (which begins: 'As in those nations where they yet adore'), is signed in a contemporary hand 'To Mrs Mary Napp'.[51]

However, whatever the alluring mysteries of the author's lost mistresses, there's no sensual fogginess about plain-speaking Ann Ayscough. The daughter of Henry, a Yorkshire gentleman, Ann was to knock Sedley's life sideways. And back again. The initial attraction of the flesh had exposed him to a mind just as agreeable.

> *Fear not, my Dear, a flame can never die,*
> *That is once kindled by so bright an eye,*
>
> ...
>
> *For though thy Beauty first allured my sight,*
> *Yet now I look on it but as the light*
> *That led me to the treasury of thy mind.*[52]

This flame clearly wasn't for snuffing. She was to become, marriage aside, his wife. Indeed a poem by Sedley ends with the sentiment that, although married and unable to give his hand, he can give more: his heart and soul:

> *My hand, alas, is no more mine*
> *Else it had a long ago been thine.*
> *Mine heart I give thee, and we call*
> *No man unjust who parts with all.*
> *What a priest says moves not the mind,*
> *Souls are by love, not words, combin'd.*[53]

It was said, however, that Sedley did marry Ann. To do so, of course, would have been bigamous, an offence punishable by death. Any such celebration would have had to have been in strictest secrecy or carried out in a mock ceremony. Ann soon provided a son who not only took the father's first name but scandalously took his last name, also – as only 'lawful' children should. Charles Jr would be knighted by William III in 1689. Another son, William, died in infancy. Interestingly, the child was buried at the family church in Southfleet on 10 October 1676, but his name was entered discreetly in the burial register in Latin (the only entry so written) – 'Wilhelmus Caroli Sedley militis et Baronet' – possibly to soften the scandal of illegitimacy.

With his heart captured, Sedley broke rank from the circle of wits and squared up to a semi-retirement. He stayed with Ann for the rest of his life.

> *And little Sidly for Similie renown'd,*
> *Pleasure has always sought, but never found:*
> *Tho' all his Thoughts on Wine and Women fall,*
> *His are so bad sure he ne're thinks at all.*
> *The Flesh he lives upon is rank and strong,*
> *His Meat and Mistresses are kept too long.*[54]

With age increasingly bolting the door to excess and with a stable (in more ways than one) partner, Sedley's fiery affair with debauchery was certainly cooling. And just in case he wasn't translating the messages, an accident in January 1680 nearly claimed his life.

Historians normally set this story in the theatre, although it much more likely occurred during a tennis match. Sedley, George Etherege and Fleetwood Shepherd, was present when the roof of the tennis court in the Clare Market collapsed, with Sedley and Etherege being seriously hurt. Indeed, Sedley suffered such severe head injuries that he was immediately thought to be dead. Two newspapers, *True Domestic Intelligence* and *The True News, or Mercurius Anglicus*, both reported the supposed fatal tragedy, although subsequent editions confessed that their intelligence of news wasn't so true after all. The false news travelled at speed. In Oxford, Anthony à Wood was sufficiently abreast of the seemingly ever-changing situation to enter into his diary that Sedley had died on 20 January 1680 and had 'left his estate to his natural son and £10,000 to his owne daughter.' Amusingly, Wood, later and clearly in receipt of more reliable information, crossed the entry out and noted at the side: 'alive again'.[55]

In a letter to his brother, Charles Hatton wrote on 15 January 1680:

Yesterday ye roof of ye Tennis Cote in ye Haymarket fell down. Sr Charles Sidley being ther had his skull broke, and is thought it will be mortall. Sr George Etheridge and severall others were very dangerously hurt.[56]

The 1722 memoir recorded the following:

It was the Acting of his Play call'd Bellamira, that the Roof of the Playhouse fell down. But what was particular, was that very few were hurt but himself. His merry friend Sir Fleetwood Shepherd told him, There was so much fire in his Play that it blew up the Poet, House, and all. He told him again, NO: the play was so Heavy that it broked down the House, and buried the Poet in his own rubbish.[57]

A lot can happen to a story in 42 years. But it is this exchange that has guided historians to believe a theatre roof caved in – as it appears they were watching the play *Bellamira, or The Mistress*. However, Sedley wrote for the King's House, which was closed during January 1680 owing to an actors' dispute. Nor have there been any corroborative accounts of a collapsing theatre roof. Plays may well have been performed or rehearsed in a tennis court (the first two Restoration theatres were converted tennis courts), but Shepherd and Sedley's talk of 'the play' might as easily be linked to sporting play as to anything theatrical. Had it been a theatre, for the roof to injure so few – and one of those being the playwright – is pushing even Restoration reality beyond belief. Also, *Bellamira* did not open until 12 May 1687 and was thus evidently not the play being watched.[58]

Nonetheless, be it tennis court or stage, for Sedley it was neither the fifth and final set nor act. His life had been granted a sequel and this time the fireworks of part one were not accounted for in the budget. Through the gaping hole above him as he lay in the debris he seems to have seen the light of redemption.

> *Sidley He started once and did return again,*
> *But now his ears are bored by his own pen.*
> *When the old tennis court fell on his back,*
> *Tho his soul fluttered and the Goose cryed Quak*
> *Devotion by compulsion is but short...*[59]

The reformed Sedley, once in league with the very devil, had relegated his past, and championed God. Naturally, the satirists wasted little time in reaching for their quills.

> *Go let the fatted Calf a Victim burn*
> *For Sidley's the loose Prodigals return*
> *Sidley the Bold, the witty and the gay*
> *Whose tongue has lead so many Maids a stray*
> *Has laid aside the Vices of the Lay,*
> *And in the Arms of Mother Church at last*
> *More than attones for All his wandrings past.*[60]

He had assumed gently the prophecy of an earlier poem, 'To a Devout Young Gentlewoman', in which he noted that:

> *Old Men (till past the Pleasure) ne're*
> *Declaim against the Sin...*[61]

In this respect, Sedley compared favourably with the playwright William Wycherley, who kept the fires burning well past the time he had the strength to stoke them. Wycherley's lifestyle pickled his memory so much that he would claim he wrote all four of his plays (*Love in a Wood, The Gentleman Dancing-Master, The Country Wife* and *The Plain-Dealer* – a small but perfectly formed body of work) between the ages of 18 and 21, although his first play opened in 1671, when he was 31, and the last in 1676. In his cantankerous old days he befriended the young Alexander Pope, who wrote about the 64-year-old Wycherley: 'He had the same single thoughts (which were very good) come into his head again that he had used twenty years before. His memory did not carry above a sentence at a time.'[62]

Sedley's later days owed little to the vanity that soaked Wycherley, and he began a more serious career in politics. Once an old mucker of Charles II, and father of the mistress of James II, Sir Charles was a man naturally wrapped in the Stuart flag. However, he quietly unfurled it and laid it to rest as he supported the 1688 Glorious Revolution. His early biographer described him 'coming out of the

House of Commons the Day they Voted King William and Queen Mary into the Throne, Sir Charles mentioning it to a Friend, 'Well, says he, I am even with King James, in Point of Civility: For as he made my Daughter a Countess, so I have help'd to make his Daughter a Queen'.[63]

Later, in a letter to Sir Richard Newdigate, dated 12 January 1699, Sedley discussed the business of the house of commons:

> ...this day we went into a Committee of the whole house upon a bill presented by Sr John Philips, entitled an act to prevent debauchery and profanes: after some pains and penatrys aggreed to against persons keeping or frequenting bawdy houses: wee came to a clause concerning such women as should bee convicted of adultery it was provided that they should pay such cases the summ of 100*l* or be publikely whipt.[64]

How securely was the gate to the past now bolted.

As the new century opened so it would soon close for both Sir Charles Sedleys. Records show that Sedley's only son was buried in St Giles-in-the-Fields on 29 May 1701. He was about 29. Father soon followed the son, no doubt grief-stricken at his loss. Falling ill, he took a cottage near the then village of Hampstead at the beginning of August. The clean air managed to keep him alive for only about three weeks. The cottage was later occupied by Richard Steele, the playwright, MP and journalist, who was knighted in 1715. He also founded *Tatler* and, with Joseph Addison, the *Spectator*. Steele wrote to the poet Alexander Pope on 1 June 1712:

> I am at a solitude, a house between Hampstead and London, wherein Sir Charles Sedley died. This circumstance set me a thinking and ruminating upon the employments in which men of wit exercise themselves...
>
> This was a happy talent to a man of the town; but dare I say, without presuming to make uncharitable conjectures on the author's present condition, he would rather have had it said of him that he had prayed
>
> > *O thou my lips inspire,*
> > *Who touched Isaiah hallowed lips with fire!*[65]

Sedley's own less hallowed lips still clearly enjoyed the smack of ale and wine, if another epitaph, citing a favoured house of entertainment, is to be believed:

> *Oh, Dog and Partridge, thou hast cause to mourn;*
> *Thy Darling Son is from thy Bosom torn;*
> *Sidley is gone and never will return.*[66]

The Dog and Partridge, a tavern and eating house, was a regular haunt among the wits. It was one of three places mentioned by the character Sparkish in Wycherley's *The Country Wife* as a possible venue for the night's entertainment. The other two were Cateline's and the Cock. Cateline's was an extraordinarily fashionable French eating house in Covent Garden run by Henry Cateline, although, as with some restaurants there today, the fare was mediocre and unforgivably overpriced. Unfortunately, it's harder to identify the Cock exactly, as the name was rather popular but could well be either the tavern for ever linked to Sedley's scandalous youth, or the popular establishment on the Strand.

Thomas Shadwell also immortalised the wits' favoured tavern some eight years before Wycherley, in his 1668 production of *The Sullen Lovers*. Bridget tells her mistress, 'Oh, Madam, we must go to the Setting Dog and Partridge to supper tonight, Master Whiskin came to invite us, there will be the Blades, and we shall have a Ball.'[67]

With Sedley's death the Ball was burst. He was said by Harry Davenant, grandson to the theatrical legend William, to have 'died like a philosopher without fear or superstition', and was buried in the family vault at Southfleet Church on 26 August 1701.[68]

JOHN WILMOT, EARL OF ROCHESTER – SO IDLE A ROGUE

'Why dost thou abuse this age so? Methinks it's as pretty an honest, drinking, whoring age as a man would wish to live in.'
— Dorimant (said to have been based on Rochester) in
The Man of Mode, or Sir Fopling Flutter by George Etherege 1676

Just as everyone painted a saint has, if not the full skeleton, a few choice bones cluttering up their closet, just so in reverse, for those drawn as the epitome of wantonness. Nobody can be *that* good or *that* bad. The portrait of words that is the life of Rochester has, on the whole, been a case of painting debauchery-by-numbers. He certainly womanised, drank and entertained with his scrapes, but his reputation is a case of battery-farm overegging. As is said of

Etherege's Dorimant, 'I know he is a Devil, but he has something of the Angel yet undefac'd in him.'

John Wilmot was born on 1 April 1647, the son of Henry, first Earl of Rochester. His father, somewhat a dandy, refused to disguise himself in labourer's clothes during the escape after the defeat at the Battle of Worcester in 1652 on the grounds that 'he should look frightfully in it'. Even the king disguised himself as a farm worker after hiding from Cromwell's troops in an oak tree in Boscobel Woods. Finally convinced by his comrades, Wilmot in the end donned the remarkable disguise of a hawk on his wrist. Foolproof. Amazingly, he escaped to France. However, in exile he would for ever remain, for he died in 1658 at Sluis, Netherlands.[69]

The second earl's only inheritance was his father's title. Indeed, money would never be in bountiful supply despite his marrying an heiress – Elizabeth Mallet – for he relied on salaried royal appointments for his subsistence. As befitting a life member of the circle of wits, he was very well read, enjoying the classics and being very fond of Boileau (whom he imitated in his poem 'Timon') and the English writers Cowley and Waller, the latter of whom he quoted repeatedly.

He had four children with his wife: Anne, baptised on 30 August 1669; his only son, Charles, who would outlive his father by a only year, on 2 January 1671; Elizabeth, on 13 July 1674; and Mallet on 6 January 1675. He would also have a daughter, in 1677, with his mistress, the actress Elizabeth Barry.

After indulging in the gentry's post-Oxford statutory grand tour of Europe, the young earl soon discovered life at court to be perfectly agreeable. The hand-me-down image of this god of hellfire, for whom men, women and children were lusty logs to stoke the flames, had a rather more mundane picture of himself: 'I have seriously considerd one thinge, that of the three Buisnisses of this Age, Woemen, Polliticks & drinking,' he wrote to his friend Henry Savile, 'the last is the only exercise att wch you & I have nott prouv'd our selves Errant fumblers.' Indeed, his drinking was of a legendary vintage. 'The natural heat of his fancy, being inflamed by Wine,' wrote Gilbert Burnet, 'made him so extravagantly pleasant, that many, to be more diverted by that humour, studied to engage him deeper and deeper in Intemperance: which at length did so entirely subdue him; that, as he told me, for five years together he was continually Drunk: not all the while under the visible effect of it, but his blood was so inflamed, that he was not in all that time cool enough to be perfectly Master of himself.'[70]

Alcohol informed, inspired and inhibited Rochester's writing.

> *Vulcan contrive me such a cup*
> *As Nestor used of old:*
> *Show all thy skill to trim it up;*
> *Damask it round with gold.*
>
> *Make it so large that, filled with sack*
> *Up to the swelling brim,*
> *Vast toasts on the delicious lake,*
> *Like ships at sea may swim.*[71]

(*Sack* – sec, white wine.)

As usual for the court wits, the classical poetry and legend were reference points for their own meanderings. In the above poem, 'Upon His Drinking a Bowl' Vulcan was the Roman god of fire and destruction, and linked to Hephaestus, the Greek god of fire and metalcraft, whose unfaithful wife was the goddess of beauty and sexual love. In Homer's *The Iliad*, Nestor's

> beautifully wrought cup…was set with golden nails, the eared handles upon it were four, and on either side there were fashioned two doves of gold, feeding, and there were double bases beneath it. Another man with great effort could lift it full from the table, but Nestor, aged as he was, lifted it without strain.

And the only thing fit for this cup was wine, naturally.[72]

In the other two businesses of the age, women and politics, Rochester has honestly admitted his failings. With the exception of the actress Elizabeth Barry, Rochester shied away from long-term mistresses, but was an embittered slave to alcohol-induced casual sex. He was on good, if in general distant (geographically at least), relations with his wife, and at times was certainly affectionate towards her. In a letter to her from Newmarket, submerging himself in the gambling spirit, he informed her: 'I'll hold you six to four I love you with all my heart, if I would bet with other people, I'm sure I could get two to one.'[73]

It has been suggested that Rochester was a repressed homosexual and needed to get drunk to face sex with women, although – as discussed in Chapter 3 – occasional acts of sodomy actually reinforced a brutish masculinity. He may well have been bisexual, but one song in particular is hashed out as indisputable proof of his extended sexual preferences:

> *Love a woman? You're an ass!*
> *'Tis a most insipid passion*
> *To choose out for your happiness*

The silliest part of God's creation.
Farewell, woman! I intend
Henceforth every night to sit
With my lewd, well-natured friend,
Drinking to engender wit.
Then give me health, wealth, mirth, and wine,
And, if busy love entrenches,
There's a sweet, soft page of mine
Does the trick worth forty wenches.[74]

Also, this stanza from 'The Disabled Debauchee':

Nor shall our love-fits, Chloris, be forgot,
When each the well-looked linkboy strove t'enjoy
And the best kiss was the deciding lot
Whether the boy fucked you, or I the boy.[75]

As for politics, Rochester contented himself looking from the outside in and sending up those laughable types who sought and exerted influence. He commented, '...they who would be great in our little Government, seem as ridiculous to me as School-boys, who with much endeavour, and some danger, climb a Crab-tree, venturing their necks for Fruit which solid Piggs would disdain if they were not starving.'[76]

He delighted in spinning off satirical quickies, such as his 'Impromptu on the English Court':

Here's Monmouth the witty,
And Lauderdale the pretty,
And Frazier, that learned physician;
But above all the rest,
Here's the Duke for a jest,
And the King for a grand politician.[77]

Monmouth, was James Crofts, the Duke of Monmouth who despite grace and dashing good looks was somewhat less well endowed with wit or intelligence. *Lauderdale* was John Maitland (1616–82), created first Duke of Lauderdale in 1672, who as secretary for Scottish affairs was basically ruler of that nation, a task he took to with stern, iron-fisted relish. However, he was not the prettiest of all his majesty's subjects. Burnet wrote, 'He made a very ill appearance: he was very big: his hair red, hanging oddly about him: his tongue was too big for his mouth, which made him bedew all that he talked to.' *Frazier* was Sir Alexander

Frasier (c. 1610–81), physician-in-ordinary to the king. Clarendon thought him 'good at his business, otherwise the maddest fool alive'. *The Duke* was the king's brother, James, Duke of York, who was remarkably humourless. The king, of course, was relentlessly lampooned as politically lazy and inept, which he took in good humour.

It was this characteristic coupled with the king's own wit and penchant for well-meant but seldom-delivered pledges that inspired Rochester's famous 'Impromptu on Charles II':

> *God bless our good and gracious King,*
> *Whose promise none relies on;*
> *Who never said a foolish thing,*
> *Nor ever did a wise one.*[78]

However, Rochester enjoyed satirising the social as well as political life of the court. And it transpired that he had a resourceful method of assembling serviceable information. 'To gain him intelligence [at court] he employed a footman,' wrote Gilbert Burnet, 'who knew almost everybody, to stand, all winter long, every night as a sentinel at such ladies' doors as he believed might be in any intrigues. By this means he made discoveries, and when he was thus furnished with materials, he retired to the country and wrote libels.'[79]

Nor was Rochester the only one to employ such schemes. Hugh, Lord Cholmondeley, similarly added such tasks to his footmen's job description, and another rake, Jack Howe, turned his sisters into social spies. The (typically) anonymous author of (typically) 'A Satyr' in 1680 pointed the finger at Ned Russell, third son of the Earl of Bedford, as one who snooped to conquer:

> *. . . Like a cur who's taught to fetch he goes*
> *From place to place to bring back what he knows:*
> *Tells who's i'th' Park, what coaches turned about,*
> *Who were the sparks, and whom they followed out.*[80]

And salacious sagas weren't exclusively about everybody else: sometimes Rochester was the victim of rip-roaring stories of embarrassment, as Pepys discovered on 2 December 1668. On visiting the Duke of York on business, he 'saw all the ladies and heard the silly discourse of the King with his people about him, telling a story of my Lord of Rochester's having of his clothes stole while with a wench, and his gold all gone but his clothes found afterward, stuffed into a feather bed by the wench that stole them.'[81]

Such stories did little to rob you of your rake-hood. Although famed for his sexual and drinking exploits and the occasional meddling in matters of the day, Rochester was less convincing on the sabre-rattling side of things. The earl rarely put his dukes up. And, while he didn't search out violence, it inevitably came a-calling, as the Epsom assaults prove.

On a balmy Saturday night of 17 June 1676, Rochester with William Jephson, Captain Bridges, Captain Downs and George Etherege (undoubtedly doing his damnedest to be rid of the title 'Gentle') were involved in an affray at Epsom. Downs was killed 'by his hurts recd from ye Rusticks.'[82]

On 29 June a letter by Charles Hatton to his brother summarised the sorry story.

Mr Downs is dead. Ye Ld Rochester doth abscond, and soe doth Etheridge, and Capt Bridges who occasioned ye riot Sunday sennight. They were tossing some fidlers in a blanket for refusing to play, and a barber, upon ye noise, going to see what ye matter, they seized upon him, and, to free himself from them, he offered to carry then to ye handsomest woman in Epsom, and directed them to the constables house, who demanding what they came for, they told him a whore, and he refusing to let them in, they broke open his doores and broke his head, and beate him very severely. At last, he made his escape, called his watch, and Etheridge made a submissive oration to them and soe far appeased them that ye constable dismissed his watch. But presently after, ye Ld Rochester drew upon ye constable. Mr Downs, to prevent his pass, seized on him, ye constable cryed out murther, and, the watch returning, one came behind Mr Downs and with a sprittle staff cleft his scull. Ye Ld Rochester and ye rest run away...[83]

With such a rapid exit, it was clear that the town wasn't big enough for these sparks, and they rapidly deserted their friend, leaving him to fight on valiantly but vainly.

...and Downs, having noe sword, snatched up a sticke and striking at them, they run him into ye side wth a half pike, and soe bruised his arme yt he wase never able to stirr it after.[84]

Downs died of his wounds ten days later. It seems Rochester's flight saved his skin. This may have been the source of a comment by Burnet concerning 'an unlucky accident, which obliged him to keep out of the way.' He was set to be tried by his peers for murder, as a letter – dated

27 June – from the Earl of Anglesey to the Earl of Essex indicated: 'Yesterday, the Lord Cornwallis was tried by his peers...My Lord Rochester's turn will be next.' But the trial, without the accused, never took place. Given the aristocratic forgiveness that permeated the House on such occasions, even if the trial had been held, he probably would have been sentenced to promise not to do it again. Or for a very good while at least.[85]

About ten days or so later, Rochester, in cathartic mood, seems to have knocked out the eighteen lines, in part suitably remorseful, and in part uncomfortably boastful, that became 'To the Postboy':

> Rochester.   *Son of a whore, God damn you! can you tell*
> *A peerless peer the readiest way to Hell?*
> *I've outswilled Bacchus, sworn of my own make*
> *Oaths would fright Furies, and make Pluto quake;*
> *I've swived more whores more ways then Sodom's walls*
> *E'er knew, or the College of Rome's Cardinals.*
> *Witness heroic scars – Look here, ne're go! –*
> *Cerecloths and ulcers from the top to toe!*
> *Frighteed at my own mischiefs, I have fled*
> *And bravely left my life's defender dead;*
> *Broke houses to break chastity, and dyed*
> *That floor with murder which my lust denied.*
> *Pox on't, why do I speak of these poor things?*
> *I have blasphemed my God, and libelled Kings!*
> *The readiest way to Hell – Come quick!*
> Boy.   *Ne'er stir:*
> *The readiest way, my Lord, 's by Rochester.*[86]

(*Bacchus* – the Roman god of wine and ecstasy; *Furies* – in Roman legend, the Furies were three winged maidens with serpents twisted in their hair; they punished crimes such as filial disobedience, murder and lack of hospitality; *Pluto* – in Greek mythology, the lord of Hades – the underworld; *Cerecloths* – wax-covered or spice-soaked cloths commonly used as plasters in surgery.)

However, Rochester may have gone away but memories of the fracas remained for viewing by appointment. They would be courted and paraded by his increasing number of enemies. After Rochester had fallen out with another one-time companion, Sir Carr Scrope, the squinting minor poet, engaged Rochester in a duel more suited to his temperament: a duel of words. He had already discharged his opening volley in reply to Scrope's criticisms in 'An Allusion to Horace':

Should I be troubled when the purblind knight,
Who squints more in judgment than his sight,
Picks silly faults, and censures what I write . . . ?[87]

Upping the ante, in 'A Defence of Satire' Scrope merrily recalled the regrettable incident at Epsom. The 'buffoon conceit' may well be 'To the Postboy'.

He who can push into a midnight fray
His brave companion, and then run away,
Leaving him to be murder'd in the street,
Then put it off with some buffoon conceit;
Him, thus dishonour'd, for a wit you won,
And count him top fiddler of the town.[88]

In the autumn of 1676, Rochester counter-thrusted with 'On the Supposed Author of a Late Poem in Defence of Satyr', part of which ran:

A lump deformed and shapeless wert thou born,
Begot in love's despite and nature's scorn,
And art grown up the most ungraceful wight,
Harsh to the ear, and hideous to the sight;
Yet love's thy business, beauty thy delight.
Curse on that silly hour that first inspired
Thy madness to pretend to be admired:
To paint thy grisly face, to dance, to dress,
And all those awkward follies that express
Thy loathsome love and filthy daintiness;
Who needs will be an ugly beau garcon,
Spit at and shunned by every girl in town,
Where, dreadfully, love's scarecrow thou art placed
To fright the tender flock that long to taste,
While every coming maid, when you appear,
Starts back in shame, and straight turns chaste for fear.
For none so poor or prostitute have proved,
Where you made love, t'endure to be beloved.
'Twere labour lost, or else I would advise
But thy half wit will ne'er let thee be wise.
Half witty, and half mad, and scarce half brave;
Half honest, which is very much a knave -
Made up of all these halves, thou canst not pass
For anything entirely but an ass.[89]

That Scrope was outcast from the Merry Gang was confirmed in one of the surviving letters of Nell Gwynne sent around June 1678. In typically chatty mode, she informs Laurence Hyde that her house at Pall Mall 'is now to me a dismale plase sinse I have so uterly lost Sr Car Scrope never to be recooverd agane for he tould me he could not live allwayes at this rate & so begune to be a little uncivil, which I could not suffer from an ugly baux garscon.' It amply shows the devastating effect Rochester could have on his enemies – some two years after 'On the Supposed Author', his labelling of Scrope as an '*ugly beau garcon*' had evidently become his moniker.

However, Scrope, although now ostracised, could not have formerly kept such company as Rochester and Nelly without displaying a fruitful wit. And it was from this that he unleashed a bustling riposte in the form of an epigram, finally making play with Rochester's non-duel with Mulgrave:

> *Rail on, poor feeble scribbler, speak of me*
> *In as bad terms as the whole world speaks of thee.*
> *Sit swelling in thy hole like a vexed toad,*
> *And full of pox and malice, spit abroad.*
> *Thou canst blast no man's frame with thy ill word:*
> *Thy pen is full as harmless as thy sword.*[90]

Understandably, Scrope decided to quit the quarrel on a personal high. Rochester, however, would spit more malice in 'The Mock Song' and 'On Poet Ninny'. The vexed toad.

It may have been this ability to spiral into a spleen-venting frenzy that caused Rochester, in 1677, to declare to his friend Henry Savile that he had become 'a man whom it is the great mode to hate'. He was clearly capable of pernicious pursuit, as one of the court ladies discovered. Goditha Price seemingly made the mistake of quarrelling with a young woman much admired by Rochester, but whose liaisons had been conducted in secrecy. Price exposed the affair and 'thereby drew upon herself the most dangerous enemy in the universe'. Every day was marked with some new song, lampoon or satire that ridiculed Price and her name. Rochester, hungry for morsels to exploit, was fed every conceivable trifling detail about her life, background, likes and so on for him to mould together in some cutting jibe.[91]

It was a festering obsession of which Scrope was only too aware. Rochester's 'The Mock Song' mocked one of his lyrics, possibly for Cary Fraiser, maid of honour to the queen and daughter of the king's physician-in-ordinary, Sir Alexander Fraiser, whom he was courting at the time.[92]

Scrope

I cannot change as others do,
Though you unjustly scorn,
Since that poor swain that sighs for you
For you alone was born.
No, Phyllis, no, your heart to move,
A surer way I'll try,
And to revenge thy slighted love,
Will still love on, will still love on, and die.

When killed with grief Amyntas lies,
And you to mind shall call
The sighs that now unpitied rise,
The tears that vainly fall,
That welcome hour that ends his smart
Will then begin your pain,
For such a faithful, tender heart
Can never break, can never break in vain.

Rochester

'I swive as well as others do;
I'm young, not yet deformed;
My tender heart, sincere and true,
Deserves not to be scorned.
Why, Phyllis, then, why will you swive
With forty lovers more?'
'Can I,' said she, 'with nature strive?
Alas I am, alas I am a whore!

'Were all my body larded o'er
With darts of love, so thick
That you might find in every pore
A well-stuck standing prick,
Whilst yet my eyes alone were free,
My heart would never doubt,
In amorous rage and ecstasy,
To wish those eyes, to wish those eyes
fucked out.'

On the grounds that the physician's daughter was associated with Scrope (whether or not she moistened his bauble) was enough for her to become a legitimate target for Rochester. The outcome: 'On Cary Frazier'.

> Her father gave her dildoes six
> Her mother made 'em up a score;
> But she loves nought but living pricks,
> And swears by God she'll frig no more.[93]

The last of his surviving apparent attacks on Scrope is 'On Poet Ninny'. Ninny was originally a character in Thomas Shadwell's *The Sullen Lovers* and supposedly based on Edward Howard, himself responsible for acutely average poetry and middling plays. The name Ninny was thus associated with hack mediocrity. Hence Rochester's choice of name for Scrope in this final attack. Unsurprisingly, it centres on Scrope's weak pen, ugly face and that ultimate badge of Restoration dishonour – pride.

> Born to no other but thy own disgrace,
> Thou art a thing so wretched and so base
> Thou canst not ev'n offend, but with thy face;

And dost at once a sad example prove
Of harmless malice, and of hopeless love,
All pride and ugliness! Oh, how we loath
A nauseous creature so composed of both![94]

Violence, however, was not Rochester's forte, as his one and only punch-up indicates. At a dinner hosted by the Dutch ambassador on 16 February 1669, the drink, as convention would have it, was little spared. Rochester, his wit somewhat watered by the wine, could only reply to Tom Killigrew's baiting of him on keeping his wife in the country by unleashing 'a box on the ear in the King's presence.' Despite this shocking display of bad form, which widely affronted the court, the whiff of offence became all the more pungent to see 'how cheap the King makes himself, and the more for that the King hath not only passed by the thing and pardoned it to Rochester already, but this very morning the King did publicly walk up and down, and Rochester I saw with him, as free as ever to the King's everlasting shame to have so idle a rogue his companion.' However, according to the Sandwich manuscripts, Rochester was banished from court and went to France.[95]

Dorothy, Lady Sunderland, confirming Rochester's less than sober state, wrote, 'This has been a quarrelsome week; before the King my Lord of Rochester forgot his duty so much as to strike Tom Killigrew. He was in a case not to know what he did, but he is forbid the Court.'[96]

One other incident, loosely linked to violence deserves the telling:

The late Lord Rochester being, upon a freak with some of his companions, at the Bear at the Bridge-foot, among their music, they had a hump-back'd fiddler, whom they called His Honour. To humour the frolic, they all agreed to leap into the Thames, and it came to Lord Rochester's turn to do it at last; but his Lordship seeing the rest in, and not at all liking the frolic, set the crooked fiddler at the brink of the balcony, and push'd him in, crying out – I can't come myself, gentlemen, but I've sent my honour.[97]

Rochester's true honour was tested by his relationship with his only known long-term mistress. Described as 'undoubtedly the greatest Restoration actress', Elizabeth Barry struggled to convince at the start of her career. She was sacked after her first year, according to the actor, manager and writer Colley Cibber. Anthony Aston wrote that the stage folk 'for some Time...could not make nothing of her. She could neither sing nor dance, no, not in a Country-Dance.'[98]

Betterton's *History of the English Stage* described a typical performance where 'several Persons of Wit and Quality being at the Play, and observing how she performed, positively gave their opinion she never would be capable of any Part of Acting.' However, one observer clearly saw that something special could be fashioned from the wood before him. Rochester 'entered into a wager, that by proper instruction, in less than six months he would engage she should be the finest player on the stage'. Rochester appears to have been the original exponent of 'method' acting, believing an actor should become the part rather than simply sing lines. He was to enable her to 'enter into the Nature of such Sentiment, perfectly changing herself as it were into the person, not merely by proper Stress or Sounding of the Voice, but feeling really, and being in the Humour, the Person she represented, was supposed to be in'. The exclusive Wilmot School of Stage & Dancing had enrolled its first and only student. It was to have a 100 per cent success rate as its star pupil would be heralded as 'the first really outstanding English actress.'[99]

Her looks appear to have been about as exceptional as her early talent, but, as Rochester detected, there was still something there. Aston thought her 'a fine Creature' though 'not handsome'. Cibber describes her as 'middle siz'd, and had darkish Hair, light Eyes, dark Eye-brows, and was indifferently plump'.[100]

An early – if not the first – part as the new, improved Mrs Barry* was the Hungarian Queen Isabella in the Earl of Orrery's tragedy *Mustapha*, for which 'the whole theatre resounded with applause.' Inevitably, given Barry's craving for career enhancement and Rochester's rakish reputation, she was soon skipping about his bedchamber as confidently as she strode the boards. The volatile actress and the earl clearly had a stormy and passionate relationship. In one letter to her, Rochester writes, 'Dear Madam, You are stark mad, and therefore the fitter for me to love; and that is the reason I can leave to be.'[101]

A lyric survives in Rochester's own hand, simply entitled 'Song', addressed to an actress mistress. The temptation to believe it was written for Barry is strong but remains circumstantial:

> *Leave this gaudy gilded stage,*
> *From custom more than use frequented,*
> *Where fools of either sex and age*
> *Crowd to see themselves presented.*
> *To love's theatre, the bed,*

---

*'Mrs' was pronounced 'Mistress' and actually referred to a single woman rather than a married woman as today.

Youth and beauty fly together,
And act so well it may be said
The laurel there was due to either.

'Twixt strifes of love and war, the difference lies in this:
When neither overcomes, love's greater triumph is.[102]

In December 1677, Henry Savile wrote to a sickly Rochester retired to the country for recuperation, of a rather significant development:

The greatest newes I can send you from hence is what the King told mee last night, that your Ld has a daughter borne by the body of Mrs Barry of which I give your honour joy, I doubt shee dos not lye in in much state, for a friend and protectrice of hers in the Mall was much lamenting her poverty very lately, not without some gentle reflexions on your Lds want either of generosity or bowells toward a lady who had not refused you the full enjoyment of her charmes.[103]

The child was named after the mother. Rochester, perhaps nudged by Savile's taunting, wrote to the new mother that same month:

Your safe Delivery has delivered me too from fears for your sake, which were, I'll promise you as burthensome to me, as your great-belly could be to you. Everything has fallen out to my wish, for you are out of danger, and the child is of the soft sex I love. Shortly, my hopes are to see you, and in a little while to look on you with all your beauty about you. Pray let nobody but yourself open the box I sent you; I did not know, but that in lying in you might have use of those trifles. Sick and in bed as I am, I could come at no more of 'em; but if you find 'em, or whatever is in my power, of use to your Service, let me know.'[104]

Rochester, later concerned for his daughter, removes her from Barry to be brought up with his other children.

Madam, I am far from delighting in the grief I have given you by taking away the child; and you, who made it so absolutely necessary for me to do so, must take that excuse from me for all the ill nature of it. On the other side, pray be assured I love Betty so well that you need not apprehend any neglect from those I employ, and I hope very shortly to restore her to you a finer girl than ever. In the meantime you would do well to think of the advice I gave you, for how little show soever my prudence makes in my own affairs, in yours it will prove very successful if you please to follow it. And since discretion is the thing alone you are like to want, pray study to get it.[105]

Betty was most probably 'the infant child by the name of Elizabeth Clerke' left £40 a year in Rochester's will, proved in London on 23 February 1681. However, the annuity would not be needed for long because it appears that young Betty died aged twelve. Barry, however, kept on going, becoming an acting legend in her own lifetime for the sheer volume of roles she played. Her final appearance came, defiantly into her fifties, on 13 June 1710 as Lady Easy (somewhat appropriately for those who sniffed at her notorious private life) in a revival of Colley Cibber's *The Careless Husband*. Off the stage she never had a husband, of her own at least, careless or otherwise. She died in Acton on 7 November 1713.

Rochester's affair may have been a one-off, but some things were more regular in his life. His actions, for example, but more often his words almost annually resulted in the ultimate sanction: expulsion from court. Commanded away from the fray would destroy or belittle most. For Rochester it became an occupational hazard.

Take, for example, the sundial incident of June 1675. The king's interest in time was well known. He had hundreds of clocks and collected sundials and chronometers. One warm, fateful night, Rochester 'in a frolik after a rant did yesterday downe the dyill which stood in the middle of the Privie [Gard]ing, which was esteemed the rarest in Europe.' The phallicism of this particular 'Pyramidical Dial', which apparently resembled 'a prick of candlesticks', was unmistakable. It was,

broken all to pieces (for they were of glass spheres) by the earl of Rochester, lord Buckhurst, Fleetwood Shephard, &c, coming in from their revels. 'What!' said the earl of Rochester, 'doest thou stand here to fuck time?' Dash they fell to worke.[106]

One correspondent worried if upon that account Rochester would be found impertinent or might be excused it as an accident. However, even this soft-eyed king would find it hard to look kindly on such a drunken caper. In any case, Rochester didn't hang about to discover his fate and made his way to Woodstock, his country estate.

Being caught up in drunken challenges added to Rochester's woes. A newsletter dated 16 March 1668 reported that five days earlier, on Tuesday night, there was a quarrel between the Duke of Richmond and Mr James Hamilton after they had dined well at the Tower with Sir Henry Savile. They had chosen their seconds, but the Lord General sent for the principals, and out them on their honours not to prosecute it. The Earl of Rochester was one of the party, who, upon his disgrace at Court, intends to go to France for some time.[107]

However, it was more likely to be a libel that would see him pack his quills. In December 1671, we're told that Rochester was 'forbid the court againe about publishing (or rather not concealing) a Libell, wherein the Duchesse of Cleveland and Mr Churchill & others were concerned.' This was probably 'Mistress Knight's Advice to the Duchess of Cleveland in Distress for a Prick'.

> *Quoth the Duchess of Cleveland to counselor Knight*
> *'I'd fain have a prick, knew I how to come 't.*
> *I desire you'll be secret, and give your advice:*
> *Though cunt be not coy, reputation is nice.'*
> *'To some cellar in Sodom Your Grace must retire*
> *Where porters with black-pots sit around a coal-fire;*
> *There open your case, and Your Grace cannot fail*
> *Of a dozen of pricks for a dozen of ale.'*
> *'Is 't so?' quoth the Duchess. 'Aye, by God!' quoth the whore.*
> *'Then give me the key that unlocks the back door,*
> *For I'd rather be fucked by porters or carmen*
> *Than thus be abused by Churchill and Jermyn.'*[108]

(*Cleveland* – Barbara Villiers, Duchess of Cleveland, the king's mistress, although out of favour; *Knight* – Mary Knight, the singer (of whom Evelyn thought incomparable and 'doubtlesse has the greatest reach of any English Woman') and minor mistress of Charles II (hence 'whore'); *Sodom* – part of London notorious for its brothels and taverns of unsavoury reputation; *black-pots* – beer mugs; *carmen* – sedan carriers; *Churchill* – John Churchill, Barbara's lover; *Jermyn* – Henry Jermyn, nephew of Earl of St Albans.)[109]

It happened again in January 1674 when he gave the king the wrong poem. Once again he did not wait for the king's wrath – but, being so well acquainted with form, departed for the country again. A letter dated 20 January read 'my Lord Rochester fled from the Court some time since for delivering (by mistake) into the king's hands a terrible lampoon of his own making against the King, instead of another the King asked for.' The poem that grievously offended was 'A Satyr on Charles II':

I'th'isle of Britain, long since famous grown
For breeding the best cunts in Christendom,
There reigns, and oh! long may he reign and thrive,
The easiest King and best-bred man alive.
Him no ambition moves to get renown
Like the French fool, that wanders up and down
Starving his people, hazarding his crown.
Peace is his aim, his gentleness is such,
And love he loves, for he loves fucking much.
　　Nor are his high desires above his strength:
His sceptre and his prick are of a length;
And she may sway the one who plays with th'other,
And make him little wiser than his brother.
Poor prince! thy prick, like thy buffoons at Court,
Will govern thee because it makes thee sport.
'Tis sure the sauciest prick that e'er did swive,
The proudest, peremptoriest prick alive.
Though safety, law, religion, life lay on't,
'Twould break through all to make its way to cunt.
Restless he rolls from whore to whore,
A merry monarch, scandalous and poor.
　　To Carwell, the most dear of his dears,
The best relief of his declining years,
Oft he bewails his fortune, and her fate:
To love so well and be beloved so late.
For though in her he settles well his tarse,
Yet his dull graceless ballocks hang an arse.
This you'd believe, had I time to tell ye
The pains it costs to poor, laborious Nelly,
Whilst she employs hands, fingers, mouth and thighs,
Ere she can raise the member she enjoys.
　　All monarchs I hate, and the thrones they sit on,
From the hector of France to the cully of Britain.[110]

(*Swive* – sexual intercourse; *Carwell* – the king's chief mistress the French Catholic Louise de Keroualle; the people had trouble pronouncing her last name and plumped generally for Madam Carwell; *tarse* – penis; *hector* – a swaggering bully; *cully* – someone who is imposed upon, a dupe.)

Rochester's annual expulsion from court probably served both him and Charles well. For Charles, it displayed that there was a line (after all) that could not be crossed and it signalled that excess was put on notice (albeit improbably enforceable). For Rochester, it provided a rest, a time to reflect and rekindle. It appears that his antics and (crucially) his drinking – the latter undoubtedly fuelling the former – varnished the image of man as debaucher. It was what he had to do to keep the heat of fame flickering – and people expected to be licked by his flames. Being Rochester the public property relentlessly took its physical and mental toll, and he needed time and space to be John Wilmot. The carnival of public disgrace became his private salvation. Back home at Woodstock it was a festival of peace.

Such was Rochester's reputation that tales were spun effortlessly to willing ears that knew not disbelief. It was known that the earl had no qualms about who might suffer at his jests. The biggest audience of all fell in with the earl, who devised a plan to cure the king of his 'nocturnal ramblings'. Theophilius Cibber is our source:

> He agreed to go out one night with him to visit a celebrated house of intrigue, where he told his Majesty the finest women in England were to be found. The King made no scruple to assume his usual disguise and accompany him, and while he was engaged with one of the ladies of pleasure, being before instructed by Rochester how to behave, she picked his pocket of all his money and watch, which the King did not immediately miss. Neither the people of the house, nor the girl herself was made acquainted with the quality of their visitor, nor had the least suspicion of who he was.
>
> When the intrigue was ended, the King enquired for Rochester but was told he had quitted the house, without taking leave: but into what embarrassment was he thrown when upon searching his pockets, in order to discharge the reckoning, he found his money gone? He was then reduced to ask the favour of the Jezebel to give him credit till tomorrow as the gentleman who had gone in with him had not returned, who was to have pay'd for both. The consequence of this request was, he was abused and laughed at; and the old woman told him that she had often been served such dirty tricks, and would not permit him to stir till the reckoning was paid, and then called one of her bullies to take care of him...
>
> After many altercations, the King at last proposed, that she should accept a ring which he then took off his finger, in pledge for her money, which she likewise refused, and told him, that as she was no judge of the value of the ring, she did not choose to accept such pledges. The King then desired that a jeweller might be called to give his opinion of the value of it, but he was answered that the expedient was impracticable, as no jeweller could then be supposed to be out of bed.

After much entreaty his Majesty at last prevailed upon the fellow to knock up a jeweller and show him the ring, which as soon as he inspected, he stood amazed, and inquired with eyes fixed on the fellow, who had he got in his house? to which he answered, a black-looking ugly son of a whore, who had no money in his pocket, and was obliged to pawn his ring. The ring, says the jeweller, is so immensely rich, that but one man in the nation could afford to wear it; and that one is the King. The jeweller, being astonished at this accident, went out with the bully, in order to be fully satisfied of so extraordinary an affair; and as soon as he entered the room, he fell on his knees, and with the utmost respect presented the ring to his Majesty.[111]

The old Jezebel and the bully, finding the extraordinary quality of their guest, were now confounded, and asked pardon most submissively on their knees. The King in the best-natured manner forgave them, and, laughing, asked them whether the ring would not bear another bottle.

Another story is the spurious Green Man tale. The evidence for this tale rests solely on a clearly fake memoir by St Evremond (who was a reliable commentator but was much forged in the eighteenth century) attached to an edition of Rochester's poetry in 1707. It certainly delivers a splash of the times but is fancy, not fact. It was believed to be biography for over a century and has contributed effectively to the demonisation of Rochester as the rake-hell. For that – and because it's a good yarn – it's worth the retelling.

In disgrace from court (well that part rings true) Buckingham and Rochester to pass the time of their banishment and to amuse themselves in the process took over the running, incognito, of an inn – the Green Man – at Six-Mile-Bottom near Newmarket. At specially hosted free nights they invited the local and travelling gentlemen who had wives, sisters or daughters who had caught their eye. Then they plied the menfolk with wine enough to drink themselves into a stupor, making it safe enough for Rochester and Bucks to pay their less than honourable attentions upon the neglected women.

However, one miserly old local with a young and pretty wife never let her out of his sight unless under the auspices of his wizened old sister. So, despite his regular and keen attendance at the inn, he could not be persuaded to bring his wife. And there was no joy to be had at the house because of the zealous chaperone, who would not leave her alone with a man. So, while the husband supped at their expense – again – Rochester, in true pre-Restoration theatrical tradition, dressed himself up as a country maid and visited the beauty and her beast.

Despite being convinced by Rochester's angelic face that the caller was indeed a woman, the suspicious sentry refused him access to the house. Cue the faint. On hearing the commotion, the protected wife insisted their caller be brought in. Solid research had informed Rochester that the miserly old curmudgeon's spinster sister enjoyed a nip or two on the quiet. Armed with a couple of bottles, Rochester aided his 'recovery' with a few sips and gradually convinced his nemesis to likewise try the healing spirit. Sips became glugs and when the second bottle was required Rochester produced it to the old lush's delight. However, this contained an opium additive.

With the defences breached and snoring loudly, Rochester advanced on the old man's treasure. Again feigning dizziness, the wife helped him to the bed. From such a fortunate position he discussed the wife's marriage and husband. Such a tale of woe and dissatisfaction was cast against the old tyrant that Rochester made himself – or rather part of himself – known. The neglected wife was delighted at the introduction.

Later he invited her back to the Green Man, to which she agreed but only after she had robbed her sister-in-law's purse. The husband, returning home, finding his sister drugged and his wife gone, did what any self-respecting person would do in such a bunkum story, and immediately went insane and hanged himself.[112]

Rochester's own and very real death was marked by penitence. On 7 June 1680, Ralph Verney noted that Rochester 'is like to dye,' but 'he hath been a most penitent and pious man in his sicknesse.' Six weeks later, on 18 July 1680 Mr Cary wrote to Ralph Verney: 'My Lord Rochester continues very weake, he is sometimes a little lively & this gives good hope of his recovery, but anon downe again, which makes us feare the worst.' The worst was wisely feared for within a week Rochester was dead.[113]

Undoubtedly, Bishop Gilbert Burnet, who was sent for by the dying Rochester, hijacked his death for a glorious lesson in contrition. The lost lamb was back with the fold. Lady Chaworth wrote to Lord Roos that the earl was 'so penitent that he said he would be an exsample of penitence to the whole world'.[114]

The damage of such a life – particularly the drinking – would eventually, he rightly feared, be irreparable. Intended as autobiographical or not, he toyed with the possibility in 'The Disabled Debauchee':

So, when my days of impotence approach,
*   And I'm by pox and wine's unlucky chance*
Forced from the pleasing billows of debauch
On the dull shore of lazy temperance,

My pains at least some respite shall afford
*   While I behold the battles you maintain*
When fleets of glasses sail about the board,
*   From whose broadsides volleys of wit shall rain.*[115]

In the prologue to Elkanah Settle's *Empress of Morocco*, Rochester had written, 'See my credentials written in my face.' They were certainly there now. The years of drinking had exacted their scandalous toll with menaces. He spent his short adult life awash with wit but drowning in abuse. He was just 33 years old. Another life misspent. And no change either.

Aphra Behn wrote the prologue to Rochester's unfinished play *Valentinian* on its first night. However, a further, anonymous, prologue was written, fittingly, for Elizabeth Barry and addressed to the women in the audience who had loved him:

Some Beauties here I see –
Though now demure, have felt his pow'rful Charms,
And languish'd in the circle of his Arms.[116]

And some, no doubt, languish there still.

6

Drink: in Imminent Peril of Sobriety

Drinke to day and drowne all sorrow,
You shall perhaps not doe it to morrow.
Best while you have it use your breath,
There is no drinking after death.

– possibly John Fletcher, 1619 (drinking song from
The Bloody Brother, or Rollo, Duke of Normandy – popular with
Restoration audiences)

Dear Friend, I fear my Heart will break;
In t'other World I scarce believe,
In this I little pleasure take:
That my whole Grief thou may'st conceive;
Cou'd not I Drink more than I Whore,
By Heaven, I wou'd not live an Hour.[1]
– Sir Charles Sedley, *Out of French*[1]

The English beer is best in all Europe ... it was necessary to drink two
or three pots of beer during our parley; for no kind of business is
transacted in England without the intervention of pots of beer.[2]
– Jarevin de Rochefort 1672

Life under the English Civil War and the Commonwealth was austere.
Puritanism demanded thrift, respect, piety and that most difficult of
commitments, sobriety. 'The puritans stood for change,' wrote Peter
Haydon, 'while the alehouse stood for continuity.' Custom and practice

146

would not wash any more. Taverns, inns and alehouses not only served the devil's juice but also served as hotbeds of daily 'mischiefs and great disorders'. As potentially was any place where people in numbers might gather including theatre and sporting events, such as horse racing,

The Puritans were no fun. The Long Parliament of 1644 didn't quite ban Christmas, but declared it a day of prayer and fasting. John Taylor, landlord, Royalist and poet, was a tad put out:

All the harmless sports, the merry gambols, dances and friscols, are now extinct... Madness hath extended itself to the very vegetables, the senseless trees, herbs and weeds are a profane estimation amongst them – holly, ivy, mistletoe, rosemary, bays are counted ungodly branches of superstition for your entertainment. And to roast a sirloin of beef to touch a collar of brawn, to take a pie, to put a plum in the pottage pot, to burn a fire for your sake, master Christmas, is enough to make a man be suspected and taken for a Christian, for which he shall be apprehended for committing high parliament treason.[4]

But was it all that bad? Not really. The Puritans may have an image of stripping away even the excesses of austerity, but Cromwell, as with many Puritans, 'had a deep love of English chamber music and songs'. Dancing was not banned, as has long been thought, and even theatre (which *was* banned) found a way through – certainly in private entertainments – and publicly with short pieces, sometimes with music, known as 'drolls' (short for droll humours or drolleries), which were one-act pieces or excerpts from known plays. They were staged at the Red Bull Theatre and anywhere deemed suitable or available.[5]

Drinking was never banned (except on Sundays) and, of course, was a hard-working and productive contributor to the tax chest. It certainly did its duty on that score. Indeed, during and after the Civil War, with either armies going into battle or standing armies later keeping the peace, drinking probably increased. During the war, the inns provided accommodation for the itinerant and fleeing combatants. King Charles stayed at the Red Lion in Hillingdon on his retreat from Oxford. Agents from either side met in an inn at Uxbridge in 1645 seeking conciliation, and, although they failed, the inn became the Crown and Treaty. Two events, in particular, demonstrated the inherent boozy nature of the country: the restoration of Charles II (the day after which the soil of England itself was hung over), and, first, the death of Oliver Cromwell.

John Evelyn saw the 'the superb Funerall of the Protector.' Somewhat ironically, it was a right royal do: 'He was carried from Somerset-house in a velvet bed of state drawn by six horses houss'd with the same: The Pall held-up by his new Lords; Oliver lying in effigie in royal robes, & Crown'd with a Crown, scepter, & Mund, like a King.' But for the old Royalist it was 'the most joyfullest funeral that I ever saw, for there was none but Cried, but dogs, which the souldiers hooted away with a barbarous noise; drinking, & taking Tabacco in the streetes as they went...'[6]

Drunkenness was, after all, a military characteristic. The regulation ration for sailors was a gallon of beer a day and two pounds (just under a kilo) of salt beef. The army garrison stationed in Tangier certainly flew the flag. A report for the Lords Commissioners in 1682 noted that 'soldiers sell most of their victuals for drink (which hath killed thousands).' One officer believed that drink had killed more men than the Moors.[7]

The soldiery merely followed the example of their officers. Henry Ball wrote to Secretary of State Williamson in 1673:

On Wednesday a drummer of the Duke of Albermarle's at Blackheath being got drunk and for it carried to the Horse, the soldiers got together and declared they saw no reason to punish him for what the officers had never been free from since their coming thither, and then took him from them and rudely treated their officers.[8]

Soldiers treated everyone rudely – mugging and abusing civilians, and joining in with (rather than breaking up) riots and disturbances. Laws were for others, and lawmakers were despised. The coachman of Sir John Coventry was beaten up by an officer because he worked for a 'parliament man'.

Wine-sodden words often made way for a flurry of fisticuffs and wig-pulling among their lordships. The first Duke of Albermarle (the father of the one mentioned above), once plain old General Monck, was much admired by the French ambassador, Comte de Cominges, for his drinking ability. 'An amusing affair happened last week in this Court,' wrote the ambassador to Louis XIV. He continued:

The Earl of Oxford, one of the first noblemen of England, Knight of the Garter and an officer of the Horse Guards, asked to dinner General Monk, the High Chamberlain of the Kingdom, and some few other Councillors of State. They were joined by a number of young men of quality. The entertainment rose to such a pitch that every person happened to become a party of quarrels, both as offended and offender; they came to blows and tore each other's hair; two of them drew their swords, which luckily had a cooling effect on the company. Each then went according as he pleased. Those who followed the General wanted some more drink, and it was given them. They continued there till evening, and therefore wanted food. Having been warmed by their morning and after-dinner doings each resolved to see his companion a-ground. The General, who is obviously endowed with a strong head, struck a master stroke; he presented to each a goblet of the deepest. Some swallowed the contents, and some not; but all peaceably remained where they were till the following morning, without speaking to each other, though in the same room. Only the General went to Parliament as usual, with his mind and thoughts nothing impaired. There was much laughter at this.[9]

Pepys also relates this story as a,

ridiculous falling-out at my Lord of Oxfords house at an entertainment of his, there being there my Lord of Albemarle, Lynsey, two of the Porters, my Lord Bellasse [Henry Belasyse], and others; where there was high words and some blows and some pulling off of perriwiggs – till my Lord Monke took away some of their swords and sent for some soldiers to guard the house till the fray was ended. To such a degree of madness the nobility of this age is come.[10]

For a society with a crush on pushing and jostling, the omnipresent periwig all too often proved too tempting a first target. During a debate in the House of Lords, the Duke of Buckingham 'leaning rudely over my Lord Marquis of Dorchester, my Lord Dorchester removed his elbow. Duke of Buckingham asked whether he was uneasy. Dorchester replied, "Yes", and that he durst [not] do this, were he anywhere else. Buckingham replied that, yes he would, and he was a better man than himself. Dorchester answered that he lyed. With this, Buckingham struck off his hat, and took him by the periwigg and pulled it a-t'o[ther]-side, and held him.'

Clarendon noted that the marquis, 'who was the lower of the two in stature, and was less active in his limbs, lost his periwig, and received some rudeness.' However, Dorchester 'had much of the duke's hair in his hands to recompense for his pulling off his periwig, which he could not reach high enough to do to the other.' After the Lord Chamberlain's intervention their two lordships found themselves languishing in the Tower of London for a three-day cooling down.[11]

Other and later French ambassadors at times got caught in the groundswell – Honore Courtin, for one. In a dispatch dated 24 May 1665, he confessed to his minister: 'Pray excuse my style, I have been writing all the night and I drank more than I ought.' The best company drank. As Sir Charles Sedley wrote, 'Thou swear'st thou'lt drink no more; kind Heaven send Me such a Cook or Coach-man, but no friend.'[12]

Although there were those who clearly thought otherwise. Sir Ralph Verney advised (or warned) his son, if he expected to inherit the estate, to 'carry yourselfe soberly' because if he kept 'lewd company, and by drinkinge, gaminge, or your own idleness loose your reputation, bee confident you will thereby also loose my affection, and your Portion too'.[13]

Count Lorenzo Magalotti, who on his travels visited England (London, largely) between April and June 1669, thought the English penchant for pot-walloping remarkable:

It is a common custom with the lower order of people, after dinner or at public-houses, when they are transacting business of any kind, to smoke, so that there does not pass a day in which the artisans do not indulge themselves by going to the public-houses, which are exceedingly numerous, neglecting their work, however urgent it may be.[14]

Possibly apocryphal, but the anecdote, involving Charles Sackville (then Earl of Dorset) and the poet Samuel Butler, from *The Tell-Tale* (1756) nonetheless emphasises drink as being at the hub of social and intellectual life:

The earl of Dorset having a great desire to spend an evening as a private gentleman with Mr Butler, author of Hudibras, prevailed with Mr Fleetwood Shepherd to introduce him into his company at a tavern which they used, in the character only of a common friend; this being done, Mr Butler, while the first bottle was drinking, appeared very flat and heavy; at the second bottle extremely brisk and lively, full of wit and learning, and a most pleasant, agreeable companion; but before the third bottle was finished sunk again into such stupidity and dullness that hardly anybody could have believed him to be the author of the book that abounded with so much wit, learning and pleasantry. Next morning Mr Shepherd asked his lordship's opinion of Mr Butler, who answered, He is like a nine-pin, little at both ends, but great in the middle.[15]

Prospective MPs, particularly those not normally associated with the area, were expected to treat the locals to a good drink-up. However, in his bid for Parliament in 1683, Sir Ralph Verney refused 'to treat the Mobile at all the Alehouses in the Parish to make them Drunke, perhaps a Month beforehand as is usual in too many places uppon such occasions, I shall not joyne in that Expence'. Even so, not all Verneys were so austere. Edmund, for one, managed to celebrate a victory in Buckinghamshire (where wine was declared the 'most acceptable treate for the aldermen') in the time-honoured fashion, having 'sate up all night in Buckingham drinking with the High Sheriff'. However, his friend Captain Pigott 'lay ill in Aylesbury after drinking too hard all through the election'.[16]

Beer is today used as a generic term for ale, lager, stout and porter. However, in the seventeenth century beer was distinguishable from ale by being hopped. Ale was brewed by the ancient Egyptians and was already part of British culture when the Romans landed. Its early popularity can be taken from the fact that it was first taxed in 1188. Continental brewers began using hops in their beer as flavouring and as a preservative in the fifteenth century. About 150 years later Britain hopped aboard.

Beer was proving hugely popular, not least because it was cheaper to produce, and thus cheaper to buy. A Restoration bushel of malt would yield eight gallons of ale, but eighteen gallons of beer. A barrel of beer (36 gallons) would cost between four and eight shillings, which works out at three pints for a penny.

Beers could be just as strong as ale, but were often weaker. Small beer, a very light beer, was a staple drink – a popular summer thirst-quenching drink also taken daily by children (it being a universally safer refreshment than water or milk). It was customary to drink in the morning – to take a morning draught. Pepys recorded suffering one day 'through having drunk so much Rheinish wine in the morning and more in the afternoon...'[17]

On another occasion, at Westminster Hall there was a traffic jam of coaches – a 'falling-out between a drayman and my Lord Chesterfield's coachman, and one of his footmen killed' – Pepys met with his colleague and work rival John Creed 'and he and I to Hell to drink our morning draught.' Hell was an eating-place in Old Palace Yard, Westminster, and was bigger than its neighbouring rival Heaven, presumably named to compete directly with Hell but also, perhaps, because it was on the first floor.[18]

Pepys mentions brands of ales and beers, including Mum, a strong and heavy ale, brewed with wheat malt and oat malt, and spiced with ginger, walnut rinds, cardamom (good for the stomach), sassafras, elecampane (a tonic), madder (a dye) and red sanders (a dye from the red sandalwood tree, also used as a tonic). Mum was a drink imported from Brunswick ('I thinke you'r drunk With Lubecks beere or Brunswicks Mum', 1640) and is thought to have been named after its brewer Christian Mummer, or from the notion that its effect was to make you mumble. On 3 May 1664, Pepys visited The Fleece in Leadenhall, which he described as 'a Mum-house', suggesting that some taverns at least specialised in certain drinks.[19]

Nottinghamshire's country folk not only made 'the strongest and the best ales, that looked very pale but exceedingly clear' but also 'consumed them with great avidity'. Other named drinks included Alderman Byde's ale and Hull ale (of which the poet and politician Andrew Marvell, who was born near Hull and served as its MP, received a barrel at the start of each parliamentary session). A couple of other ales mentioned – Lambeth ale and Northdown (or Margate) ale – were actually beers, as ales were being more associated with the bitter and lighter-quality brews from places such as Derby and Burton-on-Trent.[20]

Restoration Londoners with over 1,400 alehouses and taverns within the square mile of the city alone were never more than a stagger away from alcohol. Such a proliferation brought inevitable protest. One such open-minded, dispassionate account described a tavern as,

> an Academy of Debauchery, where the Devil teaches the seven deadly sins instead of Sciences [presumably, the Devil teaching the sciences would be an altogether more agreeable situation], a Tipling School a degree above an Ale-house, where you may get drunk with more credit and Apology... 'Tis the Randezvous of Gallants, the Good Fellowes Paradice, and the Miser's Terrour... 'Tis a Bedlam of Wits, where the men are rather mad than merry, here one breaking a Jest on the Drawer, or perhaps a Candlestick or Bottle over his Crown, there another repeating scraps of Old Plays or Bawdy Song...whilst all with loud hooting and laughing confound the noise of Fidlers who are properly called a Noise, for no Musick can be heard for them.[21]

Despite the Puritan frown upon drinking, beer and ale production continued to increase until the arrival of the great Protestant champion William III. However, its decline was not a result of religious fervour but rather overburdensome taxes. Supplies of alternatives varied in quality and availability (wine – and, indeed, brandy – from France, for example, dried up during wars and occasional embargoes, and especially after the Dutch glory boy ascended the throne). There was, however, a trade ripening to fill the gap – and King Billy thought it could be just the tonic: gin. Add a nice slice of tax breaks and our hero started a trend that within twenty years would see at any one time a quarter of the population of the capital drunk.

However, in London BG (Before Gin), just as there were an increasing variety of beers and ales, so grew up a selection of venues from which to enjoy them. Apart from being licensed to trade in alcoholic drinks, the only post-Restoration restriction in law was that drinks could not be served during service times on Sundays. Inns were larger properties that also provided accommodation for travellers resting overnight. Alehouses and taverns were distinguished by their main products, with taverns (being more upmarket) specialising in wine.

French wines dominated the reds, mainly claret, but French whites were rare. The accounts at Woburn Abbey show that a French wine – noted as 'Shably' and which came in bottles, not casks – made its appearance in 1664. The 62 bottles cost the steward about 1s. 6d. each (about £14 each in today's money). The following year the Earl of Bedford received his first order of 'Shampaigne' wine. White wines mostly came from Spain and the Canaries where 'sack' (Sec or secco) – a dry white – was by far the most popular import. There were some German, Greek and Italian whites also. Wines did not resemble what we have today: the cork stopper was not commonly used until the turn of the eighteenth century (although they were used in Restoration England), and the glass tubular bottles would appear in the 1770s. Wine was mainly kept in casks and poured into squat bottles for use at the table.[22]

Pepys was proud of his wine collection and even had his own bottles made: 'Thence to Mr Rawlinsons and saw some of my New bottles made with my Crest upon them, filled with wine, about five or six dozen.' However, he did worry about the effect of drinking too much and often abstained for periods of time. The sentiment, 'Went to bed with my head not well, by my too much drinking today' was not an isolated one. Particularly so, as wine was not meant to be sipped or savoured, but necked in one.[23]

Wine inspired many a quill ('Sack will the soul of poetry infuse/Be that my theme and muse'):

> *Hang sorrow, cast away care,*
> *Come let us drink upon our Sack;*
> *They say it's good,*
> *To cherish the blood,*
> *And eke to strengthen the back; '*

Tis wine that makes the thoughts aspire,
And fills the body with heat,
Beside 'tis good
If well understood
To fit a man for the Feat:
Then call, And drink up all,
The Drawer is ready to fill,
A pox of care
What need we to spare,
My father hath made his Will.[24]

Wine clearly wasn't only for drinking – as a story involving James Herbert, Earl of Pembroke demonstrates. Even the most disturbed of individuals thought Pembroke a nutter. In a letter dated 20 April 1676, Dr Denton related a dinner party he attended. Nobody had initially sat next to Pembroke and as events ensued it was reasonably clear why. Finally, someone unaware of Pembroke's reputation took the vacant seat. His lordship proposed a toast to the health of someone to which his table neighbour refused to pledge. Pembroke, a little put out by this, and in an eloquent display of anger, smashed a bottle of wine over the guest's head and chased him out 'his sword drawne'. However, the shocked guest, recovering some sense, managed to turn the tables and confronting Pembroke 'flew att him furiously, beate him, threw him downe in ye kennell, nubbled him and daub'd him daintily & soe were parted'.[25]

Drink, however and as ever, was more of an affliction for some. Wine was the favoured tipple of John Wilmot, Earl of Rochester, London's wittiest and grandest alcoholic. In a letter to his friend Harry Savile, he fears the worst:

Dear Savile
Do a charity becoming one of your pious principles, in preserving your humble servant Rochester from the imminent peril of sobriety, which, for want of good wine more than company (for I drink like a hermit betwixt God and my own conscience) is very likely to befall me. Remember what pains I have formerly taken to wean you from your pernicious resolutions of discretion and wisdom. And, if you have a grateful heart (which is a miracle amongst you statesman), show it by directing the bearer to the best wine in town, and pray let not this highest point of sacred friendship be performed slightly, but go about it with all due deliberation and care, as holy priests to sacrifice, or as discreet thieves to the wary performance of burglary and shop-lifting. Let your well-discerning palate (the best judge

about you) travel from cellar to cellar and then from piece to piece till it has lighted on wine fit for its noble choice and my approbation. To engage you more in this matter, know, I have laid a plot may very probably betray you to the drinking of it. My Lord ___ will inform you at large. Dear Savile, as ever thou dost hope to out-do Machiavel or equal me, send some good wine! So may thy wearied soul at last find rest, no longer hovering 'twixt th'unequal choice of politics and lewdness! May'st thou be admired and loved for thy domestic wit; beloved and cherished for thy foreign interest and intelligence. Rochester[26]

(Shop-lifting – interestingly, the first known use of this term; piece to piece – a piece is a cask of wine; intelligence – news.)

Another of the high-flying afflicted was the handsome but brutal and foul-mouthed Sir William Scroggs. He would become Lord Chief Justice of the King's Bench in 1678, replacing Sir Richard Raynsford 'who most commonly slept on ye bench'. He was, according to one contemporary chronicler, the son of a 'one-eyed butcher near Smithfield Bars, and his mother a big fat woman with a red face like an ale-wife'. The appointment of 'the Mouth' (as he was known) was scandalous, given his notorious dissolution and brutality. Nonetheless, his promotion was understandable given that he flaunted 'a bold front, handsome person, easy elocution and ready wit.' It was a character make-up built for success in Charles II's time. Although surviving an impeachment he held the top office for only three years before being pensioned off, and dying a further two years later.[27]

Scroggs had sat at the trial of Dr Wakeham, the queen's physician, and others during the Popish Plot hysteria. He opposed Oates, whose lies were being exposed in the Wakeham case, and directed the jury to disbelieve the prosecution case. This led to an inevitable acquittal, turned the hitherto ally Oates against him, and fortunately slowed the persecutions, although more by consequence than design.

'Dr' Titus Oates and William Bedloe presented articles against Scroggs. One such was 'That the Lord Chief Justice is very much addicted to swearing and cursing in his common discourse and to drink to excess.' Scroggs certainly enjoyed his wine. He wrote on 22 July 1673: 'And now you talke of wine, well remembered! the last hogshead [a large cask, usually about 50 gallons] abroach, and without a sudden supply there is no living for mee at Weald Hall [his residence]. The woemen drink in fear already, and you know all theire passions are violent.'[28]

Some of his letters, given the drunken appearance, show that wine was never too far from his lordship's lips. On another occasion he apologised to Lord Hatton: 'My Lrd, you must not take ill if I write of nothing but wine, for there is nothing I want more, nor of wch I can better write, or more willingly – with this difference only, that wine wrott for has not halfe yt elegancy as wine thankt for.'[29]

Another celebrated imbiber was Helena Gwynne, mother of the king's popular mistress Nelly. 'Old Maddam Gwynne' had spent a life saturated in prostitution and drink, and was chronically overweight and alcoholic. Indeed, while alcohol was her life it also proved to be her death: she drowned (in the Thames, a ditch or a fish pond, depending on your source) while drunk in 1679. A mock epitaph ran:

> *Here lies the Victim of a cruel Fate,*
> *Whom too much Element did Ruminate;*
> *'Tis something strange, but yet most wondrous true,*
> *That what we live by, should our Lives undo.*
> *She that so oft had powerful Waters try'd,*
> *At last with silence, in a Fish-pond dy'd.*
> *Fate was unjust, for had he prov'd but kind,*
> *To make it Brandy, he pleas'd her Mind.*[30]

Nelly seemingly gave her mother a good send-off:

> *Nor was her mother's funeral less her care,*
> *No cost, no velvet did the daughter spare;*
> *Fine gilded 'scutcheons did the hearse enrich*
> *To celebrate this martyr of the ditch.*
> *Burnt brandy did in flaming brimmers flow*
> *Drunk at her funeral; while her well pleas'd shade*
> *Rejoic'd, in the sober fields below,*
> *At all the drunkenness her death had made.*[31]

Nelly's household accounts show that, despite the very large lesson of her mother, drink played a huge part in her life, and that of well-to-do London. And what exceptionally able drinkers they were. One of Nelly's bills for ale and beer alone in one month came to £14. 3s. This is all the more remarkable when you consider that her entire food bill (which also included some alcohol) over Christmas 1675 came to about £8. A bill for ale and beer from 27 January to 4 August 1675 detailed three kilderkins (an eighteen-gallon cask) of 'strong ale', six kilderkins of ordinary ale, and 23 barrels (36 gallons each) of 'eights' (eight-shillings beer). This meant that, in just over six months some 1,008 gallons of ale and beer (or 8,064 pints) had been delivered. This equates to about five gallons – or 42 pints – a day. This is championship standard. Hardly surprising, then, that in 1688 12 million barrels of beer and ale were sold to a population not much over 5 million.[32]

There was a fear that brandy might be replacing the less damaging beer and ale as the everyday drink of choice. The practice spread alarmingly among the English sailors engaged in the Dutch wars. Indeed, the name 'brandy' itself derives from the Dutch 'brandewijn' meaning 'burnt wine'. The Dutch were undisputed European champions when it came to (if we keep the nautical imagery going) sailing several sheets to the wind. They were notorious even to the glassy-eyed English. Edmund Waller, in his 'Instructions to a Painter', wrote in 1665:

> *The Dutch their wine, and all their brandy lose,*
> *Disarm'd of that from which their courage grows.*

Hence 'Dutch courage'.[33]

Of course, for some, alcohol smoothed the way to the bedchamber. The not-so-subtle satire 'On the Ladies of the Court', 1663, informs us that one such lady of the court, probably one of the daughters of Sir Henry Waldgrave (who, incidentally, by two successive wives had eleven sons and eleven daughters), suffered with such halitosis that her opportunities for sex arose only with inebriated partners.

> *Waldgrave now is out of date*
> *For all her servants now of late*
> *Have found her breath so stinking!*
> *She mourns her luck*
> *For they'll not fuck*
> *Unless they have been drinking.*[34]

(*Servants* – lovers.)

With London seemingly awash with drink, it seemed a good idea, if only to vary it a bit, to have something to wash down. Some foodstuffs served with drink, such as Stilton – served with a spoon required for scooping out maggots – proved insufficient. Out of the taverns grew the eating houses, which could be grand affairs like Cateline's in Covent Garden, or the more modest and affordable ordinaries, which usually provided a fixed-price, two-course meal. This is not to say that taverns didn't provide meals. The subtle difference was that the tavern sold drinks, but also provided food, whereas the ordinary sold food, but also provided drinks. The speciality leaned one way or the other.[35]

An ordinary was less sophisticated and more communal than other eating houses and, as such, afforded less privacy for liaisons and business meetings. Despite this they were still attractive, as Charles Cotton described:

> An Ordinary is a handsome house, where everyday, about the hour of twelve, a good dinner is prepared by way of ordinary, composed of dishes, in season, well dressed, with all other accommodations fit for that purpose, whereby many gentlemen of great Estates and good repute make their resort, who after dinner play a while for recreation, both moderately and commonly without deserving reproof.[36]

Also, despite their name, they were still out of the financial or social grasp of ordinary people. As was the arrival of smart little venues dedicated to the drinking of a new and nonalcoholic drink.

The first cup of coffee reportedly drunk in England was dispatched in Oxford in 1637, and it was there, in 1650, that the first coffee house was opened by 'Jacob, a Jew'. London followed with the second two years later, when the Sign of My Own Head, run by one Pasquea Rosea, began trading in Cornhill. A dish or a bowl of coffee would cost a penny.

One commentator couldn't see the point: 'Useless,' they declared, 'since it serveth neither for Nourishment nor Debauchery.' Pepys was more forgiving. On 30 March 1664, he described how Lady Elizabeth Carteret (wife of the navy treasurer, Sir George) 'made us drink our morning draught there – of several wines. But I drank nothing but some of her Coffee; which was purely [excellently] made, with a little sugar in it.'[37]

Coffee houses sprang up, roasting the opposition (by 1663 there were 82, and over the next fifty years or so, their number would rise to about five hundred). Pepys frequented them to talk business, which became their attraction (as well as the beverages, of course). They were meeting places to discuss news and ideas. Owners soon made available newsletters, pamphlets and papers to stimulate debate. Indeed, such was their reputation for political intensity that occasionally there was talk of suppressing them. A proclamation to close them down was issued in December 1675, but was withdrawn.

Their air of exclusivity and the people they attracted proved equally stimulating. On 3 February, Pepys 'stopped at the great Coffee-house [at Covent Garden], where I never was before – where Draydon the poet (I knew at Cambridge) and all the wits of the town, and Harris the player'. This was probably Will's Coffee House at 1 Bow Street, which traded well off the premier playwright and poet's patronage: 'The great press was to get near the chair where John Dryden sate. In winter that chair was always in the warmest nook by the fire; in summer it stood in the balcony.' Coffee houses traditionally took the name of the owners: Will's being run by William Urwin. Others included Boodle's, White's, Garraway's and, famously, Lloyd's.[38]

Boodle's and White's both became gentlemen's clubs (it seemed the fate for the coffee houses, given their exclusivity; whereas ordinaries became chop shops; eating houses, restaurants; and with no clear focus taverns joined alehouses to become our modern pubs). Boodle's on St James's Street, had a name for gambling and food, and members have included Beau Brummell, Edward Gibbon and the Duke of Wellington.

Thomas Garraway kept a house that had been selling coffee since 1658. He moved in 1670 and it became a famous auction house (selling anything from 'damaged rice' to ships) and features in works by Charles Dickens (including *Little Dorrit* and *The Pickwick Papers*). It was also notable as the first place that sold tea – and at £10 a pound, much more an expensive drink. It did not stop being a coffee house till 1866 and closed down six years later.

Edward Lloyd ran his coffee house on Tower Street in the 1680s until moving to the corner of Lombard Street in 1692. It attracted ship owners, merchants and captains and soon became the place for reliable news and marine insurance, developing into today's insurance exchange.

But it was alcohol that dominated the market. And its consumption was compounded by the popularity of toasts, oaths and healths. These were said to have been introduced into England by soldiers serving in the Dutch revolt during the reign of Queen Elizabeth. One contemporary describes the ritual:

If he is in the act of taking something from a dish he must suddenly stop, return his fork or his spoon to its plate and wait without stirring more than a stone, until the other has drunk... after which an inclinabo, at the risk of dipping his periwig into his plate. I confess that when a foreigner first sees these manners he thinks them laughable. Nothing appears so droll as to see a man who is in the act of chewing a morsel... or doing anything else, who suddenly takes a serious air, when a person of some respectability drinks to his health, looks fixedly at his person and becomes motionless as if a universal paralysis had seized him.[39]

Pepys records a development in style:

Here Mr Moore showed us the French manner when a health is drunk, to bow to him that drunk to you, and then apply yourself to him whose lady's health is drunk, and then to the person that you drink to; which I never knew before, but it seems is now the fashion.[40]

This great wild sowing of oaths left no man of quality untouched. The king drank in moderation. For the most part. But he did occasionally let his periwig down. On 17 December 1676, the French ambassador, Courtin, wrote that he pitied Charles II, who only really wanted to be liked but found himself surrounded by jealous women: 'He had to face the anger of the Duchess of Portsmouth for drinking twice in twenty four hours to the health of Nell Gwynne, with whom he often supped, and who still made the Duchess of Portsmouth the butt of her tickling sarcasms.' Similarly, Pepys, although a lover of women, sometimes regretted being in their company, particularly as he was trying to abstain from drinking, because he would be forced to order wine with which to drink their health.[41]

The king was also recorded to have drunk the health of the newly appointed Judge Jeffreys (who would rise to national notoriety following the Bloody Assize of 1685) no fewer than seven times. It has been suggested that being drunk in front of the king was a 'crime so heinous' – although James II was less tolerant than his brother. It was bad form, all right, but no heinous crime. Harry Savile was 'high flowne in drinke' while in Charles II's company, and a suitable sabbatical away from court was punishment enough.[42]

Daniel Defoe remarked that that after the Restoration the 'King's health became the distinction between a Cavalier and Roundhead.' But it wasn't that cut and dried. There was a strong Puritan objection to the drinking of toasts. Pepys, on 23 May 1661, at a dinner at the Lord Mayor's, noted that the Presbyterian vicar of St-Dunstan-in-the-West, William Bates's 'singularity, in not rising up nor drinking the King's nor other healths at the table, was very much observed.' The vicar's objection was the alcohol not any anti-Royalism.[43]

If excuse were needed, up came the king's coronation: '... there were three great bonefyres and a great many gallants, men and women; and they laid hold of us and would have us drink the King's health upon our knee, kneeling upon a faggot; which we all did, they drinking to us one after another – which we all thought a strange frolique.' The morning after the night before brought its usual comeuppance. Pepys 'waked in the morning with my head in a sad taking through the last night's drink, which I am very sorry for'.[44]

And it didn't let up: 'Great joy all yesterday at London; and at night more bonefires than ever and ringing of bells and drinking of the king's health upon their knees in the streets, which methinks is a little too much.'[45]

On 6 June 1664, a Puritan in Pepys's company, a certain 'Mr Prin', would 'not drink any health; no, not the King's, but sat down with his hat on all the while'. Given that this was William Prynne who 36 years before had published *A compendious and briefe discourse proving the drinking and pledging of healthes to be sinfull and utterly unlawfull unto Christians*, this is perhaps understandable. As Pepys said, 'nobody took any notice of him.'[46]

At some stage, for sure, it will be time for the very last order:

> *Drunk we'll march off, and reel into the tomb,*
> *Nature's convenient dark re-tireing room;*
> *And there, from the noise removed, and all tumultuous strife,*
> *Sleep out the dull fatigue, and long debauch of life.'*[47]

7

Those Little Insignificant Creatures, *or* Unpardonable Rudenesses

Those little insignificant creatures, the players
– *Man of Mode, or Sir Fopling Flutter*, II, ii George Etherege, 1676

On his return from exile, Charles II lifted the ban on plays and so began the reign of one of theatre's greatest royal patrons. The king issued a patent to two theatre companies, giving them exclusive rights to produce plays. Charles was aware of the 'divers[e] companies' who were and have been performing without authority, and declared his 'dislike' of them and ordered 'all other company and companies...to be suppressed and silenced.'[1]

Charles granted the Drury Lane patent to 'our well trusted and well beloved Thomas Killigrew, Esquire, one of the grooms of the bedchamber.' Killigrew was born on 7 February 1612. He was page of honour to Charles I and often referred to himself as the 'illiterate courtier' because he had not, unlike everyone else in royal employ, gone to university.

Killigrew's patent granted him,

his heirs and assigns full power license and authority that...they may lawfully quietly and peaceably frame erect new-build and set up in any place within our cities of London and Westminster or the suburbs thereof where he shall find best accommodation for that purpose... one theatre or play house with necessary tiring and retiring rooms...wherein tragedies, comedies, plays, operas and other performations of the stage within the House.[2]

The other company 'to be erected and set up by Sir William Davenant' was to be 'styled the Duke of York's Company.' Davenant (or d'Avenant), was born in Oxford in February 1606, the son of a wine merchant and publican of the Crown Inn. He became, essentially, the Poet Laureate* to Charles I in 1637 on a pension of £100 a year. His father's house was frequented by William Shakespeare. As, indeed, was his mother's bedchamber if the rumours are to be believed. Davenant's mother, according to the diarist Anthony à Wood, was 'a very beautiful woman of good wit and conversation.' He adds that 'Sir William would sometimes, when he was pleasant over a glass of wine with his most intimate friends... say that it seemed to him that he wrote with the very spirit that Shakespeare [did], and seemed contented enough to be thought his son.' If not his actual father, Shakespeare certainly was his godfather.

With the curtain set to open on the two companies, the casting call sounded for actors. Fame has its own tingling sexual allure. Being known, being recognisable enhances your appeal and attractiveness. Famous actors today are also financially well rewarded. Money didn't pave the way for actors in Restoration England. Theatre was a pastime for the well-to-do. Wealth was in the audience and not on the stage. Even the most successful would be rewarded with a salary possibly less comparable with today's largely unknown, jobbing, in-and-out-of-work provincial actors. For women, permitted for the first time to appear on the stage, typically, it was worse. Top actors and actresses rarely topped 50 shillings a week (about £180 a week today).

It is not surprising, then, that the Lord Chamberlain's office was regularly petitioned for permission to sue players and other employees of the theatre for debt. On 18 May 1672 one Richard Utting gained an order for the actress Rebecca Marshall to appear on Monday morning before the Lord Chamberlain to answer a claim for £7. 9s. 6d. Leave was then given on 26 June 1672 to 'Richard Uttings [or Utting] to proceed against Mrs Marshall if she does not give an appearance at law within one week.' Even the better paid – the leading actors Jo Haines and Cardell Goodman, for example – were sued with alarming frequency.[3]

If Goodman had it tough when he was relatively famous, it was still an improvement on his first joining the King's Company, which barely afforded enough to eat. Colly Cibber recounts a story told him by the then retired Goodman about those early days with his hireling companion Philip Griffin. They were,

---

* The poet of the royal household or court poet – became the *poet laurete* because distinguished poets in ancient Greece and Rome were awarded laurel wreaths in recognition of their status.

confined by their moderate Sallaries to the Economy of lying together in the same Bed and having but one whole Shirt between them: One of them being under the obligation of a Rendezvous with a fair Lady, insisted on wearing it out of his Turn, which occasion'd so high a dispute their Pretensions to it were decided by a fair Tilt upon the spot, in the room where they lay: But whether [Griffin] or [Goodman] was obliged to see no Company till a worse [shirt] could be wash'd for him, seems not to be a material point in their History.[4]

However, once a month or so, the players would put on a royal command performance at the cockpit theatre at Whitehall Palace. The warrants for food and drink proved this to be one gig worth playing, considering that it was to be shared among just 24 of them: 'Twelve Quarts of Sack, twelve Quarts of Clarett... Eight Gallons of Beere... six dishes of Meate, twelve loaves of white Bread, __ loaves of Brown Bread... twelve white dishes to drink in, and two Bumbards [leather jugs] to fetch Beere... '[5]

The wages might have been poor but there were indirect added benefits. For impoverished actresses, their stage fame could be weighed in gold. Theatre audiences were, as said, mainly the well-to-do; out of whom actresses conspired to do well. Wealthy men, married or not, sought to advertise their status by parading a mistress. And so much the better if she was known – and thus much desired. The stage was a shop window for sex – even if the shop stocked only shabby second-hand goods. It was, as one satirical contemporary commentator noted,

> as hard a matter for a pretty Woman to keep her self honest in a Theatre, as 'tis for an Apothecary to keep his Treacle from the Flies in hot Weather; for every Libertine in the audience will be buzzing about her Honey-pot, and her Virtue must defend itself by abundance of fly-flaps, or those Flesh-loving Insects will soon blow upon her Honour, and when once she has a Maggot in her Tail, all the Pepper and Salt in the Kingdom will scarce keep her Reputation from Stinking.[6]

Not that a typical actress – or actor – had much in the way of a reputation to defend. It was a career path escaped down by those familiar with tavern, trouble and tribulation. The stage was essentially an alternative to domestic service. It was not a profession approved by persons of quality. A Lord or Lady Worthington most assuredly would not entertain the idea of putting their daughter on the stage. 'A Lady, with a real Title,' Cibber tells us, 'whose female Indiscretions had occasion'd her Family to abandon her' sought refuge in the theatre but was rejected because her family further protested. Her desire to 'get bread from the Stage' was 'look'd upon as an Addition of new Scandal to her former Dishonour!'[7]

Actors had an equally munificent press. There were the honourable exceptions, but most worked hard to be worthy of the person specification drawn up by Robert Gould in 'The Playhouse, A Satyr' of 1685:

> *To speak 'em all were tedious to discuss;*
> *But if You'll Lump 'em, they're exactly thus:*
> *A Pimping, Spunging, Idle, Impious Race,*
> *The Shame of Vertue, and Despair of Grace:*
> *A Nest of Leachers worse than Sodom bore,*
> *And justly Merit to be Punish'd more.*
> *Dieseas'd, in Debt, & every Moment dun'd;*
> *By all good Christians loath'd, and their own Kindred shun'd.*
> *To say more of 'em wou'd be a wasting Time;*
> *For it with Justice may be thought a Crime*
> *To let such Rubbish have a place in Rhime.*[8]

True pros like Thomas Betterton, 'the greatest figure of the Restoration stage', bemoaned actors who performed in 'undisguised Debauchery and Drunkenness, coming on the very Stage, in Contempt of the Audience, when they were scarce able to speak a word'. Also, the libidos of the young actors caused particular problems for the theatre's management. It seems that rather than buckle down and learn their parts they preferred to play with them. On 24 January 1669 Pepys met with the manager of the King's House, Thomas Killigrew,

> who told me and others, talking about the playhouses, that he is fain to keep a woman on purpose, at 20s a week, to satisfy eight or ten young men of his House, whom till he did so he could never keep to their business, and now he doth.[9]

The unbridled pursuit of drink and sex fearlessly inspired slurred insults and double-vision violence, which led actors frequently to feature on cast lists of detained persons at the groom porter's lodge. On 9 December 1669 two actors from the Duke's Company, Samuel Sandford and Matthew Medbourne, were arrested for being 'refractory and disorderly'. The pair had earlier, on 4 July 1662, taken part in the assault of a Revels Office messenger. Sandford played character parts for the best part of forty years until about 1698 and, unsurprisingly, given his off-stage antics, specialised in villains. His cohort, 'Mr Medburn', had a rather more short-lived career. He died in prison in 1680, although, tragically, his only crime for his incarceration in 1678 was that of being a Catholic. He was one of the earliest victims of the poppycock that was the Popish Plot. The celebrated Joseph Haines found himself charged with upbraiding the Knight Marshal on 4 November 1675 'with ill & scandalous language & insolent carriage.' However, being the king's servants meant most crimes and misdemeanours were punished by being suspended for work for a few days.[10]

Actresses were, as Dryden observed, 'made of Play-house Flesh & blood' and as such were clearly fair game. After performances their large shared changing room (known as the women's shift) would be full of male admirers who would jostle verbally and tousle physically with the actresses.[11]

Pepys often enjoyed himself backstage even though he was occasionally shocked. On 7 May 1668, he,

did see Becke Marshall come dressed, off of the stage, and looks mighty fine, and pretty, and noble – and also Nell [Gwynne] in her boy's clothes, mighty pretty; but, Lord their confidence, and how many men do hover about them as soon as they come off the stage, and how confident they [are] in their talk.[12]

Rebecca 'Beck' Marshall, however, on Saturday 5 February 1667, did at least once rebuke one loose-tongued man who had 'spoke ill of the women actors' wondering 'why he had come amongst them?' The courtier Sir Hugh Middleton, rising to the challenge, 'told her she lyed, and concluded the injury by calling her jade, and threatening that he would kick her and that his footman should kick her'. Fearful for her safety, Beck Marshall, on the Monday, requested the king's protection from any attack, 'which he graciously promised'. It wasn't enough. On Tuesday as she left work, she spied Middleton 'in the great Entrie going out of the Playhouse into Drurie Lane'. However, Middleton wasn't about to do his own – as it turned out, very – dirty work. He was there simply to identify the actress to his commissioned thug. Within seconds, 'some few doores from the Playhouse a Ruffian pressed hard upon her, insomuch that she complained first of his rudeness, and after turned about and said I thinke the fellow would rob mee, or pick my pocket. Upon wch he turned his face and seemed to slink away'. Unfortunately, he slunk back just before she reached home. And 'clapped a turd on her face and hair' and 'fled away in a Trice'.[13]

This wasn't poor Beck's debut assault, either. Two years before, in the spring of 1665, she petitioned the king for protection, complaining that she has been 'severall times barbarously and insolently affronted by one Marke Trevor of the Temple...both on and off the stage'. He had 'assaulted her violently in a Coach and after many horrid Oathes and Threats that he would be revenged of her for complaining to my Lord Chamberlaine formerly of him pursued her with his sword in his hand, and when by flight she had secured her self in a house he continued his abusive Language and he broke the windowes of the adjoining house'. Fearful of her life she requested that Trevor 'may be restrained from doing her further Injurie'. A glamorous life, indeed.[14]

However, the actors, famed for their choreographed fights on stage, were not unknown for their ability to confront Sir Violent-Flareup with a handy dose of improvised pulverisation. Even for the great and mild Thomas Betterton (admittedly with a number of accomplices) a touch of brutality, torture and false imprisonment wasn't beyond his character. As mentioned above, Thomas Killigrew and William Davenant had a monopoly on theatre production in London. However, nobody was prepared for the wounded antagonism of Sir Henry Herbert, who had been appointed master of the revels by Charles I on 20 July 1623. Or rather he had bought the mastership from Sir John Astley, who technically remained the master, until his death in 1641. But Herbert was unquestionably recognised and received as such. For example, he wrote: 'Itt pleased the King...to receive me as Master of the Revells. At Wilton, this 7th August, 1623.' Thus, upon Restoration, having not been dismissed, Herbert believed he had the right to manage the theatres, censor plays and, importantly, collect a fee for each performance licensed by him. Unsurprisingly, he opposed the 'pretended power' of the patent-holders.[15]

All sides appealed to the king. Charles acted with typically equivocal decisiveness and decreed that the matter should be looked at by Sir Jeffrey Palmer, the attorney-general. While argument and prosecution incited counterargument and counterprosecution, the actors were left bewildered as to whom they were answerable to.

Killigrew and Davenant decided at first to do battle with Herbert and won the occasional skirmish. However, the indefatigable Herbert saw his chance when (in his mind and accounts book) the two usurpers finally set up their own rival operations. He sought to divide and conquer. He pursued Killigrew, recognising astutely his lesser resolve. On 4 June 1662, ground down by the relentless, irritating pursuit, and needing to concentrate on the building of his new theatre, Killigrew capitulated. Herbert was to receive £2 (about £145 today) for each new play performed and £1 for revivals, backdated from 11 August 1660. He also paid Herbert's accrued legal costs and even added a 'noble present' of £50 in damages. In return Herbert would fain patronage and keep out of Killigrew's periwig.

Davenant was less adjusted to compromise. Unperturbed and refreshed with success, Herbert sent his messenger Edward Thomas, on 4 July 1662, to collect debts owed by the Duke's Company. The reception Thomas received was rather less than warm. Two weeks later, according to the Middlesex County Records,

> Thomas Betterton, James Noxe, Robert Noxe, Robert Turner, Thomas Lillistone, Mathew Medburne, Cave Underhill, Samuel Sandford, James Dixon, Joseph Price, Henry Harris and Francis Pavy riotously assembled together and assaulted Edward Thomas gentleman, and beat and maltreated him, and held him their prisoner for two hours. Each of the twelve riotous gentlemen confessed the indictment, and was fined three shillings and four pence, which fine he at once paid to the Sheriff of Middlesex.[16]

The details are vague but undoubtedly a deal was eventually reached between Herbert and Davenant, but it wasn't as one-sided as that struck with Killigrew. The bloodsucking Herbert retained the title of master of the revels but it became an office of little significance. Davenant and Killigrew retained control of the actors, and play censorship passed eventually and exclusively to the Lord Chamberlain. In 1737 these powers were enshrined in law – no plays could be acted without approval of the Lord Chamberlain. Also, any person acting 'for hire, gain or reward...without licence from the Lord Chamberlain of His Majesty's Household for the time being, shall be deemed a rogue and vagabond.'[17]

On Herbert's death, in 1673, Killigrew became master of the revels. It is thought that Charles II had made Killigrew his court jester in about 1661 in compensation for Herbert's keeping the mastership. Pepys recorded a conversation with John Brisbane, later secretary to the Admiralty, who told him that 'Tom Killigrew hath a fee out of the wardrobe for cap and bells, under the title of the King's foole or Jester, and may with privilege revile or jeere anybody, the greatest person, without offence, by the privilege of his place.'[18]

One of Killigrew's opposition company was no fool. The 'handsome, graceful actress' Hester Davenport (?1641–1717) was one of Davenant's early female recruits to the Duke's Company. Evelyn thought her a 'faire and famous comedian'. Her first major role, which also proved her last, was Roxolana in Davenant's own opera *The Siege of Rhodes* in June 1661. It was a role that 'she performed to such perfection...that she retained that name' – however it was spelt: for Pepys she was Roxalana, for Gramont, Roxana, and for Baronne d'Aulnoy, Roxaline.[19]

In July 1661 the company took their art and all-round bawdiness on tour to Oxford, setting up shop in the vast yard of the King's Arms in Holywell, providing a varied repertory twice daily. A shocked Oxfordian noted that 'these playes wherein women acted...made the scholars mad, run after them, take ill c[o]urses – among which Hyde of Allsouls, A.B. afterwards hanged.' Whipped up into a sexual frenzy, the undergraduates discarded their undergarments and went on a liberating rampage. The college authorities were unamused and outside entertainments were consequently banned.[20]

It wouldn't be the last time a repertory group departed that university city to a local sigh of relief. Humphrey Prideaux wrote on 28 July 1674:

> The players parted from us not having gained so much after al things payed to make a divident of £10 to the chiefe sharers which I hope will give them noe encouragement to Come again neither I suppose will the University for the future permit them here if they can be kept out since they were guilty of such great rudenesses before they left us going about the Town in the night breaking of windows and committeing many other unpardonable rudenesses...[21]

Ironically, given the unpardonable rudenesses of the theatre folk, the prologue to a Nathaniel Lee's 1675 *Sophonisba, or Hannibal's Overthrow* when staged in Oxford demonstrated the artistic relief in performing to a knowledgeable, sober and thoughtful audience than that usually experienced in the capital:

> *Free from the partial censure of the Town,*
> *Where senseless Faction runs the Poet down;*
> *Where fluttering Hectors on the Vizard fall,*
> *One half o' th' Play they spend in Noise and Brawl,*
> *Sleep out the rest then wake and damn it all.*[22]

However, it was Oxford the man as well as Oxford the city that got hot under the waistcoat at the sexually charged appearance of Hester Davenport strutting the London stage. Aubrey de Vere, twentieth Earl of Oxford, was Chief Justice in Eyre of the Forest south of the Trent (1660–73), colonel of the Royal Regiment of Horse Guards – the

Oxford Blues – (1661–88), and Lord Lieutenant of Essex, Oxfordshire and Hertfordshire. This unattached, pipe-smoking, long-chinned, so-called 'noblest subject in England' lived in a large mansion in the piazza, Covent Garden.[23]

The love affair between the two has been chronicled, if somewhat fancifully, by two contemporary memoirs: Gramont and Maria, Baronne d'Aulnoy, who, as a professional writer of fairy tales, sprinkled the dust of fiction throughout her autobiography works. However, even accounting for a lack of historical solidity, both independently written accounts agree on the core features of the romance. However, despite the earl's obvious material attractions to a poor player, Hester rejected his gifts, was unmoved by his flattery and rebuffed his advances. Nothing worked. Not even sorcery. Inevitably, the fires on his simmering passion helplessly boiled over. Hester, majestically, sought not a lover but a husband.

For eight months his lordship's obsessive urges remained unfulfilled. He even, according to Baronne d'Aulnoy, contemplated kidnapping Hester, taking her to the country and working full-time on achieving her submission. The baroness even has him admitting: 'All I care for is to satisfy myself, and when I have done that, I shall not trouble my head any further about this damned actress.'[24]

Out of a boiling cauldron of desperation rose the whiff of deceit. There was nothing for it. The earl must have his actress. And, if it was marriage that would see to it, then marriage it was. He 'presented her with a proposal of marriage, in due form, signed with his own hand'. None-theless, the ecstatic but suitably cautious Hester remained obstinately unavailable for inspection: there would be no prenuptial sampling of the goods. Her secret delights were not available on approval.[25]

Hester would happily trade in her stage title – Roxolana – for that of countess, but only in London, as she refused to leave for the country as the earl suggested. 'The next day,' said Gramont, 'she thought there could be no danger, when the earl himself came to her lodgings attended by a clergyman, and another man for a witness: the marriage was duly solemnised with all due ceremonies, in the presence of one of her fellow-players who attended as a witness on her part.' Mme d'Aulnoy, who suggests more feasibly that the ceremony took place in Oxford's London residence rather than Hester's lodgings, picks up the script:

The ceremony over he pressed eagerly toward the summit of his bliss. It seemed to him that never did a man know such joy. The night passed; it was morning & she was asleep. He pushed her rather rudely, & said: 'Wake up! Wake up, Roxaline, it is time for you to go.'

She turned & stared at him. 'Why do you call me Roxaline, my lord,' said she, 'have I not the honour today of being the Countess of Oxford?' 'Indeed you have not,' he replied.[26]

It had all been an elaborate hoax. The 'pretended priest was one of my lord's trumpeters and the witness his kettle drummer.' Screaming 'traitor!' at the earl, the violated actress drew his sword from its scabbard and chased him through the house. Unable to repay instantly the injustice – Oxford had locked himself in his grande salle – she turned the blade on herself inflicting 'a severe flesh wound, but not a vital one.'[27]

There was certainly a perception that the earl and the actress were together. Hester had left the stage soon after her performance as Roxolana – presumably to be kept by Oxford (and thus probably being more accepting of the earl's gifts than Gramont would have us believe). Evelyn thought so. He records on 9 January 1662:

I saw the third part of the *Siege of Rhodes*. In this acted ye faire and famous comedian, called Roxolana, from ye part she performed; and I think it was the last, she being taken to be the Earl of Oxford's *misse*, as at that time they began to call lewd women.[28]

Davenport had left the stage, according to Pepys, who bemoaned the 'losse of Roxalana', by February 1662. The prompter Downes confirms that she 'by force of Love [was] Erept the Stage'. The commentators soon named the source of that particular force as the Earl of Oxford. Pepys saw *The Siege of Rhodes*, Part Two, again later on 20 May 'but it is not so well done as when Roxalana was there – who, it is said, is now owned by Lord of Oxford'. Anthony à Wood, reminiscing on the actors' jaunt to Oxford in 1661, added that 'amongst which was Roxolana, married to the Earl of Oxon'. A published broadside, 'Men of Honour', 1687, castigated the earl for 'spending his estate, marrying his whore'.[29]

Although the view differed through the eyes of the law, and despite the earl's legal marriage in 1673, Hester considered herself married rather than simply a chargeable mistress. Her son, born 17 April 1664, would be buried 44 unimpressive years later as 'Aubrey de Vere, Earl of Oxford'. The name was his, the title wasn't. Indeed, it was the king's concern that a noble lineage might end that prompted the earl to marry for real. The true countess-to-be was Diana Kirke, a minor figure at court. Despite the regal prompting, their thirty-year marriage failed to deliver a son and, as a result, the title died with the earl in 1703. However, the replacement of Hester Davenport didn't end the family's theatrical connection. Oxford's daughter and only surviving child, Lady

Diana de Vere, married on 17 April 1694 the first duke of St Albans, who was the son of King Charles II and one-time star of stage, Nell Gwynne.

Interestingly, Hester didn't marry until four months after the earl's death. Aged 62, if we accept her birth date, she became Mrs Peter Hoett, and graced herself on the marriage register as 'Dame Hester, Countess Dowager of Oxford'. She outlived her legal husband and died in 1717. Defiant to the end, she signed her will confidently 'Hester Oxford'.[30]

If the players were at times outrageous outside the theatre, the audience made up their own scandalous script inside.

> *What pleasure is it to give you delight,*
> *When most of you are fit to Judge and write:*
> *Here none t'appear fantastick take great pains,*
> *Or under huge white Perr'wigs have no brains;*
> *No blustering Bullyes come in here half drunk,*
> *For Chyna Oranges and love to Punck;*
> *To fly at Vizard Masks talk Nonsense loud,*
> *And with their noise out-vye Bear-baiting Croud.*
> *Poets should be above such Judges rais'd,*
> *To be condemn'd by such is to be prais'd.*[31]

Any actor today unable to prevent a despairing eyebrow moving skyward at the mention of the audience – in America too intrusive, in Britain too detached – they would surely have diverted their skills to another profession had they lived in Restoration times. And yet the Restoration actor never had it so good compared with the centuries before or after. They never, or rather rarely, had to suffer the audience, in numbers, on the stage itself. Certainly the arrival on stage of scenery for the first time took up space once occupied by the overenthusiast, and perhaps the king's patronage inspired a rethink on that particular strand of audience participation. Any tendency towards a revival was snuffed out by an order of the Lord Chamberlain in February 1674 that unauthorised personnel, as we might say now, were not permitted behind the scenes or to sit on the stage. Any one failing to move following a warning would be 'put out' by the 'Guard of Soldiers' assigned to the theatre. However by the 1690s, after Charles II had unexpectedly exited the stage of life, such encroachment had begun again.[32]

In Thomas D'Urfey's *The Marriage-Hater Match'd*, first produced about January 1692, Berenice rebukes the antics of Lord Brainless: 'Just as he uses the Play-house, from the Box, whip he's in the Pit, from the Pit, hop he's in the Gallery, from thence, hey pass between the Scenes in a moment, when I have seen him spoil many a Comedy, by Baulking the Actors entrance, for when I have eagerly expected some Buffoon to divert, the first nauseous appearance has been my Lord.'[33]

The prologue of *The Fairy Queen*, an adaptation of Shakespeare's *A Midsummer Night's Dream* possibly by Elkanah Settle, staged in 1692, pleads:

> *But that this Play may in its Pomp appear;*
> *Pray let our stage from thronging Beaux be clear.*
> *For what e're cost we're at, what e're we do,*
> *In Scenes, Dress, Dances; yet there's many a Beau,*
> *Will think himself a much more taking show.*
> *How often have you curs'd these new Beau-skreens,*
> *That stand betwixt the Audience and the Scenes?*
> *I asked one of 'em t'other day – Pray, Sir,*
> *Why d'ye the Stage before the Box prefer?*
> *He answer'd – Oh! There I Ogle the whole Theatre,*
> *My Wig – my Shape, my Leg, I there display,*
> *They speak much finer Things than I can say.*
> *These are the Reasons why they croud the Stage*
> *And make the disappointed Audience rage.*[34]

The rage of an audience was often the desired outcome. David Garrick in his *Lethe*, first staged at Drury Lane on 15 April 1740, a Fine Gentleman talks Aesop through an evening's entertainment:

I dress in the Evening and go generally behind the Scenes of both Play-houses; not, you imagine, to be diverted with the Play, but to intrigue and show myself – I stand upon the Stage, talk loud, and stare about – which confounds the Actors and disturbs the Audience; upon which the Galleries, who hate the appearance of one of us, begin to hiss and cry off, off, while I undaunted, stamp my Foot so – loll with my Shoulder thus – take Snuff with my Right-hand, and smile scornfully – thus – This exasperates the Savages, and they attack us with Vollies of suck'd Oranges and half-eaten Pippins.[35]

'And you retire?' asks Aesop. 'Without doubt,' comes the reply, 'if I am sober – for Orange will stain silk, and an Apple may disfigure a Feature.'

The management may have been able to deploy armed security to keep the Restoration stage free of theatregoers, but the changing rooms, or tireing rooms as they were known, were a free-for-all. A prologue spoken by top-of-the-bill Charles Hart in William Wycherley's *The Country Wife*, first produced 12 January 1675, runs:

> *We set no Guards upon our Tyring-Room,*
> *But when with flying Colours, there you come,*
> *We patiently you see, give up to you*
> *Our Poets, Virgins, nay, our Matrons too.*[36]

It was, perhaps, in an attempt to reduce the invasion of the changing rooms that gave rise to the hospitality suite, the so-called green room. Its first theatrical mention is found in Thomas Shadwell's *A True Widow*, first produced (possibly) on 21 March 1678. Shadwell was a large man who enjoyed his drink. Indeed, the character Merryman in Sedley's *Bellamira*, described as having 'drunk his Gallon every day these seven years' and being 'as true a shap'd Drunkard as heart can wish, Great Belly, double chin, thick legs', may have been a nod towards Shadwell. Also, in 'Absalom and Achitophel' Dryden casts Shadwell as Og:

> *Og from a treason-tavern rolling home,*
> *Round as a globe and liquor'd every chink,*
> *Goodly and great he sails behind his link.*

Perhaps it was therefore inevitable that Shadwell would introduce posterity if not the profession to the green room. His character Selfish, 'a coxcomb conceited of his Beauty, Wit and Breeding, thinking all Women in Love with him; always admiring and talking of himself', boasts 'I am the happiest Man, I think, that ever the Sun shin'd on: I have enjoyed the prettiest Creature, just now, in a Room behind the Scenes.' Later we discover the colour of that room when Lady Busy (a 'Woman of Intrigue, very busie in Love-Matters of all kinds, too old for Love of her own, always charitably helping forward that of others, very fond of young Women, very wise and discreet, half Bawd, half Match-maker') is seeking to match Gartrude with Stanmore, when the latter replies: 'No Madam; Selfish, this Evening, in a green room, behind the Scenes, was before-hand with me; she ne'r tells of that.'

The *Shorter Oxford English Dictionary* cites the phrase's origin some thirteen years later. However, *The Female Wits: Or, The Triumvirate of Poets at Rehearsal*, first produced about 1697, Praiseall tells the actresses that 'I'll treat you all in the Green Room with Chocolate.' Also, in Colley Cibber's *Love Makes a Man; or, The Fop's Fortune*, first produced on 7 December 1700, Clodio says: 'I do know London pretty well, and the

Side-box, Sir, and behind the Scenes, ay, and the Green Room, and all the Girls and Women-Actresses there.' More than likely the green room was so-called because it was originally painted in green, or at least the hangings were that colour.[37]

With stalls having to wait until the 1840s for their own first night, the pit ruled the roost. It was not as riotous as that prescribed by popular imagination but it certainly had its moments. Those who knew best, according to the epilogue of Nathaniel Lee and John Dryden's *The Duke of Guise*, snaffled the boxes:

> *This makes our Boxes full; for men of Sense*
> *Pay their four Shillings in their own defence:*
> *That safe behind the Ladies they may stay;*
> *Peep o'er the Fan, and Judg, the bloudy Fray.*[38]

A respectful silence upon which to hang out every word was never on the cast list. The audience would chatter, repeat lines and anticipate them. Perhaps much as people watch television today – a casual, interactive and leisurely experience. A sudden thought or remembrance would interject quite normally with the viewing. The theatre, like the tavern and the coffee house, was a meeting place. In Thomas Betterton's 1670 play *The Amorous Widow; or, The Wanton Wife*, Brittle moans that his 'is grown as common as the Exchange, or Playhouses, where all sorts of Company meet to laugh and talk Bawdy.' For the audience the actors were as much competition as entertainment. Unsurprisingly, the image of sparks in the pit who are 'Noise and Nonsense full' (Aphra Behn's prologue to *The Young King; or, The Mistake*), and often alcohol-fuelled, is strongly evidenced in contemporary writings. Shadwell commentates on the corruption of youth who 'at Sixteen forsooth, set up for Men of the Town. Such as come Drunk and Screaming into a Playhouse, and stand upon the Benches, and toss their full Periwigs and empty Heads, and with their shrill, unbroken pipes, cry, Dam-me, this is a Damn'd Play; Prithee let's to a Whore, Jack.'[39]

The 'Noise and Tumult' of 'the Pratlers in the pit' rumbled on unchecked into the next century, if the 'Prologue Against the Disturbers of the Pit', dated 1709, is anything to go by:

> *Laughers, Buffoons, with an unthinking Croud*
> *Of gaudy Fools, impertinent and loud,*
> *Insult in ev'ry Corner. Want of Sense,*
> *Conform'd with an outlandish Impudence,*
> *Among the rude Disturbers of the Pit,*
> *Have introduc'd ill Breeding and false Wit.*

The boast their Lewdness here young Scowrers meet,
And all the vile Companions of the Street,
Keep a perpetual Brawling at the Door,
Who beat the Bawd last Night? Who bilkt the Whore?
They snarl, but neither fight, nor pay a Farthing;
A Play-House is become a meer Bear-Garden,
Where ev'ry one with Insolence enjoys
His Liberty and Property of Noise…
While ev'ry little thing perks up so soon,
That at Fourteen it Hectors up and down,
With the best Cheats, and the worst Whores in Town;
Swears at a Play, who should be whipt at School,
The Foplings in time must grow up to Rule.[40]

Also part of the entertainment for the more adventurous or brave (or just plain drunk) was to pit their wit against the bluntness of the women employed to sell fruit at the theatre: the so-called orange women or orange wenches. With the opening of the King's House, Brydges Street, the theatre management, on 10 February 1663, granted an exclusive licence for 39 years to the widow Mary 'Orange Moll' Meggs 'to vend, utter and sell oranges, lemons, fruit, sweetmeats and all manner of fruiterer's and confectioner's wares'. In return Meggs was required to pay 6s. 8d. for each day the theatre was open.

Oranges were a luxury item: in the prologue to Aphra Behn's *Young King* produced in 1679, we're told: 'Half Crown my Play, Sixpence my Orange, cost.' And it appears that was the price they got if the playgoers heeded the etiquette advice of the Young Gallants Academy of 1674, which informed the would-be gallant to 'give a hum to the China-Orange-wench, and to give her her own rate for her Oranges (for 'tis below a Gentleman to stand haggling like a Citizens wife)'.[41]

Although refreshing, they were also useful weapons of a crowd's displeasure with a play (because of this they were banned in the upper circle). They could, however, be hazardous to eat. Pepys records that 'a gentleman of good habitt, sitting just before us eating of some fruit, in the midst of the play did drop down as dead, being choked; but with much ado Orange Moll did thrust her finger down his throat, and brought him to life again.'[42]

In the fourth act of Thomas Shadwell's *A True Widow*, for the first time we see a take on the Restoration theatre audience. The stage directions reveal that 'Several young Coxcombs fool with the Orange-Women' and the scene opens with an Orange Woman crying:

'Oranges! will you have any Oranges?'[43]

The most famous orange woman was, of course, Nell Gwynne. In the anonymous 'A Panegyric to Nelly', 1681, the author alludes to her younger days:

> *But first the basket her fair arm did suit*
> *Laden with pippins and Hesperian fruit.*
> *This first step rais'd, to the wond'ring pit she sold*
> *The lovely fruit, smiling with streaks of gold.*[44]

The orange women needed confidence, impudence, wit and looks – as *Collin's Walk Through London and Westminster* of 1690 testifies:

> *From whence his Heart e're she can ask it*
> *Leaps into th'Orange-Wenches Basket;*
> *There pants, and Praises the damn'd Features*
> *Of that most Impudent of Creatures.*[45]

Contemporary satires routinely refer to that stage of Nelly's career (before her career became the stage). Later, her great rival as mistress to the king, the haughty Frenchwoman, Louise de Kerouaille, remarked: 'Anybody might have known she had been an orange wench by her swearing.' The repartee and language of orange women were infamously somewhat less sweeter than their wares. Successful orange women often resorted to hard-sell tactics. Pepys on 11 May 1668 ventured to the Duke's House to see *The Tempest*:

But there happened one thing that vexed me; which is, that the orange-woman did come in the pit and challenge me for twelve oranges which she delivered by my order at a late play at night, to give to some ladies in a box, which was wholly untrue, but yet she swore it to be true; but, however, I did deny it and did not pay her, but for quiet did buy 4s worth of oranges of her – at 6d a piece.[46]

The best orange women gave as good as they got. This meant indulging in banter to make sales, flirting, embarrassing people into purchases or charming them to do so. The punters didn't shy of the challenge either. The prologue to *The Debauchee: or, The Credulous Cuckold*, includes the lines:

> *You'd be so welcome here, would you but sit*
> *Like Cyphers, as you are, and grace the Pit,*

Well drest, well bred, we'd never look for Wit,
But you come bawling in with broken French,
Roaring out Oaths aloud, from Bench to Bench,
And bellowing bawdy to the Orange-wench.[47]

And it wasn't just words that struck home. In a letter from John Verney to Sir Richard Verney, attention is drawn to the scandal caused by John Churchill somewhat less illustriously 'beating an orange wench in the Duke's playhouse'. Churchill was 'challenged by Capt. [Thomas] Otway (the poet), and were both wounded, but Churchill most'.[48]

But for most the orange women epitomised bawdy London. They talked incessantly about sex (the character Mr Vaine in James Howard's *The English Monsieur*, first staged in 1663, witnessed 'the orange-wenches talk of ladies and their gallants') and acted as go-betweens for the audience and the players. One of the audience-characters in *A True Widow*, becoming bored with the play, 'sits down and lolls in the Orange-Wench's Lap'. In the prologue – 'spoken by Mr Mountford' – to John Dryden's *Clomenes, the Spartan Heroe*, the author prays that his audience is free of the usual liquor louts:

I think, or hope at least, the Coast is clear;
That none but men of Wit and Sense are here;
That our Bear-Garden friends are all away,
Who bounce with Hands and Feet, and cry, Play, Play,
Who, to save Coach-Hire, trudge along the Street,
Then print our matted Seats with dirty Feet;
Who, while we speak, make Love to Orange-Wenches,
And between Acts stand strutting on the Benches.[49]

The actor who first spoke these lines, William Mountfort, had a productive line in 'fine gentlemen' and wrote several comedies. His title role in *Sir Courtly Nice*, by John Crowne, was 'nicely Perform'd'. Mountfort had been a boy actor but tragedy struck as he blossomed into maturity, depriving the stage of a possible legend. His death, however, was anything but legendary. He was cut down in the street on Friday, 9 December 1692, before he could draw his sword to defend himself, dying the next day. His brutal murder was incited by an absurdly jealous Captain Richard Hill, who had unrequited feelings for the actress Anne Bracegirdle – that 'loveliest of English actresses.' He had suspected Mountfort of being more requited on that score than himself. Mountfort had married the successful and beautiful actress Susanna Percival on 2 July 1685. She was described in later life by

Anthony Aston as 'a fine, fair Woman, plump, full-featur'd; her face of a fine, smooth Oval, full of beautiful, well-dispos'd Moles on it, and on her Neck and Breast'.[50]

The Mountforts had a daughter, also Susanna, and a second daughter, who died after only eight days – keeping the devastated mother from the stage for eight months. She was also pregnant again at the time of her husband's murder, with their third daughter, Mary, who was baptised just over three months later. William Mountford was only 28 and his widow 25.

And the bad luck didn't end there. Susanna's father, Thomas Percival, was also an actor whose own minor career declined in the 1680s as his daughter's blossomed. He took to crime and was sentenced to death on 17 October 1693 for clipping coins. Susanna petitioned Queen Mary II for clemency and succeeded in having the penalty reduced to transportation. Nonetheless, Percival died in Portsmouth before he could board the convict ship.

The young and still handsome widow, on 31 January 1694, married another emerging actor, the altogether more volatile 'fiery Jack' Verbruggen, whose 'Sword was drawn on the least Occasion'. Inevitably, Mrs Mountfort-Verbruggen's death would be in a manner that reflected the fortune of her tragically tinged life: she died in childbirth in 1703, although the child survived. Fiery Jack was finally dowsed in 1707. The 26th of April 1708 saw a performance 'for the [benefit] of a young orphan child of the late Mr & Mrs Verbruggen'. The young Susanna followed her mother onto the stage and eked out a career as a comic actress between 1703 and 1718. Her relationships proved less amusing than her comedy talents and a string of unhappy failures drove her insane and ultimately to her death.[51]

As William Mountfort's death shows, violence in the playhouse wasn't restricted to stage directions. And, while the audience were capable of setting their wheels into commotion, the actors were not always that far behind. A production of *The Change of Crownes* by Edward Howard was cancelled at the King's House because the leading man, John Lacy, was detained in the groom porter's lodge 'for his acting his part in the late new play.' In this topical satire, Lacy played the role of Asinello, who, in a performance before the king and queen and the Duke and Duchess of York, 'doth abuse the Court with all imaginable wit and plainness, about selling of places and doing everything for money'. Lacy had added some of his own material:

Lacy, the famous Comedian, is at length by great intercession, released from his durance under the groom porter, where he stood committed by his Majesty's order for having on his own head, added several indiscreet impressions in the part he acted.[52]

But the corpulent player blamed his punishment on the playwright's words and not his additional material. Restored to liberty, Lacy,

came to the King's house and there met with Ned Howard, the poet of the play, who congratulated his release; upon which, Lacy cursed him as that it was the fault of his nonsensical play that was the cause of his ill usage. Mr Howard did give some reply, to which Lacy [answered] him that he was more a fool then a poet; upon which Howard did give him a blow on the face with his glove; on which Lacy having a cane in his hand, did give him a blow over the pate.

Howard, rather than run the impudent player through, as some suspected, merely complained of Lacy's behaviour to the king. And Lacy once again found himself in custody, this time in the knight marshal's office. And the theatre's doors were locked again.

8

Violence and Crime: Highwaymen, Duels and an Ambuscade

GENTLEMEN OF THE ROAD – RESTORATION HIGHWAYMEN

'*Les Highwaymen sont, en général, d'une classe supérieure; ils se piquent d'avoir de l'éducation et de bons procédés; aussi les appelle-t-on* gentlemen of the road.'[1]

– J L Ferri de St Constant, 1804

'Tales of their cunning and generosity were in the mouths of everybody, and a noted thief was a kind of hero.'[2]

– Abbé le Blanc, c. 1737

The wind was a torrent of darkness among the gusty trees,
The moon was a ghostly galleon tossed upon cloudy seas,
The road was a ribbon of moonlight over the purple moor,
And the highwayman came riding –
Riding – riding –
The highwayman came riding, up to the old inn door...[3]

– traditional song

We cut little slack to muggers or burglars or car thieves. But we tend to view the antics of, say, bank robbers through lenses fragrantly tinted with a swag-bag of rose. They're taking from those who have a lot. Fair game. Good luck to them. It's the same notion – but sweetly intensified by their days-of-yore existence – that tempers our perspective on highwaymen. And it's by no means a modern or even Victorian romanticism. Highwaymen were heroes throughout the seventeenth century. People delighted in tales of their derring-do even when clearly they derring-didn't.

Biographical information about Restoration highwaymen is somewhat sparse and most of what we have comes from Captain Alexander Smith, who was never overly concerned with historical reliability. As such, the stories of highwaymen given here may well be smokescreens confounding truth, but even smokescreens are born of fire.[4]

The fear of highwaymen and footpads (same as highwaymen but without the panache or the horse) was bad enough for the traveller in Restoration England, but the condition of the roads was equally criminal. Getting around wasn't easy. In 1736, Robert Philips, in his *Dissertation concerning the Present State of the High Roads of England*, especially of those near London, noted that,

> In the Summer the Roads are suffocated and smothered with Dust; and towards the Winter, between wet and dry, there are deep Ruts full of Water with hard dry Ridges, which make it difficult for Passngers to cross by one another without overturning; and in the Winter they are all Mud, which rises, spues, and squeezes into the Ditches; so that the Ditches and Roads are full of Mud and Dirt alike.[5]

Overturned or broken-down carriages or those stuck in the mud provided easy pickings for the knights of the road, who weren't exactly a rare breed. Indeed, such was their number that travellers expected to be held up and prepared accordingly. The open countryside was their natural nocturnal habitat. It seems London-based or London-bound travellers took their valuables (if not their lives) in their hands every time they plotted a course over Bagshot Heath, Hounslow Heath and Blackheath.

Sir John Reresby wrote in his memoirs that in February 1677 he went to London 'well guarded for fear of some of my back friends and highwaymen, having caused one of the chiefe of them to be taken not long before.' Similarly, when Cosmo III, Grand Duke of Tuscany, left Dorchester on 11 April 1669 he was protected from robbers by 'a great many horse soldiers belonging to the militia of the county.'[6]

John Verney wrote in 1679 that a couple of highwaymen,

> having robbed a country man & leaving him his horse, he pursued 'em with hue and cry which over took them, but they being very stout fought their way through Islington & all the road along to the town's end, where after both their swords were broken in their hands & they unhorsed, they were seized & carried to Newgate. 'Tis great pity such men should be hanged.'[7]

Standing and delivering next to his brutal counterpart on mainland Europe, who would often take your money and your life, the English highwayman was, at times at least, comparatively genteel. Violence was a last resort. Weapons were part of the regalia first, and tools of the trade, second. A German historian thought English highwaymen 'generally very polite; they assure you *they are very sorry that poverty has driven them to that shameful ordeal,* and end by demanding your purse in the most courteous manner'. Highwaymen were the aristocracy of the criminal classes and as such behaved as gentlemen.[8]

Indeed, many of them were gentlemen coming from well-to-do backgrounds, as were over half of the 59 highwaymen recorded in Smith's book. The Civil War and subsequent republican rule had forced some dispossessed Royalists to attempt to retake their wealth from the roads. One 'most notorious fellow' was John Cottingham, known as Mull-Sack because of his penchant for that drink – a spicy warm sherry – which he sank 'morning, noon and night'. Having 'a great antipathy against Committee-men and the Rump Parliament', he successfully held up a pay wagon carrying £4,000 for soldiers in Oxford and Gloucester. Unfortunately for Mull-Sack, he didn't quite see in the Restoration as he was captured and hanged in Smithfield Rounds in April 1659.[9]

It is the image of noble robber, those figures of unbridled romance, that sits with us today, and not the one of the murdering, raping thug who also 'took to the highway'. Men such as Jack Withers, for example. Fleeing a bungled assault, Withers and his accomplice, William Edwards, were forced to 'make their escape on foot through bye-lanes and over fields'. Coming across a so-called penny postman (William Dockwra's penny post began in London in 1680), they assaulted him and,

> taking from him about eight shillings, to prevent his discovery of 'em Withers (though much against the will of his comrade Edwards) took a butcher's knife out of his pocket, and not only most barbarously cut his throat, but also ripped out his guts, and filling the poor man's belly full of stones, threw him into a pond, where he was found the next day.

Withers, later condemned for another robbery, confessed to the murder of the penny postman at his execution in Thetford, Norfolk, in 1703.[10]

Patrick O'Bryan was one who combined the gentleman and the thug. The gentleman O'Bryan is depicted by his new trade's first encounter, no less distinguished a prey than the king's mistress Nell Gwynne.

O'Bryan was born in Galway, hence the approximation of a supposed Irish accent in this anecdote recounted by Smith:

> ...stopping her coach in the road to Winchester, quoth he, Madam, I am, by my Shalvation, a fery good shentleman, and near relation to His Majesty's Grace the Duke of Ormond; but being in want of money, and knowing you to be a charitable whore, I hope you will give me shomething after I've took all you have away. Honest Nell seeing the simplicity of the fellow and laughing heartily at his bull, she gave him ten guineas, with which [he] rode away without doing farther damage.[11]

The thug, though, was more in keeping with his natural impulses. On one occasion he happened across a man who had testified against him previously, when he had been sentenced to death by hanging in Gloucester. O'Bryan 'miraculously retrieved a forfeited life' after his dead body, which was handed over to relatives for internment, proved to be still alive. Now O'Bryan was faced again by his accuser, and his revenge was to rob him again, but he made sure there would be no further testimony, first by lodging a bullet in his head, and second, by using 'a sharp hanger' (a short sword) with which he 'cut his carcase into several pieces.'[12]

On another occasion, with four 'other villains', O'Bryan broke into the house of a squire, one Lancelot Wilmot outside Trowbridge, Wiltshire. The gang bound and gagged Wilmot's five servants and then did likewise to the squire and his wife as they lay in their bed. 'Next,' we're told,

> they went into the daughter's room, who was also in bed; but O'Bryan being captivated by her beauty, quoth he, Before we tie and gag this pretty creature, I must make bold to rob her of her maidenhead. So whilst this villain was eagerly coming to the bedside, protesting that he loved her as he did his soul and designed her no more harm than he did himself, the modest virgin had wrapped herself up in the bedclothes as well as time would permit. And as he took her in one arm, and endeavoured to get his other hand between herself and the sheet, she made a very vigorous defence to save her honour, for though she could not hinder him from often kissing, not only her face, but several other parts of her body, as by her struggling they came to be bare; yet by her nimbleness in shifting her posture, and employing his hands so well with her own, they could never attain to the liberty they chiefly strove for.

She neither made great noise, bit or scratched, but appeared to be resolute, and her resistance was made with so much eagerness and is such good earnest, that the lascivious villain seeing there was nothing to be done without more violence, his lust incited him to downright brutish force; and no sooner had he obtained his will, by ravishing the young gentlewoman, but such was his barbarity, that he most inhumanly stabbed her. Then, he and his companions murdered her father and mother. After this, taking away about £2,500 in gold and silver, they set fire to the house, burning it down to the ground, and in flames also destroyed all the poor servants.[13]

The story bears a remarkable similarity to that involving another highwayman, Jocelin Harwood. He, with two others, broke into a knight's house in Shropshire, and first gagged the servants and then, in their bedchamber, the master and mistress of the house. In the next room lay the two daughters, who asked to be treated civilly, 'for in case you and your comrades should be afterwards taken for what you act here, we may perhaps use you civilly, for we know you from 500 men'. It was not a wise move. Harwood replied, 'Do you so? I'll prevent that then.' He then, in a frenzied bloodlust, 'cut them into several pieces with his hanger. And then flying into a great passion into the parents' room, he swore in the midst of a thousand horrid oaths, curses and imprecations, that they should not survive their damned offspring, and stabbed them both through the heart.'

However, the murderer's comrades, sickened at his attack, as they made their escape shot Harwood's horse from under him 'and tying him hand and foot, left him in the road, with a piece of the knight's plate lying by him, saying that was but a just reward due for his barbarous murder'. Undeterred, he behaved 'very audaciously' during imprisonment in Shrewsbury gaol and even spat in the face of the judge and jury at his trial. He continued 'cursing and swearing and drinking to the very morning he was to die'. At the gallows he recanted nothing and said 'with an unchangeable countenance, that was the murder to do again, he would act it'. He was 'turned off' in 1692, aged just 23.[14]

The highwayman William Macqueer closed in on a victim, the aptly named Captain Shooter, on Hampstead Heath. Determined not to 'tamely part with his money' the good captain drew his own pistols. Once these were spent, both parties drew swords and 'pushed at one another. But Macqueer bethinking himself of another pistol he had, still charged, in his breeches pocket, he pulled it out and shot his antagonist through the head, from whom he took fifty guineas and a silver watch.'[15]

As with Patrick O'Bryan, the highwayman Bob Congden enjoyed a sideline in housebreaking and murder. His most brutal attack, however, took place in a house in which he was welcome. In need of money, he,

> went home to his lodgings one night...and with an iron bar bashed out the brains of his landlady; next, having no pity on her child which began to cry at this bloody spectacle, he most barbarously killed that. Then standing behind the street-door till the maid returned, whom he had sent out to buy some tobacco, he killed her and robbed the house of £186.[16]

The Quaker and rapist Jacob Halsey became notorious for the 'formal language of those worst of British schismatics' employed while robbing his victims. His trademark was not his looks but the religiosity of his words: 'Friend,' he declared to a country curate travelling between Oxford and Abingdon, 'taking thee to be some Philistine going to spoil an honest Israelite for tithes, I must make bold to spoil thee first; therefore thou wicked one, deliver thy mammon to the righteous, that he may convert it to a better use than to exhaust it in gluttony and fine clothes, otherways I must send thee to the bottomless pit, before thy time is come by the course of nature.' His formality did not evade him even at the point of rape. Addressing a 'very pretty gentlewoman on horseback betwixt Maningtree in Essex and Harwich,' Halsey declared, 'My pretty lamb, an insurrection of an unruly member obliges me to make use of you upon an extraordinary occasion; therefore I must dismount thy alluring body, to the end I may come in unto thee.' However, 'having surfeited himself with unlawful pleasure, he sent her about her business, without so much as searching her pockets or taking the gold watch which she had then by her side.'[17]

On meeting a beadle of St Clement Danes, Halsey was challenged to a fight with quarter-staffs:

> Jacob was handsomely thrashed, and suffered severely in the flesh, but nevertheless gaining the victory over his adversary, quoth he, *I see thou canst exercise thy long-staff pretty well, but I'll prevent thee from using thy short one to-night.* So tying his hands behind him, he pulled his member out of his breeches, and with a great nail he had in his pocket, and a great flint-stone he took off the ground, he just took the end of the skin thereof (for Jacob would do him no further damage) and nailed it to a tree.[18]

And all for 14 shillings.

After the Restoration, William Nevison from Pomfret, Yorkshire, cut his criminal teeth in Leicestershire. He soon carved out a reputation as a gallant highwayman given his favourable inclination towards the fairer sex, his charitable acts and his refusal to rob anyone allied to his preferred Cavalier party. However, it was following his capture that the inevitable romance of his story took to the breeze. Placed under close 24-hour surveillance in Leicester gaol and chained so tightly that he was unable to move, he seemed somewhat unlikely to be able to effect escape. But that was exactly what Nevison contrived.

Feigning illness, he sent for a physician and nurse, who happened to be friends. The good doctor pronounced the patient struck with the plague and declared that, unless he was removed away to solitary cell and his chains loosened to permit him to breathe more easily, he would infect the entire gaol. Worried about infection, none of the gaolers would go near Nevison, which meant his friends had freedom to paint blue plague spots on his chest, hands and face. He was then given a potion that knocked him out so that it appeared he was dead.

However, the gaoler refused to allow Nevison's body to be taken away in the coffin brought by his friends until a jury decided on the cause of death. Luckily for the plotters, the assembled jury feared infection more than the truth, and, having quickly glimpsed the body, declared it a victim of plague. Nevison was carried away to safety in his coffin. After he had returned to his illegal profession, rumours soon gathered momentum that Nevison's ghost was now plying the same trade.

Unconvinced that the dead need to be nourished by material objects, the authorities dug up Nevison's coffin and discovered it was as empty as the rumours. However, despite a £20 reward on his plague-free head, he remained at large for a little over three years until time and the authorities caught up with him in Yorkshire. Tried and sentenced to death, Nevison managed to cheat the gibbet again thanks to the intervention of a knight who engineered a reprieve in the form of transportation. Typically, Nevison failed to take his berth on board and continued his preferred career in the county of his birth. He was finally captured by a Captain Hardcastle about thirteen miles outside York. Within a week that city saw him hanged on 15 March 1684.[19]

Another gaolbreak was featured in *The London Gazette*, which reported in December 1687 that the convicted highwayman Augustine King had escaped from the gatehouse at Cambridge. King was described as 'a burly, corpulent man, about thirty-one years of age, fresh coloured, full-eyed, and lank-haired.' A real dreamboat. He had several accomplices and they were all 'well known to every inn-keeper out of London'.

However, the most famous of all Restoration highwaymen of his time was Claude Du Vall. He was born in 1643 in Domfront, Normandy, and came over from France upon the Restoration as a page in the service of the Duke of Richmond. Unable to meet his gambling expenses on a servant's wage, he took to the more lucrative but dangerous road, a trade he carried out with elaborate politeness.

On stopping one coach, which carried a knight, his wife, a female servant and, one imagines rather importantly, £420 in cash, Du Vall was intrigued to see the lady, clearly untroubled by the prospective ordeal, play a flageolet. The highwayman, in response, took out his own flageolet and played along. Impressed by her musicality, he asked the knight permission to dance with his wife which, unsurprisingly given the circumstances, was granted. Afterwards, as the entourage repaired back to the coach, Du Vall reminded the knight that he had not yet paid for the music, and the knight promptly handed over a bag containing 100 guineas. 'Sir,' he said looking upon the bag, 'you are a liberal, and shall have no cause to repent your being so; this liberality of yours shall excuse the other £300.' And with that, dripping in gallantry, he rode off into the night.

Less gallant, though, and more convincing as it appears in the *Newgate Calendar* as well as biographies of Du Vall, is the following story:

> It happened another time, as Du Vall was upon his vocation of robbing on Blackheath, he met with a coach richly fraught with ladies of quality, and with one child, who had a silver sucking bottle. He robbed them rudely, took away their money, watches, rings and even the little child's sucking bottle; nor would, upon the child's tears, nor the ladies' earnest intercession, be wrought upon to restore it; till at last, one of his companions forced him to deliver it.

Similarly, his demise was less wistful than his reputation. Spotted drunk in the Hole-in-the-Wall tavern in Chandos Street, he was arrested and taken to Newgate Prison, which was still being rebuilt after the Great Fire, 'where crowds of ladies visited him in the condemned hold; many more in masks were present at his execution', throwing flowers at his feet. He was hanged at Tyburn on Friday, 21 January 1670, and laid in outlaw state overnight 'in the Tangier Tavern in St Giles, in a room draped with black and covered with escutcheons'. He was 26.[20]

He was buried in St Paul's, Covent Garden, in the middle aisle, under a stone reading:

> *Here lies Du Vall: Reader, if Male thou art,*
> *Look to thy Purse; if female, to thy Heart.*

> *Much Havock he hath made of both: for all*
> *Men he made stand, and women he made fall.*
> *The second Conqueror of the Norman race*
> *Knights to his Arms did yield, and Ladies to his face.*
> *Old Tyburn's Glory, England's illustrious thief,*
> *Du Vall, the ladies' Joy, Du Vall the ladies' Grief.*

Samuel Butler wrote a 'Pindarick Ode':

> *... And yet the brave Du-Vall, whose name*
> *Can never be worn out by fame,*
> *That liv'd and dy'd, to leave behind*
> *A great example to mankind;*
> *That fell a public Sacrifice*
> *From ruine to preserve those few,*
> *Who through born false, may be made true,*
> *And teach the world to be more just and wise;*
> *Ought not like vulgar ashes rest*
> *Unmention'd in his silent Chest,*
> *Not for his own but public interest...*[21]

The public hanging of highwaymen, intended to discourage crime, in reality achieved almost the opposite. They became hugely popular spectacles in which the condemned were fêted as romantic heroes. As Henry Fielding wrote later,

> The day appointed by law for the thief's shame is the day of glory in his own opinion. His procession to Tyburn and his last moments there are all triumphant; attended with the compassion of the weak and tender-hearted, and with the applause, admiration and envy of all the bold and hardened. His behaviour in his present condition, not the crimes, how atrocious soever, which brought him to it, is the subject of contemplation. And if he hath sense enough to temper his boldness with any degree of decency, his death is spoken of by many with honour, by most with pity, and by all with approbation.[22]

Just as ineffective was the public hanging, or gibbeting, of dead highwaymen. The body would be left to decompose in an iron cage erected near the scene of the crime. A regular feature for centuries, gibbeting was not actually legalised until 1752. So endemic was the practice that gibbets became landmarks. It was the aim of these 'dreadful mementoes' to act as a deterrent to others who may contemplate a career following in the hoofprints of the deceased. Your life of crime leads to your death as a criminal. In order to sustain this deterrent, the body was soaked in tar. However, this practice often aided associates of the dead man to set fire to the corpse. This happened to three executed highwaymen who had robbed the North Coach. Gibbeted at the top of the Chevin, near Belper, Derbyshire, their bodies were set alight by a friend, and they burned so ferociously that when discovered only the iron cage remained.

Eventually, even the authorities realised it proved as hopeless a deterrent as hanging. The last man to be gibbeted was James Cook at Aylestone, near Leicester. Rather than repulse people, his gibbet became a meeting place for noisy crowds on Sunday afternoons.

THE DUEL IN THE CROWN – THE DEMAND FOR SATISFACTION

'And as there is not anything that makes a man more known than a duel, especially if it be one of distinction, and procures him greater applause than the managing of it with discretion as well as courage.'
– Captain Alexander Smith, 1719[23]

Duelling, or, more precisely, the duel of honour, despite royal distaste, was stunningly fashionable in Restoration England. It was equally fashionable to wear a dress sword, which must have served as constant reminder of where an argument could next go. Although the duel has been polished in custom and tradition, it has been argued that the first such recorded encounter was that between Cain and Abel. Biblical squabbles aside, historically begotten of the judicial duel (trial by combat) and the duel of chivalry (jousting tournaments), the duel of honour was essentially imported from France, in keeping with much about Restoration high society.

In 1610, John Seldon in his *The Duello, or Single Combat*, describing the ripening of the duel of honour, wrote that,

truth, honor, freedome and curtesie being as incidents to perfit chivalry upon the lye given, fame impeached, body wronged, or curtesie taxed, a custom hath bin among the French, English, Burguignons, Italians, Almans and the Northern people (which as Ptolomey notes are alwaies inclined to liberty) to seek revenge of their wrongs on the body of their accuser and that by private combat *seul à seul*, without judicial lists appointed them.[24]

The duel of honour, Seldon's 'private combat *seul à seul*', rendered redundant in England the fifteenth-century so-called 'killing affrays', where paid thugs were recruited to carry out murder. Nonetheless, we see in Restoration England their less fatal offspring, which we might term 'beating affrays', find occasional and profitable employment. Recruiting thugs to beat an adversary as a lesson or warning may be looked down upon as cowardly but was an attractive policy for women who, demanding retribution for an affront, could not fight themselves nor find a male to do so voluntarily on their behalf.

Duels were clearly fairer than killing affrays – you did the fighting yourself, the numbers were equal, and a strict code was followed. But, ultimately, they remained unsatisfactory, particularly if honour demanded satisfaction in order to resolve a dispute. The better fighter and not the better argument will, almost inevitably, win.

The first recorded duel of honour in England took place in Islington in 1609 between Sir George Wharton and Sir James Stewart, two courtiers of James I. The cause (apart from there being 'reproachful words between them') was unknown, the outcome an unhappy draw: they killed each other. Unsurprisingly, upset at the loss of two favourites, whom he supposedly buried together, James I censured the practice in his 'Proclamation against Private Challenges and Combats' in 1613. It and subsequent royal proclamations did little to stem the swell of bloody-satisfaction seekers. There was, however, a marked decrease during the Civil War and the Protectorate.

Duels were fought for any number of reasons or (for the more naturally belligerent) excuses, including females (an injury, insult or seduction), defamation, violence and lies. But mainly lies. The so-called 'giving the lie' was the most provocative cause of a quarrel, for which, naturally, only bloodshed could possibly compensate.

Once offence had been caused, the ritual of sending the challenge, nominating seconds, choosing weapons and selecting time and place got under way. It was normal to choose a friend or acquaintance to deliver the challenge and act as your second. As the seconds also fought each other, the challenged's second had to be of equal ability as that chosen by the challenger. It was also the seconds' task, if possible, to reconcile the protagonists without recourse to battle. It was with this in mind that two authorities on conduct barred the use of Irishmen as seconds on the grounds that nine out of ten of them 'have such an innate love of fighting that they cannot bring an affair to an amicable adjustment'. Occasionally, mirroring the French, each party would be accompanied by two seconds, as with the duel between the Earl of Shrewsbury and the Duke of Buckingham in 1668.[25]

Uniquely in England the choice of weapons rested with the

challenged or the offender. Naturally, this gave a precious advantage to choose a weapon in which you were most proficient or your counterpart encouragingly weak. The great duelling favourite was the sword, of which the rapier was popular in the early seventeenth century. However, it was so long and awkward that it usually had to be supplemented by a defensive weapon, either the cloak or dagger. But, by the Restoration, a smaller, lighter rapier, known as the *flamberge*, had been introduced and was capable of defensive parries also. This, in turn, gave way to the small sword, which needed a stiffer, stronger blade and thus became heavier, requiring at times two hands to wield. The sword, as the duelling weapon of choice, gave way in the eighteenth century to the pistol, leading to the chilling epithet of 'pistols for two, coffee for one'. The duel itself would be contested until one of the parties 'is well blooded, disabled, or disarmed, or until, after receiving a wound and blood being drawn, the aggressor begs pardon'.

The duel of honour was condemned by crown, church and largely ineffective proclamation (the first was on 13 August 1660). The state even appointed a Committee of Council to suppress duelling, but the contests continued until well into the nineteenth century. Only when the public finally gave it the thumbs-down did it truly do the honourable thing and fall on its own sword.[27]

In June 1671, Thomas Hickman, Lord Windsor (who was Lord Lieutenant of Worcestershire), regaled Lord Conway with a tale of unrequited violence. Windsor had, according to Conway, sent Sir William Knight (although state papers refer to Sir William Kile) to Sir John, Baron Berkeley of Stratton, Lord Lieutenant of Ireland (1670–72), whom Windsor had heard was at Kidderminster. Knight/Kile was to put Berkeley,

in mind of his promise to fight with [Lord Windsor] when he came out of Ireland; my Lord Berkeley answered him that he never challenged my Lord Winsor; the other affirmed that he did, and told him that he was farther commanded to bring him a challenge, if he had forgot the former, to which Lord Berkeley replied, that he was still the King's Lieutenant in Ireland, and would not fight with my Lord Winsor. Sir William Knight answered him that my Lord Winsor was the King's Lord Lieutenant of Worcestershire, and as good a man as himself, and that if he refused to fight with him, he was commanded to tell him that my Lord Winsor would put him up for a coward, and cudgel him wherever he met him. So they parted, and my Lord Berkeley told him he was going to Windsor, and would complain to the King.[28]

The king clearly upheld Berkeley's complaint, as the state papers on 29 June 1671 confirm:

The main business was a challenge from Lord Windsor to the Lord Lieutenant of Ireland in his passage to London. Lord Windsor was sent to the Tower and Sir Wm. Kile who delivered the challenge, sent for into custody.

Windsor was discharged on 18 July, and Knight/Kile on 5 August.[29]

The vociferously Tory Major Theophilius Oglethorpe, from Godalming, Surrey, was lieutenant colonel in the Duke of York's troop of guards. A loyal Yorkist, he was knighted by his master on his accession as James II in 1685, promoted to brigadier general and appointed Gentleman of the Horse. Oglethorpe's honour needed little incitement to action: a toast would usually do the trick. As one satire put it:

> *[Let] Oglethorpe fight*
> *And swear each common health is drunk in spite.*[30]

On 17 February 1680, upon hearing a group of Whigs talk in less than admirable terms about the king's much-unloved French mistress, Louise de Keroualle, he challenged the lot of them. They all refused. Sometime the following year he married Louise's personal maid, Eleanor Wall (died 1732), daughter of Richard Wall of Tipperary. On 10 January 1681 he killed a Captain Richardson, while his second, Cornet Colt, wounded a Captain Churchill. Convicted of manslaughter, Oglethorpe pleaded the benefit of clergy. Middlesex County Records show that the death penalty was commuted to branding. But this reduced sentence was not enforced.[31]

Duelling was a cancerous enemy to the armed forces. At a meeting with Sir William Coventry, secretary to the Lord High Admiral, on 1 April 1667, Pepys relates the conviction with which it would not be tolerated:

While we were talking, there comes Sir Tho. Allen with two ladies, one of which was Mrs Rebecca Allen that I knew heretofore, the clerk of the ropeyard's daughter at Chatham; who, poor heart, came to desire favour for her husband, who is clapped up, being a Lieutenant, for sending a challenge to his Captain in the most saucy base language that could be writ. I perceive Sir W Coventry is wholly resolved to bring him to punishment – 'For bear with this,' says he, 'and no discipline shall ever be expected.'[32]

As well as bringing the participants to punishment, the authorities tried to pre-empt danger with swift action. At home Pepys received 'a letter from Fitzgerald [a former deputy governor of the Tangier] that he is seized upon last night by an order of the Generalls by a file of musqueteers, and kept prisoner in his chamber. The Duke of York did tell me of it today; it is about a quarrel between [Fitzgerald] and Witham [a cavalry captain in the Tangier garrison], and they fear a challenge.'[33]

It was only at foreign stations such as Tangier and Dunkirk that military courts martial cut with any teeth. In England, they had no power to imprison, let alone pass sentence on loss of life or limb. During the reign of Charles II (1660–85) only 21 general courts martial were held in England. Typically, these would be charges for fighting or duelling. Indeed, in 1684 Ensign James Hilton was dismissed from the army in disgrace for wounding Captain Henry Rowe, this being the harshest punishment available to a general court martial for an officer.[34]

Despite Pepys's dislike of duelling and desires for stronger laws to curb the whole wicked practice, he was himself almost involved in a duel in 1670. He had, with Sir William Batten, surveyor of the navy, and Sir William Penn, a navy commissioner (whose elder son, William, the Quaker leader, founded the colony of Pennsylvania), leased a privateering ship, the *Flying Greyhound*. Their captain, a pirate called Hogg, set sail with zest to pick off Dutch merchant ships. Any hauls, known as prize-goods, would, if proved lawful acquisitions and plentiful enough, turn a tidy profit on their investment. Two Swedish prizes, however, proved troublesome for Pepys and co. It brought them, in 1667, into legal conflict with Sir Johan Barckmann, Baron Leijonbergh, a diplomat in the Swedish embassy, known to Pepys as the 'Swedish Resident', and who lived in the 'piatzza', Covent Garden. Despite a court judgment against them, Pepys in 1670 disputed the amount offered to Elizabeth, wife of Sir William Batten, who had recently died. He was ordered by the king and the Earl of Arlington neither to issue nor to accept a challenge. Ironically, despite Pepys's noble defence of the widow, she would later marry Leijonbergh.[35]

It was a relieved Pepys who greeted the news, on 31 October 1666, that Sir Jeremy Smith had killed the fiery-tempered Captain Holmes in a duel. He had had words with Holmes himself and frankly feared a challenge: 'I fear every day more and more mischief from that man,' he bemoaned. He had been wary of him since 'that old business which he attempted upon my wife.' Although Pepys neglected to be more explicit, it can be assumed that the less-than-gallant captain relished the opportunity of a sexual duel with Mrs Pepys. Sadly, for this jealous husband at least, the news of Holmes's demise was premature. Holmes would later feature as a second to the Duke of Buckingham in his scandalous duel with the Earl of Shrewsbury, but over time the diarist's animosity towards him would cool.[36]

At a dinner party at the Pepys' residence, on 29 July 1667, Samuel and his cousin Roger were regaled by the story of another

Duell last night in Covent-garden, between Sir H[enry]. Bellasses [Belasyse] and Tom Porter [the play-writing son of the poet, Endymion]. It is worth remembering the silliness of the quarrel, and is a kind of emblem of the general complexion of this whole kingdom at present.

They two, it seems, dined yesterday at Sir Robt. Carrs [MP for Lincolnshire], where it seems people do drink high, all that come. It happened that these two, the greatest friends in the world, were talking together and Sir H. Bellasses talked a little louder than ordinary to T. Porter, giving of him some advice: some of the company standing by said, 'What, are they quarrelling, that they talk so high?' Sir H. Bellasses hearing it, said, 'No!', says he, 'I would have you that know I never quarrel but I strike; and take that as a rule of mine.'

'How!' says T. Porter, 'strike! I would I could see that man in England that durst give me a blow!' With that, Sir H. Bellasses did give him a box of the eare and so were going to fight there, but were hindered; and by and by T. Porter went out, and meeting Dryden the poet, told him of the business and that he was resolved to fight Sir H. Bellasses presently, for he knew if he did not, they should be made friends tomorrow and then the blow would rest upon him; which he would prevent, and desired Dryden to let him have his boy to bring him notice which way Sir H. Bellasses goes.

By and by he is informed that Sir H. Bellasses's coach was coming, so T. Porter went down out of the Coffee-house, where he stayed for the tidings, and stopped the coach and bade Sir H. Bellasses come out: 'Why,' says H. Bellasses, 'you will not hurt me coming out, will you?' – 'No,' says T. Porter. So out he went, and both drew; and H. Bellasses having drawn and flung away his scabbard, T. Porter asked him whether he was ready; the other answering he was, they fell to fight, some of their acquaintance by; they wounded one another, and H. Bellasses so much, that it is feared he will die; and finding himself sorely wounded, he called to T. Porter and kissed him and bade him shift himself – 'For,' says [he], 'Tom, thou hast hurt me, but I will make shift to stand upon my legs till thou mayest withdraw; and the world not take notice of you, for I would not have thee troubled for what thou hast done.'

And so whether he did fly or no I cannot tell, but T. Porter showed H. Bellasses that he was wounded too; and they are both ill, but H. Bellasses to fear of life. And this is a fine example; and H. Bellasses a Parliament-man too, and both of them most extraordinary friends.[37]

A newsletter reported on 12 August that 'Sir H. Bellasis died of his wounds this morning. Mr T Porter is fled.' The next day 'it was found on examination that the sword had never pierced the body.' The coroner's jury, as directed, thus gave the cause of death as unknown. After Belasyse's (at that point falsely) reported death, Pepys recorded how 'pretty it is to see how the world talk of them as of a couple of fools, that killed one another out of Love.' Despite the trivial nature of their quarrel, neither had an unblemished track record. Tom Porter had killed his adversary in a duel in 1655, and Henry Belasyse, eldest son of Lord Belasyse, was one of Charles Sackville's group of friends responsible for the killing of a tanner mistaken for a highwayman in Stoke Newington on 18 February 1662.[38]

James Pearse informed Pepys on 6 August 1662 that,

Mr Edwd. Montagu [master of the horse to the queen] hath lately had a duell with Mr Cholmely, that is first Gentleman-usher to the Queene and was a messenger from the King to her in Portugall, and is a fine gentleman but hath received many affronts from Mr Montagu...Hee proved too hard for Montagu and drove him so far backward that he fell into a ditch and dropped his sword; but with honour would take no advantage over him, but did give him his life; and the world says that Mr Montagu did carry himself very poorly in the business and hath lost his honour for ever with all people in it – of which I am very glad, in hopes that it will humble him.[39]

It seemed that even trying to win the attention of a woman was enough to spark a duel. Two gentlemen, Mr Scrope and Sir Thomas Armstrong, caused a rumpus at the Duke's House theatre when both were intent on talking to Mrs Uphill, an actress who had come to watch the play wearing a vizard, as was customary for female members of the audience. In their attempts to get to the player first, Scrope twice kicked Armstrong on the shins. John Verney takes up the story: 'The gentlemen round made a ring, and they fought, Sir Thomas killed Scrope at the first pass; not the first man he had killed, said the bystanders.'[40]

Nor do the aristocracy necessarily await coming of age before drawing their swords of honour. The fourteen-year-old Lord Gerard had taken his mother to New Bedlam: viewing mad people was a popular pastime in Restoration London. Insulted by the language and antics of a drunken porter and his wife, the youngster drew his sword and ran the porter 'into the groin'. Rather than exalting him in honour, those about him – 'the rabble' – restrain him and throw him into gaol. With a mob baying for blue blood, the lord mayor does the decent thing and offers the boy protection in his own home. Outraged, the Countess of Bath is set upon by the mob and 'has her coach broke to bits & her footman knocked down, being taken for Lord Gerard's mother'.[41]

Nor did the English penchant for duelling confine itself to its own shores. On 22 September 1681, Henry Savile, the English ambassador, informed Secretary of State Leoline Jenkins, of 'an accident hapned heer amongst our owne fellow subjects.' He continued:

On Thursday night Mr Talmache, sonn to the Dutchesse of Lawderdale, and Mr Kerneggy [Carnegie], second son to the Countesse of Southaske, having a quarrell, which came to drawing of swordes, the latter was run quite through the body, of which he did not dye till last night.[42]

The punishment meted out, once again, served only to show that the crime of aristocratic men taking a life (even other aristocratic ones) was considered a minor offence. As Savile later reports – on 21 February 1682 – the quarrel's victor was dealt a not-so-severe slap on the purse:

Mr Talmache was tryed at the Chastelet heer on Wednesday last for the death of Mr Kerneggy. Hee was acquitted for a fine of 1,000 pistoles; which beeing immediately paid, the use hee made of his liberty was to goe to Flanders to avoid an appeale to the parliament, and by consequence more trouble, though I thinke little danger.[43]

In 1669, early on in a career that would see him master of the king's household, while on duty as an ensign in the King's Guard in Ireland, Henry Bulkeley fought and killed a man called Stephen Radford. Tried and convicted of the lesser crime of manslaughter, he was sentenced to be burned in the hand. However, as with that served upon Major Oglethorpe, this was discharged after a timely intervention from the time-honoured friends in high places. It wasn't Bulkeley's first experience of duelling, either. In 1665 he had been seriously wounded while acting as a second. His never-too-cool blood was overheated by James Butler, Earl of Ossory (son of the Duke of Ormond), evidently over a long-term infatuation with Mrs B: 'the old quarrel about Mr B. wiffe is the talk of the town.'[44]

Sophia Bulkeley (c. 1648–1715) was the sister of Frances 'La Belle' Stewart, later Duchess of Richmond. Pepys thought her 'very handsome'. As indeed did many others aside from the Earl of Ossory. Treasury payments and a curious grant (on 28 February 1684) of the place and precedence of an earl's daughter for unspecified services suggest that she may have been more compliant with his majesty than her sister. And, keeping the family connections tight, Sophia's daughter, Anne, would marry James Fitzjames (the future Duke of Berwick), the son of James, Duke of York and Arabella Churchill.[45]

However, it was Sidney Goldolphin whom she bewitched.

> *Not for the Nation but the faire*
> *Our Treasury provides;*
> *Bulkly's Godolphin's only care*
> *As Middleton is Hide's.*[46]

(*Middleton* – court lady, Jenny Middleton.); *Hide* – Laurence Hyde (who took the redundant title of Earl of Rochester)

Sidney Godolphin and Laurence Hyde, together with Robert Spencer, Earl of Sunderland, formed the team at the Treasury nicknamed the 'ministry of chits'. The bad-tempered Laurence Hyde was a touch arrogant and brash for most. A contemporary, Roger North, bemoaned his propensity to 'swear like a cutler' and drink like a fishmonger. Godolphin, another talented amateur writer and general all-round fixer, was described by Charles II as being 'never in the way and never out of the way.' Godolphin's political acumen saw him survive and prosper through four reigns, being called 'prime minister' by his contemporaries as Queen Anne's chief minister. He was handsome to boot, and his shoe certainly fitted the promiscuous Sophia:

> *Next in order Richmond's sister,*
> *Recipient much of ballocks' glister,*
> *But now her sins are wiped away,*
> *Goldolphin fucks her every day.*[47]

Despite Goldolphin's 'being enamoured and intoxicated with Mrs Buckly', it was the Earl of Ossory who made Mr Bulkeley's blood boil. He would twice throw down challenges to Ossory in February 1675 (for which he was imprisoned in the Tower) and again in December 1677. Bulkeley also launched into his fair share of brawls and skirmishes – most notably in the company of Charles Sackville, Lord Buckhurst, outside the King's Theatre, as Henry Ball described to Secretary of State Williamson:

> The quarrell on Monday att the King's Theatre was occasioned thus: one Mr Ravenscroft having half a yeare since received an affront from Sir George Hewitt in the playhouse, and having ever since studyed retaliation, came that day to the play, where finding him there, beate him with his cane and so went away; presently after which my Lord Buckhurst and Capt. Bulkley going out with intentions to the other playhouse, were followed by chance by Coll. Strode, so that all three being by the doore and Mr Ravenscroft and company going by, and my Lord by chance blaming the action, Mr Ravenscroft presently fell to words, and then they all drew. My Lord was hurt in the body, Capt. Bulkely in the necke, and the Colonell in his hand and eare, but all their hurts are now cured.[48]

One of the circle of wits, Bulkley sometimes fell out with his friends, brawling with George Etherege in a tavern on one occasion, with Fleetwood Shepherd acting as a peacekeeper: 'Sheapherd . . . was runn with a sword under the eye, endeavouring to part Buckly and Etherege squabbling in a taverne.' Poor Shepherd, if that wasn't enough, after this he would be 'overturned in a coach at Matt Clifford's funerall and brake his head'. Little wonder that he referred to himself as absolutely 'a man of blood'. In October 1674 Bulkeley was again injured in a duel, acting as a second this time for the Earl of Mulgrave.[49]

Quick of thought, critically discerning, quick with his fists, cuckolder and cuckolded, swift with his sword, and heavy drinker, Henry Bulkeley was almost the embodiment a Restoration wit.

THE ROSE ALLEY AMBUSCADE – DRYDEN PUMMELLED

> *Muse, let us change our style and live in peace,*
> *In our soft lines let biting satire cease.*
> *Believe me, 'tis an evil trade to rail;*
> *The angry poet's hopes do often fail,*
> *Instead of bays a cudgel oft does find.*
> *Some lines, for being praised when they were read,*
> *Were once a cause of Dryden's broken head.*
> *– 'Utile Dulce', 1681*[50]

The events that caused the petals to fly during the so-called 'Rose Alley Ambuscade' were part of a long-standing literary feud between one-time friends John Wilmot, Earl of Rochester, and John Sheffield, Earl of Mulgrave. Mulgrave was never really a contender as a poet or man of letters and this was clear to everyone except Mulgrave himself. The only characteristic he shared with Rochester, for example, was youthfulness. In his own mind he was a talented writer, politician, soldier and, naturally enough, lover. And in his own words he boasted of his haughtily self-perceived talents. From this conceit sprang his nicknames, such as 'King John' and 'Bajazet'. Rochester would later lampoon him as 'My Lord All-Pride'.

Mulgrave has been described as 'neither esteemed nor beloved' and, unsurprisingly, Rochester was somewhat critical of his lordship's looks:

> *With a red nose, splay foot, and goggle eye,*
> *A plowman's looby mien, face all awry,*
> *With stinking breath, and every loathsome mark,*
> *The Punchinello sets up for a spark.*[51]

(*Looby* – a lazy hulking fellow, a lout; *Punchinello* (or *Polichinello*) – a seventeenth-century Italian puppet character, an ancestor of Mr Punch.)

In his awe-struck-of-himself memoirs, Mulgrave related the events beginning 22 November 1669 surrounding an uncontested duel between him and Rochester.

> I was informed that the Earl of Rochester had said something of me which, according to his custom, was very malicious: I therefore sent Colonel Aston, a very mettled friend of mine, to call him to account for it. He denied the words, and indeed I was soon convinced that he had never said them; but the mere report, though I found it to be false, obliged me (as I then foolishly thought) to go on with the quarrel.[52]

Thus, a rendezvous and seconds were agreed and the duel was fought the next day,

> on horseback, a way in England a little unusual, but it was his part to choose. Accordingly, I and my second lay the night before at Knightsbridge privately, then being secured at London upon any suspicion; which yet we found ourselves more in danger of there, because we had the appearance of highwaymen that had a mind to lie skulking in an odd inn for one night; but this, I suppose, the people of that house were used to, and so took no notice of us, but liked us the better.[53]

However, according to Mulgrave, Rochester appeared at the appointed place but not with James Porter as his second, as had been notified, but 'an errant lifeguardman whom nobody knew.' This being untrue to form, especially given how 'extremely well he was mounted', it was agreed to fight on foot. However, as they rode to the next field (there was no explanation why the original field was unsuitable for foot combat), Mulgrave related that Rochester,

> had at first chosen to fight on horseback because he was so weak with a certain distemper, that he found himself unfit to fight all the way, much less afoot. I was extremely surprised, because at that time no man had a better reputation for courage; and (my anger against him being quite over, because I was satisfied that he never spoke those words I resented) I took the liberty of representing what a ridiculous story it would make if we returned without fighting, and therefore advised him for both our sakes – especially for his own – to consider better of it, since I must be obliged in my own defence to lay the fault on him by telling the truth of the matter.[54]

So be it, conceded Rochester. His adversary, keen to display Sheffield steel, made sure the town knew of Rochester's refusal to fight, and 'entirely ruined his reputation as to courage'. He was run through a coward.[55]

However, entries in the Journals of the House of Lords raise questions against the objectivity of Mulgrave's honourable account. On 23 November, Rochester is said to have been apprehended in his chamber by an officer of the King's Guard (Mulgrave, incognito in Knightsbridge, could not be found). Despite giving his word upon his honour to the officer not to escape, he did exactly that. Presumably to keep his other appointment of honour – hardly the action of a coward.[55]

The next day, with Mulgrave in custody, Black Rod brought him before his peers. The lord keeper told him that 'their lordships do expect that he should now declare and promise upon his Honour to proceed no further in this Business between him and the Earl of Rochester; as to neither give nor receive any Challenge'. Upon his honour, Mulgrave agreed, 'to observe what was now declared to him as the Pleasure of this House'. On 26 November, Rochester also found himself in 'safe custody' and was similarly admonished by the lords, and similarly agreed by stating 'I am confident that there will be no Occasion of any Difference between us.'[56]

Rochester's 'A Satyr against Reason and Mankind', written before 23 March 1676, may have stretched back in time to draw on this incident:

The good he acts, the ill he does endure,
'Tis all from fear, to make himself secure.
Merely for safety, after fame we thirst;
For all men would be cowards if they durst.[57]

On at least three other occasions Rochester found himself embroiled
in duels. Although, interestingly, no actual fighting appears to have
occurred, or at worst no blood drawn. One time, early in 1669,
Rochester was overheard chatting to his friend Henry Savile, who was
being held at the Tower, saying such 'ugly slighting thinges' of the king,
that Savile found himself duly challenged. A newsletter dated 11 March
1669 related:

On Tuesday night there was a quarrel between the Duke of
Richmond and Mr James Hamilton, after they had dined at the
Tower with Sir Henry Savile. They had chosen their seconds, but the
Lord General sent for the principals, and put them on their honours
not to prosecute it. The Earl of Rochester was one of the party, who,
upon his disgrace at Court, intends to go to France for some time.[58]

Rochester's reputation for violence, despite such advertisements for
his cowardice at duels, remained unscathed. On 5 June 1678, Henry
Savile wrote to his brother Lord Halifax:

Last night also, Du Puis, a French cook in the Mall, was stabbed for
some pert answer by one Mr Floyd, and because my Lord Rochester
and my Lord Lumley were supping in the same house, though in
both different rooms and different companies, the good-nature of
the town has reported it all day that his Lordship was the stabber. He
desired me therefore to write to you to stop that report going
northward, for he says if it once gets as far as York the truth will not
be believed under two or three years.[59]

A planned joust on 25 March 1673 between Rochester and the
belligerent Lord Dunbar was scuppered by the intervention of the earl
marshall. In December 1674, he also agreed to be Henry Savile's
second in a duel with the seeming king of satisfaction-seekers Mulgrave,
who had been embroiled in another duel two months earlier, with
Henry Bulkeley as his second.

On Sunday night last, King being at supper at Treasurer's, Harry
Savile being very drunk, fell so foully on Lord Mulgrave, that King

commanded Savile to be gone out of his presence. However, the next day Mulgrave sent him a challenge by Lord Middleton; Rochester was second to the other side. There was no harm done.[60]

However, for Mulgrave, a more serious and authenticated threat evolved around his relationship with one of the queen's maids of honour, Mary 'Mall' Kirke, daughter of a courtier who had been a gentleman of the robes for Charles I and a groom of the bedchamber to Charles II. In September 1674, Mulgrave sought a softer sense of satisfaction with Mall, who was seemingly also in ignoble trysts with the Duke of York and the Duke of Monmouth. The latter, unlike his easy father, was prone to jealousy and devised his own line of attack. Annoyed at the thrusting Mulgrave's piercing victories, Monmouth placed a soldier on guard outside Mall's Whitehall apartment in order to foil any future lusty lunges. Upon ducal orders, the sex sentry clapped the supinated Mulgrave overnight in the guardhouse.

It not being a terribly wise consideration to challenge the king's eldest son – even Mulgrave was not that impetuous – the outraged earl set his sights on one of Monmouth's entourage. The outcome, we're told, was that 'Lord Moulgrave and Mr Felton have fought; Lord Middleton and Mr Buckley [Bulkeley] the Seconds slightly wounded.'[61]

However, this was not the end of the story. Nine months later, the fruit of someone's labour was delivered by Mall Kirke, but died within hours. But whose labour? It was 'not said yet to wt father it belongs'. Mall's brother, Captain Percy Kirke, was one who wanted to know and not for any familial niceties either: he wanted a bloody revenge. A hard-bitten professional soldier, he would later achieve notoriety with his so-called 'Kirke's Lambs' for the savagery of the cold-blooded executions carried out mostly in Taunton marketplace against prisoners captured from – ironically enough – Monmouth's troops following his failed uprising at the Battle of Sedgemore in 1685.[62]

It was this harsh, brutal man who challenged Mulgrave 'for haveing debauch'd and abus'd his sister'. You can almost still hear Mulgrave's gulp today. But he went ahead. Despite being seconded by the trusty and accustomed Lord Middleton it was Mulgrave, unsurprisingly, who came off a poor second. He was severely wounded, with Kirke targeting the offending area in question. So much so that Henry Savile wrote, with no unhidden glee, 'My Lord Mulgrave yet keeps his chamber of his wounds, and Mrs Kirke persists to protest that she does not know whether he be man or woman.' Mulgrave's body might have been badly wounded but his pride was left singularly unharmed. As the poet laureate would find out.[63]

John Dryden (1631–1700) has emerged the dominant writer of the late seventeenth century, even though a lot of his theatrical work, for example, openly played to the gallery. He was a professional writer (one of those 'that write for Pence'), and so lived off his words if not necessarily by them. Capable of brilliant political satire ('Absalom and Achitophel') he also knocked out stiff plays drenched in heroic rhyming couplets, which tackled the big issues of lost chivalry and romanticism. It was what the largely well-off cavalier audience packed into the King's House to feast upon, and exactly what he served up.[64]

Dryden, discontented with his purely authorial role, thought it a wise career move (such thoughts, for sure, were never too distant from his mind) to join the circle of wits. But a lithe and healthy wit was needed to run with these hounds. He would try to copy their bark, their leaps, their thirst. Comfortable in the kennels, he struggled once the leash was off and the hunt was on. He bravely acted a man he clearly wasn't, as he himself confessed in 'Satyr to his Muse':

> *I from that Fatal hour new hopes Pursu'd,*
> *Set up for Wit and Aukwardly was Lewd,*
> *Drunk 'gainst my Stomack, 'gainst my Conscience Swore.*

Rochester, in 'An Allusion to Horace', noted how the professional writer failed to carry the confidence of the uninhibited amateur (but natural) spark:

> *Dryden in vain tried this nice way of wit,*
> *For he to be a tearing Blade thought fit.*
> *But when he would be sharp, he still was blunt:*
> *To frisk his frolic fancy, he'd cry 'Cunt!'*
> *Would give the ladies a dry bawdy bob,*
> *And thus he got the name of Poet Squab.*[65]

(*A dry bob* – sexual intercourse without ejaculation (thus he was considered unable to finish what he started); Drybob was also the conceited poet in Shadwell's 1671 play *The Humorist* (Shadwell and Dryden quarrelled a lot but it never left the printed page); *Poet Squab* – this became one of Dryden's well-turned nicknames.)

Nonetheless, early on, possibly from about 1668, Rochester struck up a friendship with Dryden, patronising his work. Later in 1673 Dryden dedicated the very successful *Marriage-à-la-Mode* to his benefactor 'the Right Honourable, the Earl of Rochester', acknowledging 'that it received amendment from your noble hands ere it was fit to be presented', thus recognising his literary as well as financial support.

However, it seems around this time that, although Dryden would always acclaim Rochester's brilliance, the friendship fizzled out.

In the same year, another of Rochester's protégés, the underwhelming Elkanah Settle, dedicated his *Empress of Morocco* to Rochester, but included an assault on Dryden, who responded the following year. The wedge was in place and set to be driven. A third writer snuggling under the earl's wing was John Crowne. In 1675 Rochester may have secured Crowne's *The Masque of Calisto* for presentation at the court. Court masques were traditionally within the privilege of the Poet Laureate and Dryden had been, if this were so, embarrassingly overlooked. With his quill leaking revenge, Dryden dedicated his next play, *Aureng-Zebe*, to Rochester's foe: John Sheffield, Earl of Mulgrave. The gloves were off.

Rochester set loose his dogs of satire in the biting 'An Illusion to Horace' and within the first three of the poem's 124 lines the teeth are sharpened on Dryden and Mulgrave ('the foolish patron').

> *Well, sir, 'tis granted I said Dryden's rhymes*
> *Were stol'n, unequal, nay dull many times.*
> *What foolish patron is there found of his*
> *So blindly partial to dent me this?*[66]

And then they are sunk in:

> *But does not Dryden find ev'n Jonson dull;*
> *Fletcher and Beaumont uncorrect and full*
> *Of lewd lines, as he calls 'em; Shakespeare's style*
> *Stiff and affected; to his own the while*
> *Allowing all the justness that his pride*
> *So arrogantly had to these denied?*
> *And may I not have leave impartially*
> *To search and censure Dryden's works, and try*
> *If those gross faults his choice pen does commit*
> *Proceed from want of judgment, or of wit;*
> *Or if his lumpish fancy does refuse*
> *Spirit and grace to his lose, slattern muse?*
> *Five hundred verses every morning writ*
> *Proves you no more a poet than a wit.*[67]

Dryden's response, with little care for camouflage, appeared in the preface to his play *All for Love*. 'They are persecutors even of Horace himself, as far as they are able, by their ignorant and vile imitations of him; by making an unjust use of his authority and turning his artillery against his friends.'[68]

Dryden's new patron now entered the fray. Mulgrave's plodding 'Essay upon Satire' began circulating in 1679 although popular perception bestowed authorship on Dryden, who may well had a hand in correcting and amending the piece. Mulgrave included it, albeit revised, in his collected works published in 1723. The satire delivers a blundering series of thumb pictures of the court wits. In the section on Rochester, Mulgrave presses his quill hard on his enemy's supposedly feeble and fading wit (which in itself paints a vivid portrait of Mulgrave's swaggering sense of self-importance), his cowardice and his poetry.

> *Rochester I despise for's mere want of wit,*
> *Tho' thought to have a tail and cloven feet,*
> *For while he mischief means to all mankind,*
> *Himself alone the ill effects does find.*
> . . .
> *False are his words, affected is his wit,*
> *So often does he aim, so seldom hit.*
> . . .
> *And his own kickings notably contriv'd*
> *For (there's the folly that still mix'd with fear)*
> *Cowards more blows than any hero bear.*
> *Of fighting sparks fame may her pleasure say,*
> *But 'tis a bolder thing to run away.*
> . . .
> *I'd like to have left out his poetry,*
> *Forgot by almost all as well as me.*
> *Sometimes he has some humour, never wit:*
> *And if it rarely, it very rarely hit.*
> . . .
> *So lewdly dull his idle works appear,*
> *The wretched texts deserve no comments here.*[69]

Of all the wits, the only one to emerge with credit from the 'Essay upon Satire' is Mulgrave. His only crime was to have exploited those 'ill arts that cheat the fair' and become the court's cuckold-maker-in-chief. And not only that but he then also shatters their dreams by escaping their plans to marry him. The bounder. Nonetheless, given that Dryden was on Mulgrave's payroll, it followed necessarily that he must have had something to do with polishing his master's voice. With such an ego to buff, gossip had rounded on the Poet Laureate and that was good enough for the time. Rochester, for one, was less than convinced of his guilt. In a letter to Savile, on 21 November 1679, he wrote:

> I have sent you herewith a Libel, in which my own share is not the least; the King having perus'd it, is in no ways dissatisfy'd with his. The Author is apparently Mr [Dryden]; his patron my Lord Mulgrave having a Panegeric in the midst, upon which happen'd a handsome Quarrel between his Lordship, and Mrs B[ulkeley] at the Dutchess of P[ortsmouth's]. She call'd him: The Heroe of the Libel, and Complimented him upon having made more Cuckolds than any Man alive. To which he answer'd, She very well knew one he never made, nor ever car'd to be imploy'd in making – 'Rogue!' and 'Bitch!' ensued, till the King, taking his Grandfather's Character upon him, became the Peace-maker.[70]

Rochester's version of events at the Duchess of Portsmouth's is echoed in a letter by Colonel Edward Cooke to the Duke of Ormond. In it, Mulgrave's role in the libel and his own unstoppable self-absorption emerge. The letter dated 22 November 1679 ran:

> If I may be permitted to play a small game I shall repeat a particular that I was informed part this week at the Dutchess of Portsmouth's, where just before the King came in a most scurrilous libellous copy of verse was read, severe upon all the courtiers save my Lord Mulgrave, whose sole accusation was that he was a cuckold maker. This brought him under suspicion to be (if not guilty of the making, yet) guilty of being privy to the making of them, who just coming in with the King, Mrs Bulkeley saluted him (in raillery) by the name of cuckold-maker, who taking it in earnest replied she knew one cuckold he never made, which she took for so great an affront that it seems her husband was entitled to revenge. But the King, it seems, came to the knowledge of it, and interfered his authority to antidote bloodshed.[71]

The satire also attacked two of the king's mistresses, Louise de Keroualle, Duchess of Portsmouth, and Barbara Villiers, Duchess of Cleveland:

> *Nor shall the royal mistresses be nam'd*
> *Too ugly, or too easy to be blam'd;*
> . . .
> *Yet sauntering Charles between his beastly brace*
> *Meets with dissembling still in either place,*

> *Affected humour, or a painted face*
> *In loyal libels we have often told him,*
> *How one has jilted him, the other sold him;*
> *How that affects to laugh, how this to weep;*
> *But who can rail so long as he can sleep?*
> *Was ever prince by two at once misled,*
> *False, foolish, old, ill-natur'd and ill bred?*

Louise was particularly upset by this satire. Her anger was heightened by the fact that, while she and Barbara were picked upon, the king's other main mistress, Nell Gwynne, was not. And didn't John Dryden write parts in his plays for little Nelly when she starred at the King's House? Louise must have believed the Poet Laureate, rather than Rochester, to be behind this outrage. Perhaps this outrage needed another.

Historical evidence that Rochester was involved had rested on a letter written to Henry Savile concerning his 'being out of favour with a certain poet': 'If he falls upon me at the blunt, which is his very good weapon in wit, I will forgive him, if you please, and leave the repartee to Black Will, with a cudgel.'[72]

Black Will be done. And on 18 December 1679 it seemingly was. Five days later *Domestic Intelligence* reported:

> On the 18th instant in the evening, Mr Dryden, the great poet, was set upon in Rose-street, Covent Garden, by three persons who called him rogue and son of a whore, knocked him down and dangerously wounded him, but upon his crying out murder, they made their escape. It is conceived they had their pay before-hand, and designed not to rob him, but to execute on him some-feminine if not popish vengeance.[73]

The *London Gazette* carried a plea for information:

> Whereas John Dryden Esq. was on Monday the 18th instant, at night, barbarously assaulted, and wounded, in Rose-street, in Covent Garden, by diverse men unknown, if any person shall make discovery of the said offenders to the said Mr Dryden, or to any justice of the peace, he shall not only receive fifty pounds, which is deposited in the hands of Mr Blanchard, a goldsmith, next door to Temple Bar, for the said purpose; but if he be a principal or an accessory, in the said fact, his Majesty is graciously pleased to promise him his pardon for the same.

However, the 'Black Will' letter was probably written in 1676 and is hardly credible evidence for the basis of an attack three years later, although it does prove that, even if only light-heartedly, Rochester was all too aware of the options open to an avenger.

Nonetheless, Rochester, not least because he was Rochester, was thought to be pulling the strings behind the scene. The Oxford antiquary, Anthony à Wood, recorded (some years after) in *Athenae Oxonienses*, despite the not unusual errors of time and place, that it was believed Rochester and Louise de Keroualle may have acted in tandem: 'in Nov. (or before) an. 1679, there being an *Essay upon Satyr* spread about the city in MS. wherein many gross reflections were made on Ludovisa Dutchess of Portsmouth and John Wilmot E. of Rochester, they therefore took it for a truth that Dryden was the author: whereupon one or both hiring three men to cudgel him, they effected their business at the said coffe-house [Will's, in Covent Garden] at 8 of the clock on 16th of Dec. 1679; yet afterwards John, Earl of Mulgrave, was generally thought to be the author.'[74]

Another contemporary account, however, makes no mention of Rochester but lays the blame with the king's French mistress: 'About the same time Mr John Dryden was sett upon in Covent Garden in the evening by three fellowes, who beat him very severely, and on peoples comeing in they run away: 'tis thought to be done by the order of the dutchesse of Portsmouth, she being abused in a late libell called *An Essay upon satyr*, of which Mr Dryden is the suspected author.' Similarly an account of the incident by Terriesi to the Grand Duke of Florence makes no mention of Rochester. It did, however, state that Dryden '*protesta sua innocenza*'.[75]

The real culprit in all this, the Earl of Mulgrave, would in 1694 become Marquess of Normanby and, in 1703, Duke of (the county of) Buckingham and Normanby. It is this latter title that has caused confusion with John Sheffield and George Villiers, the second Duke of Buckingham. It has even caused historians to allocate the inferior works of Sheffield to Villiers. And just so as to keep the interplay between the period's protagonists alive, Mulgrave would marry, for his third wife, Lady Katherine Darnley, the daughter (and only child to live to maturity) of James II and Katherine Sedley, on 16 March 1706. Katherine was legally separated by Act of Parliament on 12 June 1701 from her abusive first husband, James Annesley, third Earl of Anglesey, on the grounds of cruelty after less than twenty months' marriage. Mulgrave made a habit of mopping up the wives of earls. His first wife was Ursula, widow of the Earl of Conway, and his second was another Katherine, widow of the Earl of Gainsborough.

Mulgrave and Katherine Darnley, however, appeared well matched with both sharing an exalted view of their own status, the latter being known as 'Princess Buckingham'.

Within eight months of the Rose Alley Ambuscade, John Wilmot, Earl of Rochester, having danced on his Mulgrave, would be dead. And, despite their quarrel, Dryden and Rochester respected the abilities of each other. In 1693 Dryden, writing to Charles Sackville, then Earl of Dorset, described Rochester as 'an author of your own quality (whose ashes I will not disturb).' The hatchet, with Rochester's body, was buried.[76]

9

The Fam'd Mr Blood –
That Impudent Bold Fellow

When daring Blood, his rents to have regain'd,
Upon the English Diadem distrain'd,
He chose the Cassock, surcingle, and Gown
(No mask so fit for one that robbs a Crown)
But his Lay-pity underneath prevayl'd
And while he spares the Keeper's life, he fail'd.
With the priest vestments had he put on
Bishop's cruelty, the Crown was gone.

(*Diadem* – crown; *surcingle* – a belt that confines the cassock.)

– 'Upon Blood's attempt to steale the Crown', (1671)[1]

Here lies the man, who boldly hath run through,
More villanies than ever England knew;
And nere to any Friend he had was true,
Here let him then by all unpitied lie,
And let's Rejoyce his time was come to Dye.
– 'An Elegie on Coronel [Colonel] Blood', (1680)[2]

Ask a schoolchild about the reign of Charles II and chances are he or she will know about, or at least have heard of, the great fire of London, the plague, and the attempt to steal the crown jewels by 'Colonel' Blood. It was an exploit for which the word 'daring' was probably invented.

Thomas Blood was probably born about 1618, with his notoriously oversized thumbs (they were twice as large as normal), in Ireland, to where his grandfather, Edmund, a soldier of fortune, had moved from Duffield in Derbyshire. Little is known of his early years, but Blood

211

became a justice of the peace at 21 and married Mary, daughter of Lieutenant-Colonel John Holcroft, on 1 June 1650. Nine months later, their first son, Thomas, was born. Two more sons followed, the younger of whom, Holcroft, carved out a successful army career, rising to the rank of brigadier-general.

Starting out as a king's man during the Civil War, Blood was rewarded for his changes of heart and sides with a grant of confiscated lands by Cromwell's son, Henry. However, upon Charles II's Restoration, these lands were reclaimed, leaving Blood destitute. It may well have been this incident that caused the peaceful citizen who walked within the law to stride so boldly outside of it.

Throughout Charles II's reign there was never a shortage of people – for personal, political or religious reasons – who despised the monarchy and plotted its downfall. In 1663 Irish dissidents plotted to seize Dublin Castle and with it the foreign ruler of the country, the Lord Lieutenant of Ireland, the Duke of Ormond. Among their number was one Thomas Blood, who despite his youth was detailed with the responsibility of seizing the castle. The date was set for 21 May.

However, unbeknown to the conspirators, one of their ringleaders, Philip Alden, had betrayed them. Ormond had bided his time and waited for the allotted day before authorising early-morning raids, arrests and imprisonment. However, Blood escaped, was declared an outlaw with a price on his head, and went on the run.

Another leading figure in the plot was Blood's brother-in-law, Lackie. He had refused to confess to his involvement and was sentenced to death. Two thousand were said to have turned up to enjoy the spectacle. Suddenly, a rumour darted about the crowd that Blood and a band of men were approaching to rescue Lackie. It caused mayhem. The stricken crowd fled, as did the executioner, 'leaving the person that was to suffer in the dreadful posture of a person preparing for his untimely Death, the Rope about his Neck, and nobody to do the Office'. Unfortunately, for Lackie at least, the rumour was a bloodless one, and the hangman returned, and recomposed, completed his duty. Lackie was one of five conspirators to be executed.[3]

Disguised and touring the remote parts of Ireland, Blood still felt unsafe and travelled to Holland and then England. His wife and son, under the name of Weston, were settled into an apothecary's shop, while Blood himself (now Dr Ayloffe) set up as a physician in Romford, Essex. In 1667, under one of his favourite aliases, Allen, Blood was pursued in Lancashire by the informer William Leving, who filed reports on Blood's movements and who had been issued with a warrant for his arrest.

However, the humdrum events of life on the run were about to take a bold turn. A foiled plot in the north had resulted in Captain James Mason, a friend of Blood's, being imprisoned in the Tower of London. By a bizarre coincidence, William Leving had fallen on hard times and found himself in Newgate gaol. Both men were to be taken for trial at the assizes in York and were escorted on the four-day journey by one Corporal Darcy and a troop of seven men. The same night, aware of events, Blood and three accomplices left, without boots, riding small horses with 'their Pistols in their Trouses.'[4]

The two parties eventually met up at an inn at Darrington, near Doncaster. Waiting until Darcy and his men departed, Blood's crew set about them. The element of surprise worked well at first but they were outnumbered. A barber, who had joined Darcy's troop, presumably feeling safer travelling in armed company, also took part in the tussle, in which 'several rough blows' were dealt. Refusing advice to desist, Blood's men 'were forced to dispatch [the barber], for giving them a needless trouble'.[5]

The pitched battle, according to Blood, who was hit five times, lasted a momentous two hours, although Darcy said it was but half an hour. Blood, his men and Mason were able to escape. Leving had managed to skulk off, reappearing to surrender only after the battle's cease. Having been taken to York, he was later found dead in his cell.

Sir John Reresby, who was nearby, recorded the event in his diary:

One Mason, a prisner of state, sent down guarded by some ten troopers of the guard to be tryed at Yorke, was rescued by five men at Ferrybrig and taken from them. One Scott that commanded the guard was killed, and some of the party ill wounded. I passed ther about a quarter of an hour before the fact was done. Hue and cry, with all other endeavours, were used to take the rescuers, but all ineffectually. I gave my Lord Arlinton a speedy account of the whole matter. We since understood that one Mr. Blood . . . was the chiefe of the party.[6]

Reresby was incorrect that Scott was the commander. He was, as already noted, a barber, a citizen of York travelling in the 'safe' company of soldiers. Mason, it was said, moved to London and became a tavern keeper, undoubtedly keeping the £100 reward for his arrest out of the conversation. Blood's capture value now soared to £300 (about £22,000 today) and for the next three years he kept his head, with its heavy price upon it, very much down. But what a return to notoriety he would make.

On 6 December 1670 a pumped-up Blood coursed once again into the life of a certain English nobleman who had overseen the land settlements in Ireland. The Duke of Ormond, no longer Lord Lieutenant of Ireland but still the Lord High Steward of the King's Household, had been a guest of the lord mayor of London at a special banquet at the Guildhall as part of the celebration of the visit of the king's nephew, William, Prince of Orange.

Later that night Ormond made his way home to the magnificent Clarendon House in Piccadilly, once owned by the exiled Edward Hyde, Earl of Clarendon. The mansion, described by Pepys as 'the finest pile I ever did see in my life', was built at a cost of £40,000 (about £3.15 million today), but, forever an emblem of resentment, it would be demolished in 1683. As the duke's grand coach rattled down Pall Mall and St James's Street, it was suddenly attacked by the horse-mounted Blood and his five-man gang. Believing himself to be the victim of a robbery, Ormond sought to calm the gang by saying that, if it was money they wanted, money they should have. But this wasn't a robbery: it was a kidnapping.

Ormond was forced out of the coach and onto a horse, tied with rope behind one of the gang members, who was to carry him off down Piccadilly to a prearranged destination. The rope has led to speculation that Blood was taking Ormond to Tyburn to be hanged for ruining his life. Nonetheless, whatever the true course, things, as usual, did not go to plan. Having ridden off at speed, the gang had left the duke's coachman. He, seizing the opportunity, jumped back onto the coach and rallied his horses homeward. With the alarm sounded at Clarendon House, the duke's staff gave chase.

Meanwhile, the duke and his captor were bringing up the rear, which enabled Ormond to struggle with him unseen by the rest. He managed by kicking his foot under his enemy's to unhorse him. Both men fell into the mud. As they wrestled, Ormond broke loose. However, by this time the duke's staff had arrived and the captor fled. Such was his muddied state that the normally dignified, proud and upright Ormond was downright exhausted and unable to speak, such 'that his servants knew him rather by feeling his star, than by any sound of voice he could utter'. He had been, according to his doctor, 'bruised in the ey, and a knock over the pate with a pistoll as he ghessed, and a small cutt in his head, after all which he is like I thanke God to do well.'[7]

The news of the audacious kidnap attempt of such a person, and outside his own house to boot, trembled up and down the nation. An enquiry was launched by the House of Lords, enrolling a committee 69 strong to examine the evidence. The result was a proclamation for the surrender of three men, one Richard Halliwell (or Holloway), Thomas Hunt (an alias for Blood's son) and Thomas Allen, alias Ayloffe (Blood himself). Unsurprisingly, there was no surrender from this Irishman, his son or his associate. The duke's own investigation saw the shadow of guilt cross the face of Blood but proof was short. As far as the public were concerned, the crime was an unsolved mystery.

However, some sensed the whiff of Buckingham behind this wheeze. Ormond's son, Lord Ossory, according to Dr Turner, later Bishop of Ely, was in no doubt whom to blame. Seeing the Duke of Buckingham standing next to the king, he confronted him:

My Lord, I know well that you are at the bottom of this late attempt of Blood's upon my father; and I therefore give you fair warning; if my father comes to a violent end by sword or pistol, if he dies by the hand of a ruffian, or by the more secret way of poison, I shall not be at a loss to know the first author of it; I shall consider you such; and wherever I meet you, I shall pistol you, though you stood behind the King's chair; and I tell you in his presence, that you may be sure I shall keep my word.[8]

With such a rise in notoriety, 'Captain' Blood promoted himself to 'Colonel' and launched his daring plot to steal the crown jewels from the Tower of London. If it didn't realise enough money to restore him to his fortune, then his fortune of fame would at least be made on the pages of history. Given the informality of the guarding of the jewels, it was a wonder someone hadn't tried before.

Partly recovered and partly remade after the Restoration, the crown jewels were modestly ostentatious compared with today, but still ridiculously valuable as well as symbolically priceless. They were kept on the lowest floor of the Martin Tower, just below ground. No guards or yeoman protected them. That job fell solely to the assistant keeper of the jewels, a 76-year-old ex-soldier, Talbot Edwards, who lived with his wife and daughter in apartments above the jewel room. Although there was no specific detail for guarding the jewels, Yeomen of the Guard were billeted in the Tower along with a battalion of the King's Guard. As a fortress and prison it was also rather well endowed with huge thick walls and a none too shallow moat.

The jewels were open to the public. Edwards was a salaried employee, but, as with most civil servants, payment was often late and unreliable. His boss, Sir Gilbert Talbot, the keeper of the jewels, pleaded his case to the king and they agreed that in lieu of a salary Edwards could charge and keep a small entrance fee.

About three weeks before the robbery, Blood, disguised in a long beard, cassock, long cloak and canonical girdle, presented himself as a parson interested in viewing the jewels. He was accompanied by a woman whom he called his wife (although the real Mrs Blood was in Lancashire at the time). During their viewing, the wife was seized 'with a qualm upon her stomack'. Edwards went to fetch a cordial to ease the pain, but returned with his own wife, who took the stricken woman upstairs to rest. The clergyman and his wife left soon after, thanking the couple for their great kindness.[9]

A few days later Parson Blood returned with a gift of gloves for Mrs Edwards. A friendship was struck. So strong indeed that the parson proposed a joining of their families. 'You have,' Edwards reported the parson as saying, 'a pretty gentlewoman for your daughter, and I have a young nephew who has two or three hundred pounds a year in land, and is at my disposal; if your daughter be free, and you approve of it, I will bring him hither to see her, and we will endeavour to make a match.'[10]

The men celebrated the agreement over dinner, before which the parson piously said grace and ended with a prayer of thanks for the king, queen and royal family. Edwards was as taken with the parson as the parson seemed to be with a handsome case of two pistols, which he said would make an ideal gift for a nobleman. The keeper, flattered and enamoured, thus handed over his only weapons.

On the agreed date of 9 May 1671, Blood, his son Thomas (and not son-in-law, as is often suggested) alias Tom Hunt, a man called Parrot (or Parret) and their lookout (who was probably called Richard Holloway) arrived at Martin Tower. They were all armed with sword sticks, daggers and pocket pistols. Edwards greeted his new best friend. Explaining that he was waiting on his wife, Blood suggested that in the meantime perhaps Edwards would be kind enough to show his companions the jewels. Naturally, he was.

On entering the treasure chamber, the men grabbed Edwards, gagged him and threw a cloak over his head, saying he would not be harmed if he remained quiet. The old boy would not obey and struggled fearlessly, for which was thus administered a number of 'unkind knocks' about his head with a wooden mallet. One of the assailants was for killing him there and then, but Blood refused. Dazed and collapsed, Edwards, despite further threats, kept up the struggle but was treated to a further beating and then stabbed in the belly. One of the men called out that he was dead. Edwards, who was anything but, wisely feigned his demise. Blood put the crown under his cloak, Parrot placed the orb in his breeches and Hunt set about filing the sceptre in half for ease of carrying.

At this very time and by colossal coincidence, Edwards's son, a soldier, had returned home unexpectedly after fighting in Flanders. As the fit young man ran upstairs to greet his family, the lookout raised the alarm. The sceptre-filing was abandoned and the three men made their way out of Martin Tower. The son, being sent by his mother to surprise his father in the treasure chamber, was the one who had the surprise of seeing his father covered in blood crying 'Treason! The crown is stolen!' Young Edwards and his brother-in-law, Captain Beckman, who had arrived separately as a witness of the betrothal, gave chase.

The robbers, young Thomas Blood and Holloway in front, Blood and Parrot behind, had made their way out as fast as they dare without arousing suspicion. They got past the White Tower, through the outer gate and, despite being observed nudging each other, made it past Bloody Tower. As they approached Byward Tower, their pursuers were gaining fast and calling out to the guard to prevent their passing.

A yeoman attempted to stop them but Blood, pistol drawn, knocked him aside. With escape from the tower at their mercy, Blood and Parrot made a monumental error: instead of rushing out through Bulwark Gate to a hopeful freedom, they stayed in the grounds of the Tower and doubled back along the river wharf towards Iron Gate. A small group of bystanders witnessed the commotion. The quick-witted Blood joined in the cries of 'Stop thief!' and pointed at his pursuers, causing confusion and buying time. Unfortunately for Blood, not a great deal of time was for sale, and within minutes he had been overrun and arrested.

Blood's son and Holloway managed to escape from the Tower but, as they made their getaway on horseback, young Thomas rode into the back of a turning cart and was thrown from his horse. Before he could remount, more bad luck struck, and he was recognised for his part in the Ormond kidnapping, much to the delight of a passing constable. All four were in custody and the crown and all its jewels recovered – the 'robustious struggle' had caused the great pearl (found by 'a poor Sinder Woman') and a diamond (found by a barber) to fall out.[11]

Under interrogation from the magistrates, Sir William Waller and Dr Chamberlain, Blood remained silent, save for saying he would answer to the king alone. Three days later, remarkably, he had his chance. He sat alone with King Charles II. He may have failed to take his crown but he seemingly succeeded in stealing his affection. Blood confessed to his part in the attempted abduction of the Duke of Ormond but offered up no other names in the crime. He declared his motivation was revenge for the loss of his lands and for deaths of friends caused by the former Lord Lieutenant of Ireland.

Doubtless aware that his interview was going well, Blood then 'confessed' to having been contracted to assassinate the king (for his 'severity over the consciences of the godly') during one of Charles's regular swimming forays in the Thames by Battersea. Armed with his carbine (a firearm shorter than a musket), hidden in the reeds and with his prey within range, he suddenly gave up the plot because his 'heart was checked with an awe of Majesty.'[12]

Blood was now performing for his life. He knew, he said, that he would have the full force of the law used against him, and that was only right and proper. However, his concern lay with the hundreds of associates who had pledged to avenge his – or any of their number's – death. Thus, if 'His Majesty would spare the lives of a few, he might oblige the hearts of many.' Further, Blood said, should he be pardoned, he could use his influence with republicans and dissenters to give themselves up. He offered, in essence, to become a Restoration supergrass. Charles then asked Blood, 'What if I should grant you your life?' Blood replied, 'I will endeavour to deserve it.' If ever a comeback line saved a life, then this must surely be it. One can imagine the laid-back monarch, who delighted in a witticism, unable to resist a smile. And once you had this king's smile it was only a short soft heartbeat away from friendship.[13]

However, Blood was sent back to the Tower and awaited his fate. A fretful week later he wrote to the king, no doubt a reminder of his plight, accusing the treasurers of the navy of being behind the plot to steal the crown. He ended his letter by saying, 'But know your friends. Nott else but am your Majestie's prisoner and if life spared your dutiful subject whose name is Blood, which I hope is not that your Majesty seeks after.'[14]

On 18 July 1671, warrants for the release of Blood and Parrot were signed, although Blood's son remained imprisoned. Then, remarkably, on 1 August Blood received a grant of pardon for all treasons, murders, felonies and so on committed by him alone or together with others from 29 May 1660. Blood's son was pardoned a month later. Even more remarkably, all Blood's lands were later restored to him and he was even granted an annual pension of £500. He was, however, ordered to write a stupendously grovelling apology to the Duke of Ormond and beg his forgiveness.

Less fortunate was the old soldier Edwards. For his part he was awarded a one-off compensation payment of £200 and his son £100. However, such was the usual delay in payment that both father and son cashed in their orders for half the value in order to pay for old Edwards's medical bills. He died a year or two later.

The treatment of Blood caused a national sensation. Gossip went into overdrive. One story ran that Charles, being so short of money, had organised Blood to steal the crown jewels and sell them for him. Another that a drunken wager that the jewels could be stolen was struck and Charles had recruited Blood to prove it – and thus win the bet. Another, more politically motivated story suggested that a possible coup might have been planned. This had greater credibility with the conspiracy theorists of the day when it came to light that the Lord Chancellor's house had also been burgled with only the Great Seal taken. The story that won most appeal, however, revolved around George Villiers, Duke of Buckingham. As we've already seen, it was widely held that he had previously recruited Blood to attack the Duke of Ormond – and, it was suggested, he argued for leniency for Blood, in order to annoy the old duke.

John Evelyn records his disapproval of 'one Bloud' in a diary entry curiously dated 10 May 1671, as it was the day after the attempt on the jewels but is clearly related from a time at least two months later:

> To Lond: din'd at Mr. Treasurers where dined Monsieur de Gramont & severall French noblemen: & one Bloud that impudent bold fellow, who had not long before attempted to steale the Imperial Crowne it selfe out of the Tower, pretending onely curiositie of seeing the Regalia there, whn stabbing (though not mortaly) the keeper of them, he boldly went away with it, thro all the guards, taken onely by the accident of his horses falling. How he came to be pardoned, & even received into favour, not onely after this, but several other exploits almost as daring, both in Ireland and here, I could never come to understand: some believed he became a spie of severall Parties, being well with the Sectaries & Enthusiasts & did his Majestie services that way, which none alive could do so well as he: But it was certainely as the boldest attempt, so the only Treason of this nature that was ever pardon'd: The Man had not only a daring but a vilanous un-mercifull looke, a false Countenance, but very well spoken & dangerously insinuating.[15]

Blood seemingly set about his tasks of being a supergrass, spying and rumour-spreading with great gusto; but, after a short spate of arrests and convictions of old Cromwellians and revolutionaries, he apparently campaigned to little effect. The papers of Secretary of State Sir Joseph Williamson brim with information and reports generated by Blood, although there is little of great consequence and much of fanciful speculation.

However, one of his intrigues brought about his ruin. For so long he had been suspected of being under the protection of the Duke of Buckingham, but now, pocketing the bribery of the ex-Lord Treasurer, Earl of Danby, Buckingham became the target. Blood with seven others, including prime witnesses Philip Le Mar and his mother, Frances Loveland, accused the duke of sodomising a woman – a capital offence. He was said to have 'unnaturally and wickedly' used one Sarah Harwood, the deceased sister or wife of Thomas Harwood 'a prisoner on the common side of Newgate prison.'[16]

They further accused Bucks of sending Sarah Harwood to the Continent and having her murdered, along with other women similarly abused. The sensational action was brought in February 1680 and became 'the only discourse in the town ... and some are so confident to declare publicly that several persons of quality will be found to be encouragers or abettors in it'.[17]

Two months later, the Grand Jury rejecting the evidence as contradictory and inadequate, returned a verdict of Ignoramus ('we take no notice of [it]') and refused the case to pass to the petty jury. Le Mar and Loveland were convicted of perjury, as the court found their evidence to be 'very foul and reflected extremely upon other persons'. Le Mar died in gaol and his mother was fined and ordered to stand in the pillory on 19 June 1680 'where she was severely dealt with by people throwing dirt and rotten eggs at her'.[18]

The triumphant Buckingham smelled blood and successfully sued his notorious accuser for *scandalum magnatum*, being awarded in all up to £30,000 in damages (£2.36 million today). Dorothy Sidney, Countess of Sunderland, wrote on 1 July 1680, 'The Duke of Buckingham is come off with honour. Blood is run away; the others found guilty, and my Lord of Buckingham makes himself sure of £30,000 fine.'[19]

Blood was devastated, and while protesting his innocence had to sell his plate and beg back-payments of salary, to try to meet the debts. It wasn't enough and he found himself in Gatehouse Prison in Westminster, which had previously held Sir Walter Ralegh on the night before his execution. Blood remained there for a month while he tried to raise enough capital for his release.

Within two weeks of his return home to Bowling Green Alley, Westminster, overburdened and defeated, Blood fell sick and died on 24 August 1680. He was buried in Tothill Fields. But such was his cunning reputation that it was widely circulated that the funeral was faked. So much so, that his body was exhumed and positively identified at a public inquest. The body was his – oversized thumbs included.

10

Anna-Maria Brudenell – the Taming of the Shrewsbury

'beautiful but wicked'
– Cyril Hughes Hartmann[1]

'beautiful harpy'
– Lady Burghclere[2]

'heartless'... 'violence was as breath of life'
– Hestor Chapman[3]

'this abandoned woman'
– Gordon Goodwin[4]

A slut incarnate. A vicious whore. A selfish, grasping slattern who shocked even those who traded in the shocking. And worse. Even the word 'evil' was not too harsh. Two of the Duke of Buckingham's biographers believed so: 'In an age of scandalous depravity, Anna-Maria Brudenell, countess of Shrewsbury, achieved an evil pre-eminence.' Another thought it 'undoubted' that 'her influence over Buckingham was evil', even attributing his political and social decline solely to her. The wanton.[5]

If ever a woman's reputation has suffered it must surely be the second wife of the Catholic Francis Talbot (1623–68), eleventh Earl of Shrewsbury, whom she married on 10 January, 1659. He was 36, she was 17. Anna-Maria was a tall, buxom young woman with light-brown hair and dark eyes. Her mother, Lady Anne Savage, fourth daughter of Thomas, Earl Rivers, was second wife of Robert Brudenell (1607–1703), who became second Earl of Cardigan on 16 September 1663. Anne Savage was seemingly as respectable as her beautiful daughter was to become disreputable, despite her appearance in an early satire:

Brudenell was long innocent,
But for the time she has misspent
She'll make amends hereafter.
Who can do more
Than play the whore
And pimp too for her daughter?[6]

The long-innocent Brudenell's daughter fitted the wife-shopping Shrewsbury's bill: young with child-bearing days ahead and, equally important, Catholic. Anna-Maria and her brother Francis had been born in Paris, where the family had fled republican rule, and were naturalised English in the summer of 1661. Shrewsbury had remained in England and had retained his large estates in Worcestershire (the family seat was Grafton Manor, near Bromsgrove) by paying a fine to the government. His first wife, Anne Conyers, had died without fulfilling her chief responsibility: that of leaving a male heir. Anna-Maria proved more fruitful than her predecessor. The Shrewsburys had two sons, Charles (1660–1718) and John (1665–86). Charles, who would succeed his father as earl, went on to have a successful political career under William and Mary and Queen Anne, and was created Duke of Shrewsbury in 1694. He inherited his mother's good looks, although they were scarred by his eventual loss of an eye.

Dorothy Sidney, Lady Sunderland, writing to her brother, Henry, on 6 January 1680, commented that 'My Lord Shrewsbury has so great a blemish of one eye, that 'tis offensive to look upon it.' She later wrote that his eye 'is out and with great deformity yet, and the other in danger'. He volunteered for the expedition to Tangier that summer 'but the doctors say the sea sickness will put out his other eye, therefore the King has commanded him not to go.' However, despite the loss he remained charismatic and bisexual enough to emulate his mother's reputedly strident bedchamber success. He was described as a 'great man, attended with sweetness of behaviour and easiness of conversation which charms all who come near him ... And although but one eye, yet he has a very charming countenance, and is the most generally beloved by the ladies of any gentleman in his time.' Their second son, born in 1665, also inherited a vibrant gene of promiscuity, outrage and tragedy. He was killed in a duel with Henry, Duke of Grafton (son of the king and Barbara Villiers), on 2 February 1686.[7]

Anna Maria's introduction to court was particularly well received by those (and there were many) with an eye for pretty young things. And she quickly got into the swing of scandal. For that you could count on the countess. While she drew breath from flirting courtiers, they drew swords with each other. She played the game well, as Gramont hinted:

> ... this beauty, less famous for her conquests than for the misfortunes she occasioned, placed her greatest merits in being more capricious than any other. As no person could boast of being the only one in her favour, so no person could complain of having been ill received.[8]

But in truth most things happened around her rather than through any instigation on her part. Her first brush with a scandal that spoke her name is a case in (a rather sharpened) point. Nephew to the hopelessly rich Earl of St Albans, and youngest son of Thomas (the earl's older brother), Henry Jermyn was riotously successful at seduction, even by Restoration court standards.

He first appeared at Charles II's court in exile. The king's sister, Mary (1631–60), mother to the future William III of England, had married the Prince of Orange. And it was to her Dutch court that Jermyn entered the arena. None of the king's impoverished courtiers, nor, indeed, the king himself, could compare with Jermyn when it came to his grand appearance and horse-drawn carriage. Clearly, some things seldom change, for what you wear and what you drive, as Gramont wryly commented, 'produce as much success in love as real merit.'[9]

Gramont conceded Jermyn to be a gentleman but found him, his uncle's wealth aside, monumentally unremarkable:

> ... he had neither brilliant actions nor distinguished rank to set him off; and as for his figure, there was nothing advantageous in it. He was little: his head was large and his legs small; his features were not disagreeable, but he was affected in his carriage and behaviour. All his wit consisted in expressions learnt by rote, which he occasionally employed in raillery or in love. This was the whole foundation of the merit of a man so formidable in amours.[10]

Jermyn's formidability soon flew into action. It is said that Charles's sister 'was the first who was taken with him' followed closely by one of her ladies-in-waiting, Anne Hyde, later Duchess of York. With two such notable and efficient conquests, Jermyn's reputation would sail to England before him. The boy was made. As Gramont noted, winning the minds of women was 'sufficient to find access to their hearts; Jermyn found them in dispositions so favourable to him, that he had nothing to do but to speak.'[11]

And, incredibly, even when, in sober repossession of their senses, they realised the flimsiness upon which Jermyn's reputation was founded, borne out by an all too expedient sexual experience (or 'weakly sustained', as Gramont puts it), they continued to fall and fawn. Under his spell huddled the likes of the king's mistress Barbara Villiers, who 'undeceived in a reputation which promised so much, and performed so little', was one who continued to comply with her infatuation.[12]

Thus the all-conquering Jermyn, all wounded pride that Lady Shrewsbury hadn't sought out his well-traversed credentials, moved to claim her from all rivals. Chief of these was Thomas Howard, brother of the Earl of Carlisle. It might have been considered that there was 'not a braver, nor a more genteel man in England' than 'Northern Tom', but he also polished a fiery temper and roasted a taste for duelling. Howard had set up a rendezvous with Anna-Maria at the Spring Gardens, Charing Cross, a public 'place of amusement' set behind the site today occupied by the Admiralty, previously Wallingford House, on Whitehall. Howard, for his prey's entertainment, had brought along a bagpipe player from his regiment of guards.[13]

Having wind of the meeting, the bustling and confident Jermyn turned up at the Spring Gardens as if by chance, and within moments had 'gained the soft looks of the fair one'. Shoehorning himself into the company, Jermyn, already stepping somewhat indelicately on Howard's toes, laced up the insult by 'railing at the entertainment, and ridiculing the music'. A seething Howard struggled to contain his fury at this upstart's overt trespass, flirting and mockery. Jermyn 'went to bed, proud of his triumph' only to be 'awakened next morning by a challenge'. However, despite seconds being agreed, no time and place were fixed.[14]

A few days later, on 18 August 1662, tired of kicking his spurred heels, Howard and his second, Colonel Cary Dillon, sought out Jermyn and his second, Giles Rawlins. Ambushing them as they left the tennis court at St James's Park, Howard issued his demand for honour. Jermyn complained that he and Rawlins had only their dress swords. Howard demanded his fight. They requested that at least they be permitted to change swords with their footmen. Howard, blood up, refused and unleashed his heavy duelling sword easily overpowering them. Rawlins, however, managed to strike Howard but his lancet virtually bent double against Howard's ox-hide leather jerkin – known as a buff. Upon the first flurry, Rawlins was left 'stone cold dead'. Jermyn suffered three severe wounds and 'was carried to his uncle's, with very little signs of life'.[15]

The incident certainly caused a stir. Pepys, at work on 19 August, was informed by Sir William Coventry, secretary to the Lord High Admiral:

By and by to sit at the office; and Mr Coventry did tells us of the duell between Mr Jermin, nephew to my Lord St Albans, and Collonell Giles Rawlins, the latter of whom is killed and the first mortally wounded as it is thought. They fought against Captain Tho. Howard, my Lord Carliles brother, and another unknown – who they said had armor on, that they could not be hurt, so that one of their swords went up to the hilt against it. They had horses ready and are fled. But what is most strange, Howard sent one challenge, but they could not meet, and then another; but did meet yesterday at the old Pall Mall at St James's, and would not to the last tell Jermyn what the quarrell was. Nor doth anybody know. The court is much concerned in this fray; and I am glad of it, hoping that it will cause some good laws against it.[16]

Having pronounced that justice was done, Howard and Dillon rode to a port and then on to France to escape the authorities. They returned three months later with the situation cooled, surrendered themselves and were duly acquitted of manslaughter. About the same time, Jermyn recovered his health and was back wreaking marital havoc and etching his mark on the bedpost of the king's mistress, Barbara Villiers, for which he would find himself banished. And thus the business of life, for the three surviving protagonists, went on as usual.

In a curious coincidence, given subsequent liaisons, Tom Howard would later marry Mary Villiers, dowager Duchess of Richmond and Lennox, the older sister of the Duke of Buckingham. In a letter to his wife Catherine ('Deerest Kytt'), dated 26 November 1664, Sir Charles Lyttleton, the returning Lieutenant-Governor of Jamaica, wrote:

Northern Tom Howard is married to ye Duchesse of Richmond, and they say [they] are the fondest couple that can be. I heare she will have a considerable joynture, above 4[0?],000li. Duke of Buck., they say, was mightily troubled at ye match[17]

Given the scandal of the Jermyn–Howard duel, it was taken as read that Anna-Maria must have graced 'le petit Germain' with her soft favours, but there is no evidence. Not that that would trouble the satirists:

> *Shrewsbury hath sounding fits,*
> *You'd think she'd almost lose her wits,*
> *She so on the ground, sir;*
> *But Jermyn's tarse*
> *Will claw her arse*
> *And make her soon rebound, sir*[18]

(*Tarse* – penis.)

Henry Jermyn had a long association with James, Duke of York, for whom he was master of the horse (1660–75). Within two months of his accession as King James II, Jermyn was created Baron Dover on 13 May 1685, and granted many offices by his royal benefactor: he became a privy councillor in 1686, colonel of the 4th Horse Guards (1686–88), lieutenant-general of the Royal Bodyguard, one of the lords of the Treasury, and a gentleman of the king's bedchamber. He accompanied James into exile after his fall in 1688 and for his loyalty was created Earl of Dover on 9 July 1689 (which, of course, could only be a courtesy title, being officially unrecognised). Married but childless, Jermyn died on 6 April 1708, his titles dying with him.

Although for the next couple of years Anna-Maria managed to keep out of news letters, her currency at court was minted in gold. Gramont 'would take a wager [Lady Shrewsbury] might have a man killed for her every day, and she would only hold head the higher for it: one would suppose she imported from Rome plenary indulgences for her conduct: there are three or four gentlemen who wear an ounce of her hair made into bracelets...'[19]

In the late summer of 1665 (Gramont, whose dates are unreliable, records it a few months after the Duke of Monmouth's marriage, but that was April 1663 and obviously too early), a succession of events that would end in a scandalous tragedy was triggered by Harry Killigrew, who, 'having nothing better to do', fell in love with Anna-Maria. Harry Killigrew (1637–1705), a groom of the bedchamber to the Duke of York, was the son of Thomas, would-be master of the revels, dramatist and patent holder of the King's Theatre. The delight Killigrew felt to be in the arms of his cousin (he was married to Anne Savage, a daughter of John, Earl Rivers) was tempered by a lack of jealousy in other potential suitors. This, however, may also have had something to do with young Harry's fanciful imagination: not without cause was he labelled 'Lying' Killigrew.[20]

Nonetheless, he set about the task of whipping up envy manfully. He boasted of Anna-Maria's prowess, ability and all-round amenity. He trumpeted the beauty of her body to all who would listen and to many more who wouldn't. Browbeaten by raging praise, one man 'resolved at last to examine into the truth of the matter himself'. And that man 'was both the father and the mother of scandal' – George Villiers, the second Duke of Buckingham.[21]

Buckingham was born on 30 January 1628, the son of the first duke, a great favourite of James I and, subsequently, Charles I. Indeed, after the first duke's assassination, Charles met with his widow and told her that he would care for her as a husband and her children as a father. So the young George Villiers grew up virtually a brother to the future Charles II. In even these vivid times, the Duke of Bucks beamed Technicolor. 'He was extremely handsome,' thought Gramont, 'and still thought himself so much more so than he really was: although he had a great deal of discernment, yet his vanity made him mistake some civilities for his person, which were only bestowed on his wit and drollery.'[22]

He was a man of many parts, but never quite the part, as Dryden memorably depicted in his epic 'Absalom and Achitophel', in which Buckingham was cast as Zimri:

> *Some of their Chiefs were Princes of the Land;*
> *In the first rank of these Zimri did stand:*
> *A man so various, he seem'd to be*
> *Not one, but all Mankind's Epitome.*
> *Stiff in Opinions, always in the wrong;*
> *Was Everything by starts, and Nothing long:*
> *But, in the course of one revolving Moon,*
> *Was Chymist, Fidler, States-man and Buffoon.*
> *Then all for Women, Painting, Rhiming, Drinking,*
> *Besides ten thousand Freaks that died in thinking.*
> *Blest Madman, who coud every hour employ,*
> *With something New to wish, or to enjoy!*
> *Railing and praising were his usual Theams;*
> *And both (to shew his Judgment) in Extreams:*
> *That every Man, with him, was God or Devil.*[23]

In his prose 'Character of a Duke of Bucks', Samuel Butler concurred that the sums of his parts outweighed the whole. He was,

one that has studied the whole body of vice. His parts are disproportionate to the whole, and like a monster he has more of some, and less of others than he should have. He has pulled down all that fabric that Nature raised in him, and built himself up again after a model of his own...His appetite to his pleasures is diseased and crazy...Perpetual surfeit of pleasure has filled his mind with bad and vicious humours (as well as his body with a nursery of diseases) which makes him effect new and extravagant ways, as being sick and tired of the old. Continual wine, women and music put false values upon things, which by custom become habitual and debauch his understanding so, that he retains no right notion or sense of things.[24]

However, it was his buffoonery – his wit and ability to make people laugh – that brought universal admiration. Gramont, no mean purveyor himself, considered Bucks 'full of wit and vivacity'. Bishop Burnet, no ally, thought him 'a man of noble presence. He had a great liveliness of wit, and a peculiar faculty of turning all things into ridicule, with bold figures, and natural descriptions...He had no principles of religion, virtue, or friendship: – pleasure, frolic, or extravagant diversion was all that he laid to heart. He was true to nothing; for he was not true to himself.'[25]

Sir Henry Bennet wrote to the Duke of Ormond, 'My last told your grace I was going into the country to pass my Christmas at my Lord Crofts', and when I tell you that the Duke of Bucks and George Porter were there you will not doubt but we passed it merrily.' George Porter was a gentleman of the privy chamber to Queen Henrietta Maria and later groom of the bedchamber to Charles II. Politically inert, he was, nonetheless, in demand for his company. In her memoirs, Baronne D'Aulnoy noted Porter's 'charming joyous humour, his regularity of feature, and his address, which was above all the others, saving the Duke of Buckingham'. He left his wife for the actress Jane Long in about 1673 and moved to Berkshire. Jane Long was one of the original players in William Davenant's company at the Duke's House. Not a noted beauty, she was lampooned as 'Malicious Witch Long' with 'damn'd stinking breath'. There was no great suspicion that many envied him.[26]

Before the arrival of Anna-Maria, we have little evidence of any affairs of note for the all-conquering, handsome Buckingham. However, Gramont recalled that among the queen's Portuguese retinue was a handsome man 'but a greater fool than all the Portuguese put together' called Taurauvedez, who styled himself Don Pedro Francisco Correo de Silva and was 'more vain of his names than of his person'. Faced with such a pompous appellation, Buckingham helpfully translated it to mean Peter of the Wood. 'He was so enraged at this,' Gramont informs us, 'that, after many fruitless complaints and ineffectual menaces, poor Pedro de Silva was obliged to leave England, while the happy duke kept possession of a Portuguese nymph more hideous than the queen's maids of honour, whom he had taken from him, as well as two of his names'.[27]

A social animal he may have been, but politically he was a beast, and that was how he made his mark. Indeed, one lampoon on the so-called Cabal thought this rake-hell the very devil:

> *How can this nation ever thrive,*
> *Whilst 'tis governed by these five:*
> *The Formal Ass, the Mastiff Dog,*
> *The Mole, The Devil and the Hog?*[28]

(*Dog* – Clifford; *Ass* – Arlington; *Devil* – Buckingham; *Mole* – Ashley (Earl of Shaftesbury); *Hog* – Lauderdale.)

An example of the duke's bizarre political thinking is recounted by Burnet. Buckingham was convinced that his nemesis Clarendon had stitched up the succession in favour of his own son-in-law, James, Duke of York, by selecting a queen who was unable to have children. Unable to persuade Charles to admit to having married his mistress-in-exile Lucy Walter, thus legitimising James, Duke of Monmouth, Buckingham employed his fertile deviousness to hatch another scheme. Simple, he thought: with his majesty's permission he would kidnap the queen and hold her prisoner on a plantation. In a belated attempt to allay the king's disbelief at such a scheme, he added that she would be well looked after. Such a humdrum assurance took little of the sting out of this tale and the king 'rejected the contrivance with horror'.[29]

His only other solution was to persuade the queen's confessor to prevail upon her to leave this corrupted world and seek peace in a convent. Such an action would surely cause Parliament to see that Catherine, bride of Christ, could not also be the bride of an earthly king and thus dissolve the marriage. But Catherine had been in England too long. A convent may have appealed on her arrival but no longer: 'The Queen, in short, had no mind to be a nun.'[30]

Nor, in 1665, had the luscious Countess of Shrewsbury. Indeed, with the Duke of Bucks setting about his task, she didn't have a prayer. He even collected phrases in his commonplace book to melt hearts:

I desire all, hope little, and dare ask nothing.
It would content me if you did but dream of me, or if I could dream that you did so, but I shall never sleep enough for thinking of you to dream at all.
You are in everything a goddess, but that you will not be moved by prayers.
Her face is so smooth that the eye slides off it – smooth as Waller's verse – smooth as the path of day that's beat in Heaven by the swift wheels of the ever-travelling sun.[31]

However, somewhat more roguish and less enlightened quotes can also be found:

A wench is good flesh when she is fresh, but she's fish when she's stale.
Wenches are like fruits, only dear at their first coming in; their price falls a-pace after.

Her chamber is the centre of all my goods; they'll never rest till they are there.
Neither her purse nor her cunt could ever be filled by anybody.
Her whole morning is nothing but the preparation of herself, and her afternoon her preparation of others, for her sins at night.
Her impudence spoiled the relish of it: it tasted too much of brass.[32]

In sending his quarry a love poem, he followed the conventions of the time by addressing Anna-Maria with a classically derived name (in this case Phyllis, while his wife became Celia). In it he seeks her kindness – her sexual surrender. Anthony à Wood found that the text below was 'written in a spare leaf before the romance called "Eliana"' and noted that it was 'Made by the duke of Buckingham one the 20 of Julii 1665, addressed to his mistris.'

> *Though, Phyliz, youer prevailinge charmes*
> *Hath forct my Celia's frome my armes,*
> *Thinke not youer conquest to maintaine*
> *By rigor or unjust disdayne.*
> *In vain, fare nimph, in vaine you strive,*
> *For love douth seldom hope survive.*
> *My hearte may langish for a time,*
> *As all beautyes in theire prime*
> *Cane justifye such crueltye*
> *By the same fate that conquerd mee.*
> *When age shall come, att whose command*
> *Those troopes of beautye must disbande,*
> *A tirant's strength once tooke away,*
> *What slaves soe dull as to obey!*
> *But if you will learne a nobler way*
> *To keepe this empire frome decay,*
> *And theire for ever fix youer throne,*
> *Bee kinde but kinde to me alone.*[33]

Defying her reputation, Anna-Maria proved no easy conquest. However, a chance meeting at Hull in July 1666 opened the gate upon that 'fatall amour'. Anna Maria's father, the Earl of Cardigan, had travelled north with his family 'and a great retenue' to meet with some relations. The duke 'prevailed on that company to make some stay in Yorke, wher he entertained all the company at a vast expence in my Lord Erwins hous for a whole month'. Bucks had hired Henry Ingram, Viscount Irvine's mansion at Minster Yard, because his own base at Fairfax House was too small.[34]

Sir John Reresby, a deputy lieutenant of the West Riding, in his diary recorded the frolics: 'The days were spent in visits and play, and all sorts of diversions that place could afford, and the nights in dancing sometimes till day the next morning.' Although 38, Buckingham was still youthful, vigorous and game. The 24-year-old Anna-Maria revelled in the party atmosphere. Her husband and her father 'not being men for those sports, went to bed something early'. Kindness was in the air. It was, however, made thin by their increasingly indiscreet behaviour.[35] Reresby was told by Anna-Maria's brother, Francis, Lord Brudenell, that,

> one day over a bottle of wine that comming hastily thorow the dineing room the evening before he saw two tall persons in a kind posture, and he thought they looked like the Duke and his sister, but he would not be too inquisitive for fear it should proove soe.

Her husband, evidently, proved more inquisitive:

> And one night my Lord Brudnall was sent for from the tavern very late to his sisters chamber to [make] her and my Lord Shrewsbury friends, they haveing had a great quarrell of jealousie concerning the Duke; and yet the Countesse had soe great a power with her lord, that he stayed some time after that.

Such was their infatuated recklessness that of all the company gathered only the duchess 'percieved nothing at that time of the intrigue that was carrying on between her husband and the Countesse of Shrewsbury'.[36]

One of Buckingham's biographers believes he sowed the seeds of his downfall from the time he planted himself in Anna-Maria's affections. An excess of her stimulated other excesses. From October 1666 to July 1667 he was involved in brawls or challenges on five separate occasions, and found himself languishing in the Tower three times 'for insufferable rowdiness and general belligerency'.[37]

Buckingham's loss of influence may have been a long-term effect of his affair, but the short-term loser was Harry Killigrew, who, outraged at being 'ousted' by Bucks, made the mistake of insulting Anna-Maria. Perhaps anticipating the portrait most historians and biographers would paint, he 'let loose all his abusive eloquence against her ladyship: he attacked her with the most bitter invectives from head to foot: he drew a frightful picture of her conduct; and turned all her personal charms, which he used to extol, into defects.'[38]

On seeing Killigrew at the theatre, Buckingham quickly ensured that the action and drama shifted off stage to the auditorium. Recounting the 'fray', Pepys enjoyed that the Duke of Bucks 'did soundly beat [Killigrew] and take away his sword and make a fool of, till the fellow prayed him to spare his life.' Buckingham's actions were greatly admired, Pepys himself being 'glad of it'. Killigrew must have taken a solid beating because, although initially he was sent to the Tower, two days later he 'was so much hurt in the head by the Duke', that he obtained leave to remain at his own house. The king ordered a committee of the council to enquire upon and 'report to him a full account of the quarrel'. This they did on 9 August, although Killigrew failed to appear before them. Nursing his head injuries seemingly cleared his mind and he 'resolved to leave the country until he be reconciled to all parties.' He fled to France. The king, unimpressed, 'gave order that when taken he should be sent to the Tower, and that he should be for ever banished from the Court'. This went the way of many of Charles's pronouncements: it held good until it didn't.[39]

Soon after, Anna-Maria was also reported as leaving for France, but in hot pursuit. Henry Savile commented on 16 September that,

> my Lady Shrewsbury, with only one chambermaid, took her heels, and they say is gone either into a monastery or to kill Harry Killigrew herself, since none of her relations will undertake it, but her Lord has sent to Dover and Rye [a popular port at this time] to stop her if it be possible.[40]

While in France, Killigrew found himself mentioned in dispatches between the king and his sister, Minette. Typically, Charles, in a letter dated Whitehall, 17 October 1667, although reportedly set to ban his errant friend from court for ever, confirms his sister 'may see him as you please', while adding:

> though I cannot commende my Ldy Shrewsbury's conduct in many things, yett Mr Killigrew's carriage towards her has been worse then I will repeate, and for his démêlé with my Ld of Buckingham, he ought not to brag of, for it was in all sorts most abominable. I am glad the poor wrech has gott a meanes of subsistence, but have one caution of him, that you beleeve not one word he sayes of us heere, for he is a most notorious lyar, and does not want witt to sett forth his storyes pleasantly enough.[41]

It wasn't the first time Killigrew's mouth, aimed at a courtesan, had caused him discomfort and shame. About a year earlier he found himself banished from court for using 'raw words' against 'a lady of pleasure'. The subject of this outburst was Barbara Villiers. He declared her 'a little lecherous girl when she was young, and used to rub her thing with her fingers or against the end of forms, and that she must be rubbed with something else'. Barbara complained to the king, who, in turn, instructed his brother (in whose employ Killigrew was) to send him away. James, for his part, and so stunningly in keeping with his dour character, felt undermined because he believed Barbara should have approached him first, and with her failure to do so, the duke had 'ill-blood' towards her.[42]

Meanwhile, Anna-Maria and Bucks continued their relationship,

> until Lord Shrewsbury, who never before had shewn the least uneasiness at his lady's misconduct, thought proper to resent this: it was public enough, indeed, but less dishonourable to her than any of her former intrigues. Poor Lord Shrewsbury, too polite a man to make any reproaches to his wife, was resolved to have redress for his injured honour: he accordingly challenged the Duke of Buckingham.

But why challenge now? Why not over her previous affairs? Perhaps because she hadn't had any. This was the only affair that undoubtedly took place. The earl was a quiet, reserved man with no history of violence. Even if affronted would he seriously risk all and issue a challenge? Buckingham later believed he was goaded into action by his family: 'If the earl had been left to the goodness of his natural disposition, and had not been exasperated by others,' he argued, no challenge would have been issued. Shrewsbury's family were political enemies of the duke. Did they see this as their chance to be rid of him? Certainly, for his seconds, the earl looked no further than two of his kinsmen, both adept swordsman, Bernard Howard, brother to the Duke of Norfolk, and Sir John Talbot, closely allied with Henry Bennet, Earl of Arlington, Buckingham's keenest rival.[43]

For his part, the Duke of Bucks must have caught the whiff of a planned assassination, and rather than call upon his boon companions, the usual form, he looked to the armed forces for his appointed seconds. Sir Robert Holmes, the naval commander, and Captain William Jenkins, an officer in the Horse Guards and supposed fencing instructor, were to stand by him on the field of honour.

The date was settled for 16 January, and the venue was a close near Barn Elms, the former manor house of Barnes in southwest London, renowned for its fashionable gardens and popular with the well-to-do on relaxing river trips. Formerly owned by the statesman Sir Francis Walsingham, where he entertained Elizabeth I, the house survived until

1954, when it was demolished following a fire, having been derelict since World War Two.

A newsletter of Henry Muddiman, dated 16 January, related the outcome:

> ...about 2 or 3 in the afternoon, near Barne-Elmes, a duel was fought betwixt the Duke of Buckingham and the Earl of Shrewsbury (upon a challenge for the Earl) as principals...In the engagement betwixt the Duke and the Earl, the Earl is run through under the pap [nipple], but it is judged not mortally, the Duke 'tis said only having a scratch on his shoulder. In that betwixt Sir Robert Holmes and Sir John Talbot, Sir John was wounded through the arm, and Sir Robt. 'tis said, hurt in the hand. In that betwixt the others, Mr Jenkins was killed, and Mr Howard was not hurt.[44]

The day after, Pepys recorded,

> all the discourse of the Duell yesterday...and all about my Lady Shrewsbury, who is a whore and is at this time, and hath been for a great while been, a whore to the Duke of Buckingham; and so her husband challenged him, and they met yesterday in a close near Barne Elmes and there fought; and my Lord Shrewsbury is run through the body from the right breast through the shoulder, and Sir Jo. Talbot all along one of his arms, and Jenkins killed upon the place, and the rest all in a little measure wounded.

Pepys continued mournfully: 'This will make the world think that the King hath good councillors about him, when the Duke of Buckingham, the greatest man about him, is a fellow of no more sobriety then to fight about a whore.'[45]

And then came the titillation of shameless garnish. Lord Peterborough (Henry Mordaunt, second Earl of Peterborough, who authored a fanciful history of his own family, and therefore not over-packed with credibility) added the anecdote of Anna-Maria disguising herself as a page in order to relish the carnage while holding her lover's horse. And as if that weren't enough:

> The witty Duke of Buckingham was an extreme bad man. His duel with Lord Shrewsbury was concerted between him and Lady Shrewsbury. All that morning she was trembling for her gallant, and wishing the death of her husband; and, after his fall, 'tis said the duke slept with her in his bloody shirt.[46]

This story, reputedly by Alexander Pope, was also soaked up by Macaulay: 'Some said that the abandoned woman witnessed the combat in man's attire, and others that she clasped her victorious lover to her bosom while his shirt was still dripping with the blood of her husband.' One of the spurious letters of St Evrémond, in Langhorne's eighteenth-century collection, squeezed a further acidic twist by declaring that Anna-Maria 'had pistols concealed, and that she had pledged her honour to shoot both Shrewsbury and herself, if her husband proved victorious.'[47]

However, Buckingham in his testimony at his arraignment in 1674, claimed that at the time of the duel Anna-Maria was in a French monastery. Admittedly, he may have been protecting her. But at that trial he was subjected to his enemies baying for every drop of blood they could get. His claim was not challenged.

The affair took the exclusive attention of the nation and its government. 'The whole House full of nothing but the talk of this business,' wrote Pepys, 'and it is said that my Lord Shrewsbury's case is to be feared, that he may die too, and that may make it much the worse for the Duke of Buckingham; and I shall not be much sorry for it, that we may have some soberer man come in his room to assist in the government.'[48]

The Earl of Shrewsbury was carried to a house in Chelsea. Five days later he moved to Arundel House in the Strand, the home of the Duke of Norfolk. Henry Muddiman believed that the earl's condition was thought worse than it was:

The Earl is very dangerously wounded, insomuch that we have had here (though he lies at Putney) several reports of his death. And yet the chirurgions make no question of his life, saying his wound doth well digest, and that his spitting blood was a good sign of his recovery, in that it expectorated that which otherwise might have ulcerated in the cavity of the breast.[49]

However, blood spitting notwithstanding, any recovery would be short-lived. But not if you listened to his doctors. Muddiman reported two days later that the earl 'is so well recovered that it was judged without danger to bring him up to town, where he is'.

With a scandal smouldering, Bucks was not without danger of his own. But on 27 January, eleven days after the fight, he was granted his political absolution against any charges for 'all treason, misprision of treason, felony, &c, especially concerning the killing of Wm. Jenkins, and assaults on Francis Earl of Shrewsbury, or Sir John Talbot.' This pardon was, as Henry Muddiman discoursed and believed, 'in consideration of the high provocation given to the Duke!' Up until this time, if the rumours are to be believed, Bucks was keeping a low profile. Muddiman thought that he received his warrant 'whilst he was at the Duke of Albermarles, under the concealment (as I am informed) of a black periwigg.'[50]

However, given the earl's condition a thoughtful addition was supplied to the duke's pardon: 'whether or not they have died or shall die of the same; with non-obstante [notwithstanding] of the statutes requiring security for good behaviour.' Muddiman, for one, was unsure why:

> And yet I cannot find that the addition was made upon any suspicion that either the Earl of Shrewsbury or Sir John Talbot may miscarry, but out of prudent care of security against all accidents. For, upon enquiry, I find that Sir John's wound, though it be painful is not dangerous, and the Earl of Shrewsbury sits up, and has such promising signs of recovery that the care is now left to the managery of one chirurgion, which before was committed to two.[51]

As a deterrent, the law required that following a death in a duel all those involved must be tried for murder. And, with Buckingham spared the force of law, so clemency smiled upon the surviving protagonists. Shrewsbury was pardoned on 28 January and the others three days later.[52]

The high bailiff of the City of Westminster, John Bennett, was outraged at the decision to pardon the duke and the others. However, this indignation sprang from a financial rather than moral imperative. With the Duke of Bucks out of custody, poor old Bennett the bailiff was out of pocket. For his part in the duel, Buckingham had forfeited his goods, chattels, and personal estate to the king, a considerable part of which, being in Westminster, would come to Bennett. Hard done by, Bennett petitioned the king, begging leave to sue Buckingham for compensation. Having been denied his slice of the considerable action, Bennett's begging bowl was equally ignored.[53]

Lawsuits and murder charges may have been flung at Bucks but he wasn't in the political stocks for long. But then, just as the dust of scandal was settling, the earl died, and blew it all back in the duke's face. Three days later on Thursday 19 March the 'body of the Earl of Shrewsbury was opened at Arundel House before several noblemen and persons of quality, and certain physicians and surgeons of good note.' Henry Muddiman numbered the onlooking medical staff as seven 'of the most eminent physicians and 3 chirurgions'.[54]

'It was certified that the wound was perfectly cured' and 'that no impostumed or congealed blood was found in all his lungs or the chest of his body.' Muddiman's information corroborated the findings: 'it was found that the wound was well, and fairly cured, without any appearance of ulcer or virulent matter in the lungs or cavity of the breast'. However, it was noted that 'his heart had grown very flaccid, and his liver and entrails much discoloured and decayed.' It has been suggested that Shrewsbury's death may have been caused by a traumatic aneurysm.[55]

Gossip traders, scandal merchants and purveyors of high-quality rumour knew little about the medical findings and certainly cared less. Whatever the true cause, diseased liver or heart, or even medical malpractice, the earl's death had followed the wounding dished out by the duke; therefore Buckingham had killed him. This delicate situation called for another explicit pardon. It appeared on 19 May 1668: 'Warrant for a grant to George Duke of Buckingham of pardon for and concerning the killing of Francis late Earl of Shrewsbury, with restitution of lands and goods.'[56]

Nonetheless, such an action clearly carried armfuls of potential for outcry against the abuse of power. Charles thus justified his pardon by saying no more of the same will be issued: 'on no pretence whatsoever any pardon shall hereafter be granted to any person whatsoever for killing of any man in any duel... but that the cause of law shall wholly take place in all such cases.'[57]

And yet the whole sorry affair might never have happened. Pepys tells us that,

> the King had some notice of this challenge a week or two ago, and did give it to my Lord Generall [George Monck, Duke of Albemarle] to confine the Duke, or take security that that he should not do any such thing as fight; and the Generall trusted to the King that he, sending for him, would do it, and the King trusted to the Generall; and so between both, as of everything else of the greatest moment doth, doth fall between two stools.[58]

In keeping with the Restoration spirit – with food so expensive and life so cheap – things soon slotted back into a familiar groove. Buckingham, a week later, was seen at the first night of George Etherege's *She Wou'd if she Cou'd* and sat 'openly' in the pit. The whole episode a mere glitch. The body politic had blinked, that's all. 'The public,' as Gramont observed, 'was at first shocked by the transaction; but the public grows familiar with everything by habit, and by degrees both decency and even virtue itself are rendered tame and overcome.'[59]

Back in England, Anna-Maria became the grieving widow. Buckingham remained stoically cynical: 'He died out of necessity,' he wrote in his commonplace book, 'and she grieves out of custom.' He added stingingly, 'She weeps and beats herself; aye, she had need strike the rock to get water out of it.' And yet some of the melodramatic tingles of love rippled temptingly outwards: when she dried her tears, he wrote, they 'seemed like crystals returning to its first principle', and that he thought her 'sadness became her so well, that it bred delight in everybody else.'[60]

'The Duke of Buckingham and Lady Shrewsbury,' wrote Gramont, 'remained for a long period both happy and contented. Never before had her constancy been of so long a duration; nor had he ever been so submissive and respectful of a lover.' Indeed, according to Pepys, within a couple of months of Lord Shrewsbury's death, the perhaps not-so-grieving widow seeking comfort moved into Buckingham's house:

> I am also told that the Countesse of Shrewsbery is brought home by the Duke of Buckingham to his house; where his Duchess saying that it was not for her and the other to live together in a house, he answered, 'Why, Madam, I did think so; and therefore have ordered your coach to be ready to carry you to your father's; which was a devilish speech, but they say true; and my Lady Shrewsbry is there it seems.[61]

As he noted in his commonplace book, wives are chosen for 'our posterity, mistresses for ourselves.' He was all for himself now. 'Buckingham runs out all with the Lady Shrewsbury,' wrote Andrew Marvell, and they very much became part of Restoration London society. Both were good friends of the king's most popular mistress, the wonderfully mischievous Nell Gwynne. In a letter to the Earl of Essex, Lord Conway wrote that he had attended a party at Anna-Maria's house in King Street, Westminster, commenting:

> Last night my Lord Treasurer carryed me to my Lady Shrewsberryes where there was Nell Gwyn, the Duke of Buckingham, and Mr Speaker [Edward Seymour, speaker of the House of Commons] about three o'clock in the morning we went to Supper, were very merry, and drank smartly.[62]

Buckingham had often sought to influence the king through the installation of mistresses. He fished the fertile waters of the theatre to catch first Moll Davies and second, and most spectacularly and enduringly, Nelly. 'The former,' Burnet tells us, 'did not keep her hold long; but Gwynne, the most indiscreet and the wildest creature that ever was in a Court, continued in great favour to the end of his life, for she acted all persons in a lively manner, and was such a constant diversion to the King, that even a new mistress could not drive her away.'[63]

Indeed, when he was out of favour (again) and imprisoned in the Tower (again) in 1677, it was Nelly who acted as go-between for the duke and the king. Buckingham wrote to Charles, 'I am so surprised with what Mrs Nelly has told me, that I know not in the world what to say... What you have been pleased to say to Mrs Nelly is ten thousand more times more than ever I can deserve...' He went to on to do his usual and appeal to their shared past.

Nelly and Bucks also performed hilarious send-ups together when the so-called 'merry gang' met at Nelly's house in Pall Mall. Both were gifted impersonators and Charles II particularly enjoyed their acting as the Lord Treasurer, Thomas Osborne, Earl of Danby, and his wife:

'tis certain that Buckingham passes a great part of his time with Nelly, who because the Lord Treasurer would not strive to make her a countess, she is at perfect defiance with him, so that the treasurer's lady is there acted, and the King looks on with great delight.

Gramont considered Buckingham's,

particular talent consisted of turning into ridicule whatever was ridiculous in other people, and in taking them off, even in their presence, without their perceiving it: in short, he knew how to act all parts with so much grace and pleasantry, that it was difficult to do without him, when he had a mind to make himself agreeable.[64]

However, as Henry Savile tells us, Bucks wasn't the most discerning of house guests, nor a keen student of periwig maintenance:

Mrs Nelly, who is [Buckingham's] great friend and faithfull councellour, advised him not to lay out all his stock upon the christning but to reserve a little to buy him new shooes that hee might not dirty her roomes, and a new periwigg that she might not smell him stinke two storeys high when hee knocks att the outward door.[65]

Remarkably for a member of the Restoration court, Nelly was a faithful creature – although, of course, Charles was anything but to her. She was a serial monogamist. However, such a quality (or failing) aroused the curiosity of the naturally rakish Buckingham. Intent on seeing Charles on business, he happened across Nelly alone in the king's private apartment. He 'pressed her hard to grant him the favours she accorded to his master; and as he rumpled her collar in trying to snatch kisses, she boxed his ears'. He certainly didn't trespass again. One other story has it that as Nelly was preparing for a party at Pall Mall for the king's birthday, Charles asked if my Lady Shrewsbury might be invited. Nelly refused saying that 'one whore at a time was enough for his Majesty'.[66]

The king also made typically light mention of Anna-Maria in his correspondence with his sister. On 14 June 1668, he joked on the news that Hortense Mancini, Duchesse Mazarin, had deserted her husband: 'The suden retreate of Madam Mazarin is as extrarordinaire an action as I have heard; she has exceeded my Ldy Shrewsbury in point of discresion, by robbing her husband.'[67]

Having clawed their way back into what the times masqueraded as respectability, the duke and his countess were together and loving it, starring on a social progress from party to party. The poet Edmund Waller, into his sixties, wrote to his wife from the front line:

> The Duke of Buckingham with the Lady Shrewsbury came hither last night at this time and carried me to the usual place for supper, from whence I returned home at four o'clock this morning, having been earnestly entreated to sup with them again tonight, but such hours cannot always be kept.[68]

Buckingham's wife, Mary, now wickedly referred to as 'the dowager duchess', was not entirely abandoned. She had a friendly relationship with Anna-Maria, having on at least one occasion nursed her through an illness. Everything seemed to be going swimmingly until a ripple from the past broke the stillness and threatened to capsize the whole enterprise. Pepys's friend, the actor Henry Harris, told him how he was with 'some young blades' – the so-called Ballers – who joined up with 'my Lady Bennet and her ladies, and there dancing naked, and all the roguish things in the world'. Pepys had a troubling evening, because he and Harris,

> fell into the company of Harry Killigrew, a rogue, newly come back out of France but still in disgrace at our Court, and young Newport [Richard, later second Earl of Bradford] and others, as very rogues as any in the town, who were ready to take hold of every woman that came by them ... but Lord, their mad bawdy talk did make my heart ake.[69]

Yes, Harry Killigrew was back. He had been in voluntary exile since his embarrassing clash with the Duke of Buckingham the previous summer at the Duke's Playhouse. He wasted little time in resuming his vitriolic broadsides against Anna-Maria. Despite being cautioned about his behaviour, he clearly regretted nothing and carried on bleeding the same vein. However, he was soon to feel regret – and it stung with sharpened steel.

Pepys on 19 May 1669 had ventured to 'Hyde-Park' to watch the Duke of York muster seven companies of Foot Guards and two troops of Horse Guards. Suitably impressed by the turnout, although thinking they hadn't really been put through their paces, he first heard the news of

Harry Killigrew's being wounded in nine places last night by footmen on the highway going from the park in a hackney-coach toward Hammersmith to his house at Turnam-greene – they being supposed to be my Lady Shrewsbury's men – she being by in her coach with six horses. Upon an old grudge, of his saying openly that he had lain with her.

Pepys also believed Killigrew's servant was killed in the attack, but this seems incorrect.[70]

This incident was top-drawer morning-draught gossip. Even the king was caught up in it all. In a letter to his sister, dated 24 May, he wrote:

The accident which befell the Prince of Toscane [Cosmo de' Medici, Prince of Tuscany] and the french ambassadore heere made a great noise, but my Lady Shrewsburyes businesse with Harry Killigrew has quite silenced the other. My Ld cheefe Justice is enquireing after the matter and what the Law will do I cannot tell; but the Lady is retired out of her house and certainly not knowne where she is.[71]

The French ambassador, Colbert de Croissy, wrote of the incident to Lionne on 20 May 1669:

Infuriated against Killigrew because he boasted that she denied him no favour, [the Countess of Shrewsbury] nursed her anger against him until she could wreak vengeance. She was able to do this yesterday. Killigrew had arranged to visit her at her house, which is six miles from London. He went alone in a coach, and on the way fell asleep. He was awoke by the thrust of a sword which pierced his neck, and came out at the shoulder. Before he could cry out, he was flung from the vehicle, and stabbed in three other places by varlets of the

Countess. The lady herself looked on from her own coach and six, in which she was with her three daughters [in fact she had two sons and a step-daughter], and cried out to the assassins to 'kill the villain'. Nor did she drive off until he was thought dead. He was but badly beaten and wounded, and has sworn informations. You may fancy the noise the attempt to murder him causes, and the worry and anxiety of the Duke of Buckingham, who is still passionately in love with this virago, whose husband he killed in a duel for having resisted her brow-beatings.[72]

The day after the incident, and to his audience's amazement, Buckingham, in front of the duke, the king and Harry Killigrew's father, Thomas, confessed his knowledge of the attack. In the queen's bedchamber, Buckingham said 'that they did not mean to hurt, but beat him, and that he did run first at them with his sword – so that he doth hereby clearly discover that he knows who did it, and is of conspiracy with them, being of known conspiracy with her [Anna-Maria]'. The Duke of York thought Buckingham's admission 'the most impudent thing, as well as foolish, that he ever know a man to do all his life,' and rubbed his hands at the thought that such an outburst 'might perhaps cost him his life in the House of Lords'. The king had told his sister he did not know what the law might do about the attack. In the event, the law did nothing. Neither duke nor mistress was charged for any involvement.[73]

Three days after the incident, Buckingham recorded in his commonplace book that 'H Killigrew is better this morn, so as the countess (if he continue thus) may leave her retreat and appear again.' Within a few months it was all troubled water under the rickety bridge. A newsletter dated 14 September 1669 relayed that 'Mr Henry Killigrew, who was formally in disgrace upon his quarrel with the Duke of Buckingham at the play-house, is said to have reconciled himself to the Duke and to the Countess of Shrewsbury.'[74]

As Buckingham, the great coordinator began to lose his touch and see events, once so controlled, now take over him, he became more surly and prone to violent mood swings. In July 1673, a fight between two 'gentlemen of the horse guards' near the Court Gate attracted the interest of Lady Shrewsbury's coachman, who horsewhipped one of the guards across the face. The guard, a Mr Ayne, 'was so far provoked as with one thrust to run the fellow through the body, and broke his sword in him, with which he presently died'. Ayne was arrested and brought before the duke, who was very angry over the coachman's death, and proceeded to 'beat the man very much and broke his head'. However, his vow to see him hanged was not carried out. The coachman was but a commoner with the sufferance to lift his hand against a gentleman and the result was inevitable. A newsletter reported on 30 July:

> Yesterday morning was the trial at the King's Bench Bar of Mr Ayne of the Guards, for having killed the Countess of Shrewsbury's coachman in an accidental quarrel near the Court Gate. The Duke of Ormond, as steward of the House, sat as judge, assisted by Judge Littleon. The jury acquitted him.[75]

Dogged as it was with a baggage of violence, the affair was, nonetheless, purring along nicely. In the summer of 1670 Anna-Maria became pregnant and duly delivered her deliriously happy lover a son in late February. A son at last. The child was christened, like his father and grandfather, George Villiers. The birth was eyebrow-lifting enough, but what followed was an act of jaw-dropping scandal. Buckingham decided to confer upon his son the title he himself had received at birth, that of the Earl of Coventry. This was not within his gift, but, as the king agreed to be George Jr's godfather, perhaps it was but a formality. We may never know for, tragically, within a few days of his christening, the son Bucks had craved above all else was dead. The distraught parents – blind in their grief – then rubbed etiquette's face in the sand by burying the infant with unbridled pomp and ceremony at Westminster Abbey. He was buried on 12 March 'by the title of Earl of Coventry, with all the solemnities, rites and formalities of such an internment'. Andrew Marvell noted that Buckingham's son 'to whom the king stood godfather: it died young Earl of Coventry, and was buried in the sepulchre of his fathers'. The boy had arrived a bastard and departed a prince.[76]

The restrained recorder at Westminster Abbey noted simply that 'a young male child was laid in the Duke of Buckingham's vault, being part of that family.' There was nothing restrained, however, about the offence dug up by the burial. This cut to the heart of the peerage as deep and as painful as Buckingham's sword had through the chest of the Earl of Shrewsbury just three years before. A further three years on all that resentment would cause the end of his relationship with Anna-Maria. He so nearly had it all. And yet fate, all itchy feet and malice, set to work on his decline. It would be slow but in the end it would be complete. Once rich, handsome, and powerful, Bucks would die broke, flabby and without influence or friends. His cause of death – a chill caught from sitting on damp land after a foxhunt – was, given his slump, fittingly unromantic.

His end on 16 April 1688, when he was 61, was immortalised by Alexander Pope in *Moral Essays*, Epistle iii, who although incorrect over his actual place of death – it was in a bedroom in a tenant farmhouse at Kirkby-Moorside, near Helmsley – stingingly captures the desperation of decline:

> *In the worst inn's worst room, with mat half hung,*
> *The floors of plaster, and the walls of dung,*
> *On once a flock-bed, but repair'd with straw,*
> *With tape-tied curtains, never meant to draw;*
> *The George and garter dangling from that bed,*
> *Where tawdry yellow strove with dirty red,*
> *Great Villiers lies: – alas! how chang'd from him,*
> *That life of pleasure, and that soul of whim!*
> *Gallant and gay, in Clivedon's proud alcove,*
> *The bower of wanton Shrewsbury and love;*
> *Or, just as gay, at council, in a ring*
> *Of mimic'd statesman, and their merry king.*
> *No wit to flatter, left of all his store!*
> *No fool to laugh at, which he valued more.*
> *There, victor of his health, of fortune, friends,*
> *And fame, this lord of useless thousands ends.*

Political power, wealth and land – he contrived to lose it all. As Bishop Burnet noted, 'He could never fix his thoughts nor govern his estate, though then the greatest in England.' Dryden, also, was only too aware:

> *In squandering wealth was his peculiar art;*
> *Nothing went unrewarded but desert.*
> *Beggar'd by fools, whom still he found too late;*
> *He had his jest, and they had his estate.*[77]

To raise funds, he sold York House in the Strand – a splendid house, which he would let to foreign ambassadors – to the developer Nicholas Barbon, who demolished the site in the 1670s. However, Bucks insisted that Barbon name the new streets after his name and title (even the 'of'). This resulted in George Street, Villiers Street, Duke Street, Of Alley (later renamed York Place), and Buckingham Street. This has been used to demonstrate the ego of the man, but was surely just Bucks having his fizzy jest.

Penniless – even his wit was overdrawn – the duke who was once the most sought-after destination for good company had become the man to bypass: 'since at last he became contemptible and poor, sickly and sunk in his parts, as well as other respects; so that conversation was as much avoided as ever it had been courted.' Two lines from his own pen eloquently capture the loss and regret:

> *Methinks I see the wanton hours flee,*
> *And as they pass, turn back and laugh at me.*

After Buckingham's fall from office the Shrewsbury family, in 1674, seized the moment, and drew their trusty sword of revenge. They, through the brother-in-law of Anna-Maria, the 'idiotic' (as the French ambassador Ruvigny called him) Earl of Westmoreland, petitioned the House of Lords on behalf of the young Earl of Shrewsbury. They were concerned that 'the unhappy lady and her complice' had not demonstrated 'the usual care of such offenders to cover actions of Guilt and Shame' which was to the detriment of the boy earl and both Talbot and Brudenell families. The boy, the petition declared, became,

every day more and more sensible of ye deplorable death of his unfortunate father, Ffran: the late Earle of Shrewsbury, upon ye honor of his family not only by ye occation thereof, but even at ye continuance of ye wicked and scandalous life led by George, Dk of Buck: & wth Anna Maria, relict of ye sd Earle Ffrancis, multiplying every day new provocations to two soe noble families by that insolent & shameless manner of ye co-habitating together since ye death of ye said Earl.[78]

In short, it wasn't the 'shameless course of life' of the lovers or that they had 'shown no shame or quiet' that moved the Lords to take action on the allegations. No, it was the rumbling indignation felt over the burial of 'a base son of theirs in ye Abby Church in Westminster by ye title of Earle of Coventry with all rites & formallityes of such an internment' – as the petitioners well knew. Buckingham was called to account. He admitted 'that his life has not been so regular nor so free from blame as that he should be willing that the House should be troubled with a revelation of all his faults against temperance and the strict rules of morality'. In his deposition he stated that the Countess of Shrewsbury had left her husband and sought refuge in Paris 'and afterwards into a monastery'. He added that 'the Earl, upon the groundless jealousy of the Duke's being the cause of her going away, was much incensed against him.' He said that, far from its being his influence, Anna-Maria had travelled abroad because it was 'generally known' that she 'parted from her husband because she thought her honour was not vindicated upon one [Harry Killigrew] who had done her a public and barbarous affront'.[79]

He claimed to have felt as much grief as the earl's family at his death. Upon Anna-Maria's return to England she found herself ostracised by family and friends and came to him for support: what 'man of honour,' he asked, 'could deny a lady in her condition?' He ended by solemnly promising 'to avoid any reproach of the same nature for the future'. The Duke of Ormond, drawing on his hatred of Buckingham, passionately supported the petition. With the accused discovering more than the occasional ally in the house, the debate generated some heat. Reconvened for 30 January, it was taken up with Anna-Maria's father, the Earl of Cardigan, taking her side, saying that he had received a 'letter of submission' from her and 'begged she might not be made desperate'. Buckingham received support from his new ally, the anticourt leader of the Country Party, the Earl of Shaftesbury.[80]

In the end their lordships agreed the couple should be forced to separate and a deed, drawn up by a committee of bishops, bound them to the decision upon forfeiture of £10,000 each. And that was that. The most notorious relationship in the Restoration court was over. Their comet had burned itself out. Anna-Maria retired, albeit for only two years, to a convent in Dunkirk. Buckingham had, in addition, to beg the house's forgiveness, and acknowledged,

> the lewd and miserable life he had led; and though it was a very heavy burthen to lye under the displeasure of the House and the sense of transgressions, yett he had reason to give God thanks for it, since it had opened his eyes and discovered to him the foulness of his past life, which he was resolved for the future to amend; and having added severall patheticke expressions of his repentance, the House at last absolved him.[81]

However, breaking up with Anna-Maria, and publicly resuming his role of husband once again, was not to save his career. The political walls he had so expertly constructed now began to close in on him. Suffocated by his enemies, he had his last breath as a statesman taken from him when the king, his childhood friend, sacked him from the Privy Council, the Council for Trade and Plantations, and the Admiralty Commission. He was also dismissed from his other public posts – Lord Lieutenant of the West Riding, and Chancellor of Cambridge University. The surrender of his two other posts was sweetened only, for the debt-ridden duke, by his being given permission to sell them. He received £6,000 (from the Earl of Lindsay) for the position of gentleman of the bedchamber, and an annual grant of £2,400 for 21 years and a £1,500 annual pension for life for the post of master of the horse (which Charles himself purchased for his eldest son, Monmouth). Fortunately for her, amid this mini-flurry of largesse, Charles did not forgot Anna-Maria. She was awarded an annual pension of £1,600.

Outcast, Buckingham ventured north to make Yorkshire his home. Although he was good to his word and never saw Anna-Maria again, his heart was another matter. He wrote a poem, 'The Lost Mistress, a Complaint against the Countess of _____', in which he mourns being left 'forsaken and forlorn':

> *In love the blessing of my life I closed,*
> *And in her custody that love disposed.*
> *In one dear freight all's lost! Of her bereft,*
> *I have no hope, no second comfort left.*
> *If such another beauty I could find,*
> *A beauty too that bore a constant mind,*
> *Even that could bring [no] med'cine for my pain;*
> *I loved not at a rate to love again.*[82]

In her memoirs, part romance, part fact, Madam D'Aulnoy hit believability when recounting Buckingham's reminiscing about an incident inspired by Anna-Maria. It, she wrote,

> caused the Duke to sigh, he fixed his eyes on the ground for some while in silence. Presently he reverted with a start to where he was. 'If you wish,' he said, 'to see me in the profoundest melancholy, you have but to recall to me that happy time when I was so tenderly loved by one of the most beautiful people in the Universe.'[83]

The universal beauty herself, once again, sought sanctuary abroad in the convent of Benedictine nuns at Pontoise, near Paris. She returned in early 1674 to live with her parents at Cardigan House in Lincoln's Inn Fields.

About a year or so later Anna-Maria took a fancy to another George, although one less colourful. She secretly married George Rodney Bridges, a gentleman from Somerset but waited, evidently with good reason, until the summer to announce the match. Henry Savile wrote from Whitehall to his brother Viscount Halifax on 24 June 1677:

'Yesterday my Lady Shrewsbury [keeping her title] own'd her match with Mr Bridges, so much to the dissatisfaction of her parents that she left Cardigan House, and is now at my Lady Elizabeth Thimisbyes.' She seemingly remained faithful to her comparatively undistinguished husband and bore him a son, also George, who would become a long-standing MP for Salisbury. Her husband would outlive her, dying on 9 September 1713.[84]

Anna-Maria's last years were spent in scandal-free obscurity. Despite the spiteful attacks rummaging in a past that simply wasn't there. One such satire was 'Colin' or 'Cullen':

> *Shrewsbury offered for the place*
> *All she had gotten from his grace;*
> *She knew his ways and could comply*
> *With all decays of lechery;*
> *Had often licked his amorous sceptre*
> *Until the aged stallion leapt her;*
> *But long ago had the mishap*
> *To give the King Dick Talbot's clap.*
> *Though for her all was said that can be*
> *By her lean drudge the Earl of Danby,*
> *She was dismissed and told*
> *Where a tall page was to be sold.*[85]

(*His grace* – George Villiers, Duke of Buckingham; *aged stallion* – Charles II, nicknamed Old Rowley after his favourite old stallion (however, there is no evidence that Charles and Anna-Maria were lovers); *Dick Talbot* – Colonel Richard Talbot (1630–91), her brother-in-law, created Earl of Tyrconnel in 1685 by James II (Gramont suggested that he had an affair with Anna-Maria); *Danby*, possibly suggesting that Thomas Osborne, Earl of Danby pimped for her).

Anna-Maria Shrewsbury (as she signed herself) died on 20 April 1702. She was buried in St Giles-in-the-Fields, London. St Giles, fittingly, is the patron saint of outcasts.[86]

There is little contemporary evidence to conclude safely that Anna-Maria Brudenell was the voracious sexual libertine that historians have accusingly picked out on a Restoration ID parade of wantonness. That Jermyn and Howard fought over her was not at her request, but at the rage of a bully who was outflirted and slighted. The only people known to have had sex with Anna-Maria were her two husbands and the Duke of Buckingham. Hardly a back catalogue of disgrace. Harry Killigrew claimed a conquest, but he was a notorious liar and was twice publicly attacked for boasting such – the motivation being convincingly an affront of character and not an angry retribution on an embarrassingly indiscreet kiss-and-tell blabbermouth. The second attack, seemingly at Anna-Maria's instigation and with her to witness a job well done, prevents any complete character purification. But it was, nonetheless, in keeping with the occasional and casual bitterness of the times. No angel, but no demon, either.

Had she really been as notorious as we have been eagerly fed, why was she so often absent from newsletters, scandal sheets and satires? And sometimes for years? Unfortunately, her reputation revolves around the notion that her lover killed her husband in a duel. But that is wrought with trouble. Duelling, as we have seen, was a regularised part of a Restoration gentleman's culture. And it was the earl, although probably responding to family political (more than social) pressure, who demanded the duel, and not Anna-Maria or Buckingham. Evidence shows that it was not Buckingham's sword that finished off the earl, but rather a diseased liver or heart. The stories about Anna-Maria's being there to witness the spectacle, being armed with a pistol in case the result went against her and sleeping with Buckingham afterwards in a shirt stained with her husband's blood are as groundless as they are spiteful.

We need our monsters. And a male-dominated history particularly needs to scratch out its female ones. In truth, we know little of Anna-Maria Brudenell's character, so we outline a reputation and colour in the detail as best, that is as worst, as we can. It's a pity the dead can't sue.

References

Introduction

1 Dixon Hunt, J, *Andrew Marvell*, p. 178
2 Gray, R, *The King's Wife*, p. 180
3 Wilson, J H, *Court Satires of the Restoration*, p. 3; Pepys, vol 6, p. 41; Wilson, J H, (ed.) *The Rochester-Savile Letters*, p. 73; North, Roger, *Lives of the Norths*, II, p. 164
4 Pinto, V, *Sir Charles Sedley*, p. 52
5 Green, G, *Lord Rochester's Monkey*, p. 142
6 Ibid.
7 Hill, C P, *Who's Who in Stuart Britain*, p. 314; Wintle, S, in Treglown, J, (ed.), 'Libertinism and Sexual Politics' in *Spirit of Wit*, p. 139
8 Wilson, J H, *The Court Wits of the Restoration*, pp. 32–33
9 Wilson, J H, *Court Satires of the Restoration*; Veith, D, *The Complete Poems of John Wilmot, Earl of Rochester*, p. 32

Chapter 1

1 Pepys, vol 9 p. 20
2 Lord Halifax, Quoted in Chapman, H, *The Tragedy of Charles II*, p. 362; Pepys, 8 August 1667 – vol 8, p. 377 & 16 October 1665 – vol 6, p. 267
3 Wheatley, D, *Private Life of Charles II*, p. 80
4 Pepys, vol 8, pp. 181–182
5 Fraser, A, *King Charles II*, p. 37
6 Cronin, Vincent, *Louis XIV*, p. 84
7 Norrington, R, *My Dearest Minette*, p. 59
8 Masters, Brian, *The Mistresses of Charles II*, p. 18; Cronin, Vincent, *Louis XIV*, p. 51
9 Bedoyere, G de la, *The Diary of John Evelyn*, pp. 76 & 325
10 Pepys, vol 3, p. 238
11 Ibid., vol 5, p. 56
12 Ibid., pp. 58 & 16 December 1666 – vol 7, p. 411

13 Masters, p. 24; Bedoyere, G de la, *The Diary of John Evelyn*, p. 210
14 Masters, p. 29
15 Diary of Henry Sidney; Forneron, *Louise de Keroualle*, p. 232
16 Verney Memoirs; McGregor-Hastie, R, *Nell Gwyn*, p. 157
17 *A Panegyric*, Harley MS 7319
18 Hatton Correspondence, i, p. 225; Cartwright, J, *Sacharissa*, p. 260
19 *The London Gazette; An account of what passed at the execution of the late Duke of Monmouth*
20 Fraser, A, *King Charles II*, p. 137
21 Ibid., p. 154; Masters, p. 34
22 Fraser, p55
23 Masters, p. 39
24 Ibid., p. 40
25 Ibid., p. 42
26 Fraser, p. 154
27 Browning, A, *Memoirs of Sir John Reresby*, pp. 35-6
28 Hartmann, C H, *Charles II and Madame*, pp. 42 & 167; Jusserand, J J, *A French Ambassador* p. 90; Gramont, i, p. 96
29 Pepys, 13 July 1663 – vol 4, p. 230; Gramont, i, p. 107
30 Gramont i, pp. 106–107
31 Wilson, J H, *Court Satires of the Restoration*, p. 3
32 Lansdowne MS 852, f43
33 Pepys, 8 February 1663 – vol 4, p. 38; 17 February 1663 – vol 4, p. 48
34 Jusserand, p.90: 5 July 1663
35 Pepys, 24 June 1667 – vol 8, p. 288
36 Gramont, ii, p. 147; i, p. 136
37 Ibid., i, p. 137
38 Ibid., ii, p. 147
39 Courtin to Lionne, 23 August 1665, Jusserand, p. 170
40 Pepys, 18 May 1663 – vol 4, p. 142; 4 June 1663 – vol 4, p. 174; 30 June 1663 – vol 4, p. 206
41 Ibid., 6 November 1663 – vol 4, p. 366; The members of the so-called cabal, their initials spelling the word, were the king's leading ministers in the 1670s. They were Thomas, Lord Clifford of Chudleigh, Henry Bennet, earl of Arlington, George Villiers, Duke of Buckingham, Anthony Ashley, earl of Shaftesbury, and John Maitland, Duke of Lauderdale.
42 Ibid., 6 November 1663 – vol 4, p. 366
43 Ibid., 4, p. 371
44 Jusserand, p. 88
45 Wheatley, D, *The Private Life of Charles II*, pp. 77–78
46 Pepys, vol 5, pp. 20–1
47 Ibid., pp. 107 & 139
48 Ibid., pp. 209 & 254; 21 April 1666 – vol 7, p. 106
49 Ibid., 7, p. 306
50 Hartmann, C H, *La Belle Stuart*, p. 143

51 Poems on the Affairs of State, I, p. 73

52 Fraser, p. 240

53 Gramont, ii, p. 145

54 Ibid., p. 156

55 Ibid., pp. 157–158

56 Pepys, vol 8, p. 119; 9 September 1668 – vol 9, p. 302; 19 March 1667 – vol 8, p. 120

57 Ibid., 3 April 1667 – vol 8, pp. 145 & 169

58 Hatton Correspondence, i, p. 52; Add MSS 21947, f55

59 Hartmann, C H, *La Belle Stuart*, pp. 134

60 Ibid., pp. 137–139

61 Hartmann, C H, *Charles II and Madame*, p. 193

62 Hill, C P, *Who's Who in Stuart Britain*, p. 304

63 Pepys, vol 9, pp. 134–5; Hartmann, C H, *La Belle Stuart*, p. 153

64 Norrington, p. 149

65 Ibid., p. 151

66 Weinreb, B, & Hibbert, C, *The London Encyclopaedia*, pp. 795–796

67 Fleming, p. 66

68 Pepys 19 May 1668 – vol 9, p. 205

69 Hatton Correspondence, i, p. 64

70 Ibid., p. 83

71 Hartmann, C H, *La Belle Stuart*, p. 189

72 Ibid.

73 Ibid., p. 197

74 Ibid., p. 205

75 Ibid., p. 206

76 Treasury Minute Book V, p. 59

77 Wilson, J H, *Court Satires of the Restoration*, pp. 281 & 52

78 Ibid., p. 106

79 Ibid., p. 24

80 Hartmann, C H, *La Belle Stuart*, p. 219

81 Carlwright, J, *Sacharissa* p. 219

82 Blencoe, R W, (ed.) *Diary of Henry Sidney*, I, p. 100; – An Answer to Court Ladies, Wilson, J H, *Court Satires of the Restoration*, p. 42

83 Add MS 23,722, f15; Wilson J H, *Court Satires of the Restoration*, p. 211

84 Gramont, ii, 36

85 Wilson, J H, *A Rake and His Times*, p. 14

86 Gramont, (Sonneschein edition) p. 247

87 Pepys, 8 February 1663 – vol 4, p. 37

88 Ibid., p. 48 & 15 January 1669 – vol 9, p. 416

89 Ibid., 22 June 1662 – vol 3, p. 117; Rimbault, EF (ed.) *The Old cheque-book of Chapel Royal*, Quoted in Pepys, vol 3, p. 117, n1

90 Gramont, ii, pp. 104–5

91 Ibid., p. 78

92 Pepys, 12 June 1666 – vol 7, p. 162 & vol 9, p. 563

Chapter 2

1 Ashley, M, *Stuarts in Love*, p. 181

2 Hamilton, A, *Memoirs of Count Grammont*, p. 114; Gramont, i, p. 92

3 Browning, A (ed.), *Memoirs of Sir John Reresby*, p. 36; Pepys, 24 June 1667 – vol 8, p. 286

4 Hamilton, ibid; Gramont, i, p. 173

5 Pinto, V, *Sir Charles Sedley*, p. 138; Gramont, i, p. 121

6 Pepys, 19 August 1665 – vol 6, p. 198; 20 April 1661– vol 2, p. 80

7 Gramont, i, p. 160 & ii, p. 107; *The Works of Andrew Marvell*, p. 132

8 Jesse III, p. 479; Gramont, ii, p. 107

9 Pepys, 2 September 1661 – vol 2, p. 170; vol 3, p. 64; 27 January 1668 – vol 9, p. 38; Burnet, i, 237

10 Pepys, 24 June 1667 – vol 8, p. 287; 27 January 1668 – vol 9, p. 38

11 Pepys, 30 July 1667 – vol 8, p. 368

12 Gramont, ii, p. 108 & p. 111; Hill, CP, *Who's Who in Stuart Britain*, p. 348; Browning, p. 55; *The Works of Andrew Marvell*, p. 132

13 Pepys, 9 January 1666 – vol 7, p. 8; 15 October 1666, 7, p. 323; Browning, p. 55

14 *The Works of Andrew Marvell*, p. 132

15 Ashley, M, *Stuarts in Love*, p. 179; Miller, J, *James II – A Study in Kingship*, p. 44; Pepys, vol 1, pp. 260–261

16 De Beer, E, *The Diary of John Evelyn*, p. 412

17 Clarendon MS 74 f138

18 Gramont, i, pp. 162 & 164

19 Love, H (ed.), *Restoration Verse*, p. 112

20 Ollard, R, *Clarendon and His Friends*, p. 228

21 de la Bedoyere, G, (ed.) *The Diary of John Evelyn*, p. 128

22 Gramont, i, p. 167

23 Ibid., p. 169

24 Pepys, 6 April 1668 – vol 9, pp. 145–155

25 Gramont, ii, p. 170; *The Works of Andrew Marvell*, p. 166

26 Burnet, i, p. 319

27 Lawson, O (ed.), *Aubrey's Brief Lives*, p. 184; Pepys, 8 & 15 October 1666 – vol 7, pp. 315 & 323

28 Lawson, p. 182; Gramont, i, p. 173

29 Lawson, p. 183

30 Ibid, p. 184; Melville, L, *Windsor Beauties*, p. 165

31 Pepys, 10 June 1666 – vol 7, pp. 158–159; 26 September 1666 – vol 7, p. 297

32 Ibid, 29 August 1667 – vol 8, p. 406; De Beer, E, *The Diary of John Evelyn*, p. 877 (28 March 1688); Gramont, ii, p. 89

33 Pepys, 29 August 1667 – vol 8, p. 406; Gramont, ii, p. 89

34 Pepys, vol 7, p. 365; CSPD 1666–7, pp. 262-3

35 Pepys, 12 November 1666, vol 7, p. 366

36 Ibid.,12 December 1666 – vol 7, p. 405

37 Ibid., vol 8, p. 6

38 Lawson, p. 184
39 Pepys, 8 January 1667 – vol 8, p. 8
40 Ibid., vol 4, p. 19
41 Gramont, ii, pp. 6–7
42 Ibid., ii, pp. 107 & 110
43 Pepys, 12 January 1669 – vol 9, p. 413
44 De Beer, E, *The Diary of John Evelyn*, p. 587
45 HMC 12th Report, Appendix, Part V, Vol II, p. 3: Letters from Lady Chaworth to Lord Roos
46 Harris, B, *Charles Sackville*, p. 82
47 Newdigate-Newdigate, Lady, *Cavalier and Puritan*, p. 86
48 Pinto, p. 136; Thomson, G M, *The First Churchill*, p. 27
49 Harris, B, *Charles Sackville*, p. 83
50 Pinto, p. 139, n3
51 *The Ladies March*, Harleian MS 7317, f31
52 Cartwright, J, *Sacharissa*, pp. 273 & 276
53 Harris, p. 82
54 Burnet, *History of His Own Time*, p. 224
55 Ashley, M, *Life in Stuart England*, p. 99; Burnet, p. 233
56 de la Bedoyere, p. 336
57 Burnet, *History of His Own Time*, p.249
58 Pinto, pp. 346–347
59 Ibid., p. 217
60 Ibid., p. 218
61 Ibid., p. 216
62 Ibid., p. 237; Quoted in G.E.C. Peerage, *Countess of Dorchester*, IV, p406n

Chapter 3

1   Cartwright, J, *Sacharissa*, p. 216
2   Weales, G, *The Complete Plays of William Wycherley*, p. 271
3   Gramont, i, p. 116
4   Thomson, George Malcolm, *The First Malborough*, p. 15
5   Walker, John, *The Queen has been Pleased*, p. 27
6   There are many sources for this story: the letter, dated September 1671, from John Muddyman to the earl of Rochester; and a letter dated 12 September 1671 from the Attorney-General Sir Heneage Finch to his son, both quoted in Treglown, J, *Letters of John Wilmot*, pp. 68–70; Hatton correspondence, 1, pp. 68–9
7   Pepys, 6 December 1665 – vol 8, pp. 320–21
8   Ibid., 24 January 1667 – vol 8, p. 29
9   Ibid., pp. 27–8
10 Ibid., vol 9, p. 170
11 Ibid., p. 172
12 Ibid., 8 January 1666 – vol 7, p. 2
13 Ibid., p. 120

14 Ibid., vol 8, pp. 448 & 477
15 Ibid, 22 December 1676 – vol 8, p. 585; vol 9, pp. 143 & 282 (18 August 1668)
16 Ibid., 25 October 1668 – vol 9, p. 337
17 Ibid., p. 337–8
18 Ibid.
19 Thompson, R, *Unfit for Modest Ears*, pp. 67–8
20 Ibid.
21 Ibid.
22 Pepys, 24 March 1668 – vol 9, pp. 29–30
23 Ibid., 25 March 1668 – vol 9, p. 132
24 Ibid., 24 March 1686 – vol 9, pp. 29–30
25 Calendary State Papers, Domestic, 1668, p. 306
26 Sargeant, P, *My Lady Castelmaine*, pp. 161–162
27 *Impartial Protestant Mercury, No. 64, 29 November to 2 December 1681*; Hayward, A L (ed.), *Tom Brown's amusements, Serious and Comical*, p. 442
28 Thompson, p. 64
29 Pepys, 6 April 1668 – vol 9, p. 154
30 Sargeant, pp. 162–163
31 Bedoyere, G de la, *Diary of John Evelyn*, p. 186
32 Zimbardo, R, *At Zero Point*, p. 104
33 Thompson, p. 124
34 Veith, D, *The Complete Poems of John Wilmot*, pp. 60–1
35 Shorter OED, ii, p. 1896; Wilson, J H, *A Rake and His Times*, p. 256
36 Pepys, vol 4, p. 210
37 Veith, D, *The Complete Poems of John Wilmot*, p. 51
38 Wilson, J H, (ed.) *The Court Satires of the Restoration*, p. 124
39 Zimbardo, p. 104
40 Trumbach, Randolph, *The Birth of the Queen*, in Zimbardo, p. 104
41 Taylor, *Sex in History*, p. 189; J Dunton, *Athenianisme*, 1710, pp. 93–8. Thompson, p. 124
42 *Narrative of the Plot*, 1680: Petherick, M, *Restoration Rogues*, pp. 183–4
43 Kenyon, J, *The Popish Plot*, p. 47; Downes, *Roscius Anglicanus*, p. 49
44 Veith, D, *The Complete Poems of John Wlmot*, p. 45
45 Ibid., p. 54
46 Ibid., p. 29
47 Ibid., p. 58
48 Sharp, Jane, *The Midwives Book*, pp. 43–44
49 Gramont, i, p. 104; Wilson J H, (ed.), *Court Satires of the Restoration*, p. 57
50 Pepys, 3 October 1665 – vol 6, p. 251
51 Wilson, J H (ed.) *Rochester–Savile Letters*, p. 102
52 Ibid., p. 55–56
53 Ibid., p. 57
54 Sharp, Jane, p. 85; Wilson, J H, (ed.), *Court Satires of the Restoration*, p. 295
55 Ibid.

56 Veith, D, *The Complete Poems of John Wilmot*, pp. 137–138
57 Anthony Wood, *Athenae Oxonienses*; Farley-Hills, David (ed.), *Rochester – The Critical Heritage*, p. 172
58 Thompson, p. 127
59 Summers, M, *Restoration Theatre*, p. 296
60 Thompson, p. 126
61 Treglown, Jeremy (ed.), *Spirit of Wit – Reconsiderations of Rochester*, p. 64
62 Ibid.
63 Veith, D, *The Complete Poems of John Wilmot*, p. 40
64 Ibid., pp. 40–41

Chapter 4
1   Seargeant, P, *My Lady Castlemaine*, p. 1
2   Veith, D, *The Complete Poems of John Wilmot, earl of Rochester;* 'Signior Dildo' is generally credited to Rochester but was more than likely to be the co-work of other authors, also.
3   Pepys, 15 August 1665 – vol 6, p. 191; 6 February 1662, – vol 3. p. 24
4   Ibid., 21 May 1662 – vol 3, p. 87
5   Browning. A (ed.), *Memoirs of Sir John Reresby*, p. 41; Huehns, G (ed.), *Selections from Clarendon*, p. 396
6   Clarendon, *History VII*, 133; Viscount Grandison was the son of the first Viscount, a half brother to George Villiers, the first duke of Buckingham – 'Christ has his John, I have my George' James I would say – and father of the second duke, also George Villiers, who figures so prominently in this book. Thus Barbara and the Duke of Bucks were cousins.
7   Gramont, i p. 156
8   Add MSS 19, 253 f29 – Letters of Philip Stanhope, second Earl of Chesterfield
9   Ibid., f204 v
10 Ibid., f12
11 Boyer, A, *History of the Life and Reign of Queen Anne*, p. 48 (appendix); Andrews, A, *The Royal Whore*, p. 12
12 Add MS 19, 253, f15
13 Ibid., f33v
14 Ibid., f16
15 Calendary State Papers, Domestic 1660–1, p104; Lansdowne MSS 1236, f128 – letter from Sir Allen Broderick
16 Rugge's Diurnal; Add MSS 10,116–117; Pepys, 17 January 1660 – vol 1, p. 20; CSPD 1657 – 8, p. 290
17 Gramont i, p. 97
18 Ibid., p. 264
19 Fraser, A, *King Charles II*, p. 182; Pepys, vol 1, p. 199; The poem 'An Historicall Poem' has been attributed to Andrew Marvell, although this is unsure.
20 Huehns, pp. 396–397

21 Pepys, 7 December, 1661 – vol 2, p. 229
22 Ibid., vol 3, p. 139
23 Ibid., 26 July 1662 – vol 3, pp. 146–147
24 Ibid., 23 August 1662 – vol 3, p. 175
25 Ibid., 22 February 1664 – vol 5, p. 56
26 Ibid., vol 3, p. 87
27 Ibid., 31 December 1662 – vol 3, p. 302; 26 July 1662 – vol 3, p. 146
28 Fraser, A, *King Charles II*, p. 208
29 Browning, p. 41; Seargeant, p. 49
30 Huehns, p. 398; Gramont, p. 123; Bedoyere, G de la (ed.), *The Diary of John Evelyn*, p. 141–30 May 1662
31 Gramont, p. 124; Evelyn, p. 141
32 Huehns, p. 399; Seargeant, p. 47
33 Pepys, 26 July, 1662 – vol 3, p. 146–7
34 Huehns, pp. 401, 405 & 406
35 Ibid., p. 400
36 Norrington, R (ed.), *My Dearest Minette*, p. 56
37 Love, H (ed.), *Restoration Verse*, p. 112; Huehns, pp. 402, 404 & 405
38 Huehns, p. 407; Seargeant, pp. 61–62
39 Huehns, p. 407
40 Jusserand, J J, *A French Ambassador in the Court of Charles II*, p. 91
41. Ibid., p. 95
42 Pepys, 15 May 1663, vol 4, p. 137
43 Ibid., 27 July 1667 – vol 8, p. 355
44 Ibid., 29 July 1667 – vol 8, p. 366
45 Ibid., 30 July 1667 – vol 8, p. 368
46 *An Essay of Scandal*, 1681
47 Seargeant, p. 102; Pepys, vol 5, p. 21 & vol 4, p. 38
48 'A Lampoon', Anonymous, Quoted in Love, H (ed.), *Restoration Verse*, p. 113
49 Airey, O (ed.), *History of My Own Time*, Gilbert Burnet, i, p. 476
50 Andrews , *The Royal Whore*, p. 170; Savile Correspondence, p. 49
51 Manley, Mary de la Rivière, *Secret Memoirs...from the New Atlantis*, 1709; Andrews, p. 170–171; Seargeant, P, *My Lady Castlemaine*, pp. 189–190
52 Andrews, ibid; Seargeant, ibid.
53 Weales, Gerard, *The Complete Plays of William Wycherley*, pp. 9 & 28
54 Ibid., p. 113
55 Ibid., pp. 123–124
56 Ibid., p. 6
57 *Commonplace Book*, Sir Frances Fane
58 Gramont i. p. 108
59 Gramont i. p. 78
60 *Dictionary of National Biography*; Pepys, 21 September 1668 – vol 9, p. 313
61 Andrews, p. 147
62 Burnet, *History of His Own Time*, i, p. 160; Hamilton, E, *The Illustrious Lady*, p. 206

63 HMC, Second Report, Appendix, p. 22
64 Wilson, J H, *Mr Goodman the Player*, pp. 74–75
65 Downes, J, *Rosicus Anglicanus*, p. 41
66 *Oxford Companion to the Theatre*, p. 77; Gildon, C, *Life of Thomas Betterton*; Wilson, J H, *Mr Goodman the Player*, p. 2
67 Lucas, T. *Lives of the Gamesters*, 1714; Smith, A Capt, *The School of Venus*, ii, p. 17; Wilson, J H, *Mr Goodman the Player*, pp. 1–2
68 Hopkins, G, *Nell Gwynne – A Passionate Life*, p. 126
69 Harleian MS 7006, ff281–94
70 Lucas, T, *Lives of the Gamesters*, p. 266
71 Wilson, J H, *Mr Goodman the Player*, p. 3
72 Stowe MS 969. f45
73 CSPD, 1684–5 p. 172
74 Wilson, J H, *Mr Goodman the Player*, p. 94
75 HMC Rutland MS, ii, 104; Evelyn, 6 February 1685, p. 312
76 Seargeant, pp. 304–308
77 Ibid., p. 300
78 Ibid., pp. 301–302
79 Ibid., p. 310
80 Ibid., p. 300
81 Ibid., p. 308
82 Ibid., pp. 314–316
83 Ibid., p. 320
84 Oxford Satire, p. 75; Pepys. vol 3, p. 175
85 *Pindarick* Harl MS 6913; Love, H (ed.), *Penguin Book of Restoration Verse*, p. 224; *Poems on the Affairs of State*, 1705, p. 65

Chapter 5
1   Pinto, V de Sala, *Sir Charles Sedley*, p. 77
2   Veith, D, *The Complete Poems of John Wilmot, Earl of Rochester*, p. 126
3   Stowe MS 969, f67
4   Wilson, J H, *The Court Wits of the Restoration*, p. 7
5   Wood, Anthony, *Athenae Oxonienses*, IV, p. 627
6   Veith, D, *The Complete Poems of John Wilmot, Earl of Rochester*, p. 53
7   Ibid., p. 228
8   Weales, G, *The Complete Plays of William Wycherley*, p. 268
9   Veith D, *The Complete Poems of John Wilmot, Earl of Rochester*, p. 72
10 Ibid., pp. 124–124
11 Historical Manuscripts Commission, 6th Report, Appendix, p. 367
12 *The Works of the Honourable Sir Charles Sedley, Bart, with Memoirs of the Author's Life by an Eminent Hand*, Briscoe, London, 1722; Pinto, p. 51
13 *The Works of the Honouble Sir Charles Sedley. . .* pp. 3–4
14 Pepys, 4 October 1664 – vol 5, p. 288
15 Pepys, vol 8, p. 72
16 Burnet, *History of his Own Time*, p. 102

17 Pepys, 16 November 1667 – vol 8, p. 533

18 Pepys, vol 8, pp. 334, 336–7

19 Fell-Smith, Charlotte, *Mary Rich, Countess of Warwick*, p. 195

20 Lyson's *Historical Account of the Parishes of Middlesex not included in the Environs of London*, p. 109: Pinto, *Sedley*, p. 53; Pinto, Vivian de Sola, *The Restoration Court Poets*, p. 26; *The Works of the Honourable Sir Charles Sedley*...pp. 8–9

21 Pepys, 15 March 1669 – vol 9, p. 483 & 7 April 1669 – vol 9, p. 511; *Wit and Drollery*, 1661, p. 66; Harris, Brice, *Charles Sackville*, p. 27

22 Clarke (ed.), *Anthony à Wood, Life & Times*, i, p. 476; ii, p. 213

23 Lee, M H (ed.) *Diaries and Letters of Philip Henry*, p. 158; Clarke, pp. 476–7

24 Clarke, Wood, ii, pp. 476–7

25 Burnet, G, *Life and Death of Rochester*, p. 28; Pepys, 1 July 63 – vol 4, pp. 201–10

26 Pepys, 1 July 63 – vol 4, pp. 209–10

27 Clarke, Wood, ii, pp. 476–7

28 Ibid.

29 Pepys. 1 July 63 – vol 4, pp. 209–10

30 Burnet, *History of his Own Time*, p. 101

31 Pinto, *Sedley*, pp. 307–11

32 Ibid., Les Reports des Divers Specials Cases, Colligees par Tho Siderfin Esq. La Second Edition: London, MDCCXIV I, 168

33 Clarke, *Wood*, ii, pp. 476–7

34 Calendar of State Papers Domestic, Bk 16, p. 118

35 Pepys, vol 9 – pp. 335–6

36 House of Commons Journals IX, pp. 251 256, 264

37 Pepys, 23 October 1668 – vol 9, p. 336; CSPD 1668–9, p. 8

38 Ibid.

39 Pepys, 1 February 1669 – vol 9, p. 435

40 Pepys, 2 February 1669 – vol 9, p. 436 and note; *Annals of English Drama*, p. 112 & p. 168

41 Genest, J, *Some Account of the English Stage*, I, pp. 80, 81, 93; Pepys, 2 February 1669 – vol 9, p. 436 & 9 February 1669 – vol 9, p. 441

42 Pepys, 6 March 1669 – vol 9, p. 471

43 Zimmerman, Father B, *Carmel in England*, p. 236

44 Ibid., pp. 235–6

45 Ibid., pp. 236

46 Ibid., p. 237

47 Ibid.

48 Ibid.

49 Pepys, 29 July 1667 – vol 8, p. 364

50 Pepys, 7 May 1668 – vol 9, p. 189

51 Pinto, *Sedley*, p. 126

52 Ibid., p. 131

53 Ibid., p. 129

54 Ibid., pp. 144–145: *An Essay Upon Satire* by Mulgrave
55 Clarke (ed.), *Anthony a Wood, Life & Times*, ii, p. 477
56 Hatton Papers, I, p. 216
57 *The Works of the Honourable Sir Charles Sedley*, p. 10
58 *Annals of English Drama*, p. 186
59 Add MS 28,644 f57b
60 Ibid.
61 Pinto, *The Restoration Court Poets*, p. 27
62 Dictionary of National Biography, vol 63, p. 199
63 *The Works of the Honourable Sir Charles Sedley*, p. 11
64 Pinto, *Sedley*, p. 223
65 Ibid.
66 Add MS 28,644
67 Weales, G, *The Complete Plays of William Wycherley*, p. 365
68 Pinto, *Sedley*, p. 234
69 Fraser, A, *King Charles II*, p. 115
70 Treglown, J (ed.), *The Letters of John Wilmot, Earl of Rochester*, p. 67; Burnet, Gilbert, *Some Passages of the Life and Death of Rochester*, Farley-Hills, D (ed.) *Rochester, The Critical Heritage*, pp. 50–51
71 Veith, *Complete Poems*, p. 52
72 Ibid., translation by Richard Lattimore
73 Greene, G, *Lord Rochester's Monkey*, p. 159
74 Veith, *Complete Poems*, p. 51
75 Ibid., p. 117
76 Wilson, J H, *Rochester-Savile Letters*, p. 41
77 Veith, *Complete Poems*, p. 135
78 Ibid., p. 134
79 Greene, p. 101
80 Wilson, J H, *Court Satires of the Restoration*, p. xv
81 Pepys, vol 9, p. 382
82 Claydon Papers, letter of John Verney to Edmund Verney, 29 June 1676
83 Hatton Papers, I, pp. 133–34
84 Ibid., p. 34
85 Greene, p. 108
86 Veith, *Complete Poems*, p. 130
87 Ibid., p. 126
88 Ibid., p. 132
89 Ibid., p. 133
90 Ibid., p. 132
91 Treglown, *The Letters of John Wilmot*, p. 158; Gramont, ii, pp. 38–39
92 Veith, *Complete Poems*, pp. 136–137
93 Ibid., p. 137
94 Ibid., p. 141
95 Pepys, 17 February 1669 – vol 9, p. 451–452; Add MS 36916, f127; Bulstrode Papers: i, p. 91

96 Greene, p. 77
97 Ibid., p. 70
98 Wilson, J H, *All The King's Ladies*, p. 110; Cibber, Colley *An Apology for the Life of*, I, p. 159 & II, p. 303
99 Oxford Companion to the Theatre, p. 60
100 Cibber, Colley, *An Apology*, II, p. 303
101 Lamb, J, *So Idle a Rogue*, p. 154; Treglown, *The Letters of John Wilmot*, p. 98
102 Veith, *Complete Poems*, p. 85–6
103 Treglown, *The Letters of John Wilmot*, p. 174
104 Ibid., p. 172
105 Ibid., pp. 216–217
106 Laing MS, p. 405
107 Le Fleming MS, p. 62
108 Veith, *Complete Poems*, p. 48
109 Bedoyere, G de la, (ed.) *The Diary of John Evelyn*, 2 December 1674, p. 230
110 Veith, *Complete Poems*, pp. 60–61
111 Greene, pp. 95–6
112 Lyle, R C, *Royal Newmarket*, pp. 25–6
113 Verney, M (ed.) *Memoirs of the Verney Family*, ii, 336
114 HMC, 12th Report, Appendix V, Pt II, p. 50
115 Veith, *Complete Poems*, p. 116
116 Farley-Hills, D, (ed.), *Rochester, The Critical Heritage*, p. 136

Chapter 6
1   Love, H, (ed.), *Penguin Book of Restoration Verse*, p. 45
2   Haydon, Peter, *The English Pub – A History*, p. 69
3   Ibid., p. 64
4   French, R V, *Toasting*; Haydon, pp. 69–70
5   Fraser, A, *Cromwell, Our Chief of Men*, p. 464; *Oxford Companion to the Theatre*, p. 69–70
6   Bedoyere, G de la, (ed.) *The Diary of John Evelyn*, pp. 119–120
7   Bryant, A, *Restoration England*, p. 101; Childs, J, *The Army of Charles II*, pp. 127–128
8   Childs, p. 217
9   Jusserand, J J, *A French Ambassador in the Court of Charles II*, p. 96
10 Pepys, 15 May 1663 – vol 4, 136
11 Ibid., 19 December 1666 – vol 7, p. 414; Clarendon, Life, iii, 153–4, Quoted in Pepys, vol 7, p. 415
12 Jusserand, p. 152; *To Julius*, Sir Charles Sedley, quoted in Love, Harold, *Restoration Verse*, p. 60
13 Verney Papers, 16 January 1662
14 Picard, L, *Restoration London*, p. 157
15 Harris, B, *Charles Sackville*, p. 26
16 Verney Papers, ii, pp. 381 & 387
17 Pepys, 9 August 1660 – vol 1, p. 218

18   Ibid., p. 303 (27 November 1660)
19   Shorter OED, ii, p. 1371; Pepys, vol 5, p. 142
20   Celia Fienne's Journal, pp. 56–7; Sydney, *Social Life in England, 1660–1690,* pp. 78–79
21   *The Character of a Tavern,* 1675, Quoted in Pinto, *Sir Charles Sedley,* pp. 57–58
22   Thomson, G S, *Life in a Noble Household,* pp. 191–192
23   Pepys, 23 October 1663 – vol 4, p. 346 & 8 February 1660 – vol 1, p. 46; Bryant, p. 109
24   Academy of Compliments, 1671: *Oxford Book of Seventeenth Century Verse,* p. 898
25   Verney Papers ii, 314–5
26   Treglown, J, (ed.), *The Letters of John Wilmot,* pp. 91–92
27   Hatton Correspondence, i, pp. 60 & 164
28   Ibid., p. 220
29   Ibid., p. 117
30   *An Elegy upon that never to be forgotten Matron, Old Maddam Gwinn, who was unfortunately drown'd in her own fishpond on the 19th of July 1679*
31   *A Panegyric,* Harley MS 7319
32   *Memorials of Nell Gwynne,* University of Leeds; Croker-Crofton Collection; Bryant, p. 101
33   Ammer, C, *The Methuen Dictionary of Cliches,* p. 90
34   Wilson, J H, *Court Satires of the Restoration,* p. 6
35   Bryant, p. 105
36   Haydon, p. 81
37   Latham, R, *The Pepys Companion,* p. 107; Pepys, vol 5, p. 105
38   Pepys, vol 5, p. 37; Weinreb, B & Hibbert, C, *The London Encyclopaedia,* pp. 964–965
39   R V French, *Nineteen Centuries of Drink in England;* Haydon, p. 84
40   Pepys, 19 June 1663 – vol 4, p. 189
41   Forneron, *Louise de Keroualle,* p. 168
42   Greer, G, *John Wilmot, Earl of Rochester,* p. 7; Hatton Correspondence i, p. 128
43   Pepys vol 2, p. 105
44   Ibid., p. 87 (23 April 1661)
45   Ibid., 2 May 1660 – vol 1, p. 122
46   Ibid, vol 5 p. 172
47   John Oldham, *A Dithyrambic,* 1677

Chapter 7

1   The Drury Lane Patent
2   Ibid.
3   Wilson, J H, *Mr Goodman, The Player,* pp. 74-75
4   Ibid, p. 35; Cibber, *An Apology,* ii, p. 316
5   Wilson, J H, *All the King's Ladies,* p. 41
6   *The works of Mr Thomas Brown,* ii, p. 303; Wilson, *All the King's Ladies,* p. 26

7   Cibber, *An Apology*, I, p. 75; Wilson, *All the King's Ladies*, p. 9

8   Summers, M, *Restoration Theatre*, p. 314

9   Oxford Companion to the Theatre, p. 77; Wilson, *All the King's Ladies*, p. 30; Pepys, vol 9, p. 425

10   Milhous, J & Hume, R (eds), *A Register of Theatrical Documents 1660–1737*, I, p. 35; Wilson, *All the King's Ladies*, p. 31; Kenyon, J, *The Popish Plot*, pp. 47, 63, 82

11   Dryden, J, *Marriage à la Mode*, prologue, p. 7

12   Pepys, vol 9, p. 189

13   Milhous & Hume, I; CSPD, 1667, p. 502

14   SP 29/142, no. 160; CSPD 1665–1666, p. 157; Milhous & Hume, I, p. 73

15   Summers, M, *Playhouse of Pepys*, p. 55

16   Milhous & Hume, I, p. 35

17   *Oxford Companion to the Theatre*, p. 94

18   Pepys, 13 February 1668 – vol 9, p. 67

19   Gramont, ii, p. 53; *Evelyn's Diary*, 2 January 1662; Summers, *Restoration Theatre*, p. 141

20   Summers, *Restoration Theatre*, p. 126

21   Thompson, E M, *Letters of Humphrey Prideaux*, p. 5

22   Summers, *Restoration Theatre*, p. 69

23   Browning, *Memoirs of Sir John Reresby, p. 487; Savile Correspondence*, p. 164; Wilson, *All the King's Ladies*, p. 13; Adamson, D, and Beauclerk-Dewar, P, *House of Nell Gwyn*, p. 18

24   Gilbert, G D, *Baronne D'Aulnoy, Memoirs of the Court of England*, p. 274

25   Gramont, ii, p. 52

26   Gramont, ii, p. 54; Gilbert, G D, *Baronne D'Aulnoy*, p. 276

27   Gramont, ibid; Gilbert, G D, *Baronne D'Aulnoy*, p. 277

28   Gilbert, G D, *Baronne D'Aulnoy*, p. 130

29   Pepys, 18 February 1662 – vol 3, pp. 32 & p. 86; Downes, *Roscius Anglicanus*, p. 74; Wilson, *All the King's Ladies*, p. 13

30   Wilson, All the King's Ladies. p. 14

31   Prologue at Oxford. *A Collection of Poems Written upon several Occasions By several Persons.*

32   Milhous & Hume, I, p. 192

33   Summers, *Restoration Theatre*, p. 57

34   Ibid., p. 58

35   Ibid., p. 60

36   Weales, Gerald (ed.), *The Complete Plays of William Wycherley*, p. 256

37   *Shorter Oxford Dictionary*, i, p. 888 Summers, *Restoration Theatre*, p. 57 & p. 92

38   Summers, *Restoration Theatre*, p. 69

39   Shadwell, Thomas, *The Virtuoso*, I, i

40   Epilogue to Thomas Otway's *The Cheats of Scapin*; Dryden, *To The King And Queen, At The Opening Of Their Theatre Upon The Union Of The Two Companies In 1682*; Summers, *Restoration Theatre*, pp. 68–69

41   Summers, *Restoration Theatre*, p. 84

42 Pepys, 2 November 1667 – vol 8, pp. 516–7
43 Borgan, A S, Thomas Shadwell, p. 181
44 Hopkins, Graham, *Nell Gwynne*, p. 20
45 Summers, *Restoration Theatre*, p. 82
46 Pepys, vol 9, p. 195
47 Summers, *Restoration Theatre*, p. 71
48 Ibid., p. 78
49 The Poems of John Dryden, p. 257; Borgman, *Thomas Shadwell*, p. 182
50 Downes, p. 85; *Oxford Companion to the Theatre*, p. 92; Wilson, *All the King's Ladies*, p. 181
51 Summers, *Restoration Theatre*, p. 81; Wilson, *All the King's Ladies*, pp. 180–181
52 Pepys, 20 April 1667 – vol 8, p. 172; 15 April 1667 – vol 8, p. 168; Summers, *Restoration Theatre*, p. 182

Chapter 8

1   Hibbert, C, *Highwaymen*, p. 13
2   Ibid., p. 97
3   Ibid., p. 121
4   Smith, A, *A Complete History. . . of the Most Notorious Highwaymen*
5   Ibid., p. 14
6   Browning, A, *Memoirs of Sir John Reresby*, p. 110; Sydney, W C, *Social Life in England*, p. 213
7   *Verney Memoirs* ii, pp. 341–2
8   Hibbert, p. 15
9   Smith, pp. 321–326
10 Ibid., pp. 63–66
11 Ibid., pp. 165
12 Ibid., p. 166
13 Ibid., pp. 166–7
14 Ibid., pp. 462–3
15 Ibid., p. 334
16 Ibid., p. 338
17 Ibid., pp. 458–459
18 Ibid., p.459
19 Ibid., pp. 42–47; Sydney, p. 217
20 Smith, pp. 42–44; Hibbert, pp. 38–40
21 *Walter Pope's Memoires of M. du Vall*, 1670, pp. 7–9, 22; Hibbert, p. 90
23 Smith, p. 180
24 Baldick, Robert, *The Duel – A History of Duelling*, p. 32
25 Ibid., p. 38
26 *The 26 Galway Commandments*, Ibid., p. 35
27 *Steele, no 3245; HMC Le Fleming*, p. 55
28 Conway papers, p. 338
29 Calendar of State Papers Domestic 1671, pp. 346, 387 & 416

30 *Utile Dulce*, 1681, Quoted in Wilson, J H, *Court Satires of the Restoration*, p. 49

31 Middlesex County Records (IV, 150)

32 Pepys, vol 8, pp. 140–1 CSPD 1666–7, pp. 458–9

33 Pepys, 6 August 1668 – vol 9, p. 273

34 Childs, J, *The Army of Charles II*, p. 82

35 Pepys, 8, p. 22; Bryant, A, *Years of Peril*, p. 46

36 Pepys, 22 December 1661 – vol 2, p. 237

37 Ibid., 8, pp. 363–4

38 le Fleming MS, p. 52; Pepys, 8 August 1667 – vol 8, p. 377

39 Pepys, 3, p. 157

40 Verney Memoirs, ii,320–1

41 Ibid.

42 Savile Correspondence, p. 239

43 Ibid.

44 Wilson, J H, *The Court Wits of the Restoration*, p. 30; HMC Tenth Report, part V, pp. 57–68; Rutland MS, II, p. 42

45 Pepys, 30 August 1668 – vol 9, p. 294

46 *The State of the Nation* (1680), Anon, Add MS 34362; Love, H (ed.), *Restoration Verse*, p. 125

47 Hill, C P, *Who's Who in Stuart Britain*, p. 337; Wilson, J H, *Court Satires of the Restoration*, p. 57

48 Ormond MS, N.S. V, 561; Christie W D (ed.), *Letters addressed from London to Sir Joseph Williamson*, I, 87

49 Treglown, J (ed.), *Letters of John Wilmot*, p. 173

50 Wilson, J H, *Court Satires of the Restoration*, p. 49

51 *Memoirs of the Secret Service*, Quoted in Greene, G, *Lord Rochester's Monkey*, p. 81; Vieth, D (ed.), *The Complete Poems of John Wilmot*, p. 143

52 *Memoirs*, Q in Lamb, J, *So Idle a Rogue*, pp. 119–20; Pinto, V, *Enthusiast in Wit*, pp. 93–96; Greene, pp. 191–5

53 Ibid.

54 Ibid.

55 Ibid.

56 Pinto, *Enthusiast in Wit*, p. 95

57 Veith, D (ed.), *Complete Poems*, pp. 99–100

58 Greer, G, *John Wilmot, Earl of Rochester*, p. 16; HMC 7th Report, appendix 531 a, 488b; Greene, p. 77

59 Savile Correspondence, p. 58

60 Greene, p. 83

61 HMC Rutland II, 27; Essex papers I, 261; Wilson, J H, *The Court Wits of the Restoration*, p. 30

62 Bulstrode Papers, I, 303

63 Ibid., p. 304; Savile Correspondence, p. 39

64 Weinreb, B, & Hibbert, C, *London Encyclopaedia*, p. 965

65 Veith, D (ed.), *Complete Poems*, p. 124

66 Ibid., pp. 120–121

67 Ibid., pp. 124–25
68 Dryden, Mermaid Series, vol 2, p. 15
69 Greene, p. 193–4
70 Wilson, J H, *Rochester-Savile Letters*, p. 73; Treglown, J (ed.), pp. 233–234
71 Pinto, p. 178
72 Greene, p. 194
73 Ibid, p. 195
74 Pinto, p. 181
75 Ibid., p. 182; Luttrell, N, *A Brief Relation*, I, p. 30
76 Pinto, p. 183

Chapter 9
1   Love, H (ed.), *Restoration Verse*, p. 116: attributed (?) to Andrew Marvell
2   Kaye, W, *The Romance & Adventures of the Notorious Colonel Blood*, p. ix
3   Petherick, M, *Restoration Rogues*, p. 16; *Remarks on the Life and Death of the Fam'd Mr Blood*, 1680
4   Ibid., p. 18
5   Ibid., p. 19
6   Browning, A (ed.), *Memoirs of Sir John Reresby*, p. 70
7   Petherick, p. 24; Burghclere, Lady, *George Villiers*, p. 240; Carte, *Life of Duke of Ormond*, iv, p. 443
8   Carte, vol iv p. 443; Burghclere, Lady Winifred, *George Villiers*, p. 240
9   Petherick, p. 26; *Remarks on the Life and Death of the Fam'd Mr Blood*, 1680
10 Ibid., p. 26
11 Ibid., p. 29
12 Ibid., p. 30
13 Ibid.
14 Ibid., p. 31
15 Bedoyere, G de la, *The Diary of John Evelyn*, pp. 206–7
16 *A True Narration of the Design Lately Laid by Philip Le Mar and Others, against George Duke of Buckingham*, 1680; Chapman, H, *Great Villiers*, p. 262
17 Chapman, pp. 262–263
18 Ibid, p. 263
19 Cartwright, J, *Sacharissa*, p. 268

Chapter 10
1   Hartman, C, *Madame*, p. 194
2   Burghclere, *Buckingham*, p. 226
3   Chapman, H, *Great Villiers*, p. 126 & p. 132
4   Goodwin, Charles (ed.) Gramont, vol I, p. 240
5   Burghclere, *Buckingham*, p. 151; Chapman, *Great Villiers*, p. 126
6   *On the Ladies of Court*, Satires, p. 4
7   Cartwright, Julia, *Sacharissa*, pp. 225, 257 & 260; John Macky, *Memoirs*, p. 15: Q in *Satires*, Wilson, J H (ed.), p. 286/7
8   Gramont, i, p. 109

9   Gramont, i, p. 95
10 Ibid.
11 Gramont, i, p. 96
12 Ibid.
13 Ibid., p. 110
14 Ibid.
15 Ibid., p. 111
16 Pepys, vol 3, pp. 170–1
17 Hatton Correspondence, i, p. 42
18 *On the Ladies of the Court, 1663* Court Satires, p. 4
19 Gramont, ii, p. 3
20 Ibid., p. 135
21 Ibid., ii pp. 135 & 162
22 Ibid., pp. 163–44
23 *The Poems of Dryden*, p. 56
24 Q in Chapman, H, p. 295
25 Gramont, i, pp. 117 & 137
26 Wilson, J H, *A Rake and his Times*, p. 18; D'Aulnoy, p. 231; Wilson, J H, *All the King's Ladies*, p. 167
27 Gramont. i, p. 97
28 Add MSS 23,722, f15
29 Burnet, p. 100
30 Ibid., p. 101
31 Wilson, J H, *A Rake and his Times*, p. 44
32 Ibid., pp. 16–17
33 *Life and Times of Anthony Wood*, i, pp. 42–43
34 Reresby, pp. 58–59
35 Ibid.
36 Ibid.
37 Chapman, p. 126
38 Gramont, ii, p. 137
39 Pepys, 22 July 1667 – vol 8, p348; Le Fleming MS, Report 12, Appendix VII, pp. 51–52.
40 Savile correspondence, p. 22
41 Norrington, R, *My Dearest Minette*, p. 139
42 25 October 1666 HMC 7/1/485; Pepys, 21 October 1666 – vol 7, pp. 336–37
43 Gramont, ii, p. 138
44 *Notes & Queries*, 15 July 1933, p. 22
45 Pepys, vol 9, p. 27
46 Singer, S W (ed.), Rev. Joseph Spence, *Anecdotes*, p. 124
47 Macaulay, *History of England*, II, p. 318; *The Court Wits of the Restoration*, p. 44; Langhorne, John, *Letters Supposed to have passed between M. De St. Evrémond and Waller*, Letter IV
48 Pepys, 17 January 1668 – vol 9, pp. 27–8

49 *Notes & Queries*, 15 July 1933, p. 22
50 Ibid.
51 Ibid.; CPSD, 1667–8, p. 192
52 CSPD 1667–8, pp. 193 & 205
53 CSPD, 1667–8, p. 192
54 Le Fleming, Report 12, Appendix VII, p. 55; *Notes & Queries*, 15 July 1933, p. 22
55 Ibid.; Wilson, J H, *A Rake and his Times*, p. 267
56 CSPD. 1667–8, p. 400
57 CSPD, 1667–8, pp. 192–3
58 Pepys, 17 January 1668 – vol 9, p. 27
59 Gramont, ii, p. 138
60 Chapman, H, p. 148
61 Gramont, ii, pp. 137–8; Pepys, 15 May 1668 – vol 9, p. 201
62 Letter by Andrew Marvell, *Marvell's Works*, vol i, p. 406, p. 338; Nicolson, Majorie Hope, *The Conway Letters*, p. 377
63 Burnet, p. 101
64 *Robert Southwell to duke of Ormond 22 September 1677*; Gramont, ii, p. 337
65 Wilson, J H, *Rochester–Savile letters*, p. 48; Treglown, *Letters of John Wilmot, Earl of Rochester*, p. 161 The christening that Buckingham was set to attend was that of the daughter of William Fanshaw, who epitomised the incestuousness of the court. He had an affair with Charles II's early mistress Lucy Walter and later married her daughter Mary.
66 Forneron, *Louise de Keroualle*, Colbert to Pomponne, p. 83; Fane, Sir Francis, *Commonplace Book*, p. 346
67 Hartmann, C H, *Madame*, p. 211
68 Thorn-Drury, G, *Poems of Waller*, London, 1893 1 lxvi
69 Pepys, 30 May 1668; 9 p. 218–19
70 Pepys. vol 9, p. 557
71 Hartmann, C H, *Charles II and Madame*, pp. 249–50
72 Forneron, pp. 50–51
73 Pepys, 19 May 1669 – vol 9, p. 558
74 Wilson, J H, *A Rake and his Times*, p. 151; Le Fleming, p. 66
75 Wilson, J H, *A Rake and his Times*, pp. 220–221
76 Letter by Andrew Marvell, *Marvell's Works*, vol i, p. 406; Wilson, J H, *A Rake and his Times*, p. 180
77 *The Poems of Dryden*, p. 56
78 Stowe MS 182, f36
79 Hist MSS Rep IX, House of Lords, Cal., 1673–74, p. 36
80 Ibid.
81 *Essex papers, Lord Angier to Lord Essex*, vol i, p. 174
82 Wilson, J H, *A Rake and his Times*, p. 252
83 Gilbert, G D (ed.), D'Aulnoy, Baronne, *Memoirs*, p. 145
84 Savile Correspondence, p. 62
85 Wilson, J H, *Court Satires of the Restoration*, p. 25
86 Stowe MS755, f8

Bibliography

Dictionary of National Biography, London, Smith, Elder & Co, 1897.

Abbot, Wilbur Cortez. *Conflicts with Oblivion*, New Haven, Yale University Press, 1924.

Adamson, Donald and Beauclerk-Dewar, Peter. *The House of Nell Gwyn, The Fortunes of the Beauclerk Family 1670–1974*, London, William Kimber, 1974.

Airy, Osmund. *Charles II*, London, Longmans, 1904.

Andrews, Allen. *The Royal Whore*, London, Hutchinson, 1971.

Anonymous. *Prologue at Oxford. A Collection of Poems Written upon several Occasions By several Persons*, London, Tho. Collins, 1673.

— *Remarks on the Life and Death of the Fam'd Mr Blood*, London 1680.

— *The Works of the Honourable Sir Charles Sedley, Bart, with Memoirs of the Author's Life by an Eminent Hand*, London, Briscoe, 1722.

Ashley, Maurice. *Charles II*, St Albans, Panther, 1973.

— *Life in Stuart England*, London, Batsford, 1967.

— *The Stuarts in Love*, London, Hodder & Stoughton, 1963.

Baldick, Robert. *The Duel – A History of Duelling*, London, Chapman and Hall, 1965.

Barber, Richard (ed). *John Aubrey: Brief Lives*, Woodbridge, Boydell, 1982.

Bédoyere, de la, Guy, (ed). *The Diary of John Evelyn*, Bangor, Headstart History, 1994.

Betterton, Thomas. *History of the English Stage from the Restoration to the Present Times*, London, Curll, 1741.

Blencoe, R W, (ed.). *Diary of the times of Charles the Second by Henry Sidney*, London, Henry Colburn, 1843.

Borgman, Albert S. *Thomas Shadwell*, New York, Benjamin Bolm, 1969.

Boyer, Abel. *History of the Life and Reign of Queen Anne*, London, 1722.

Browning, Andrew (ed.). *Memoirs of Sir John Reresby*, London, Offices of the Royal Historical Society, 1904.

Bryant, Arthur. *Restoration England*, London, Collins, 1960.

Bryant, Arthur. *The England of Charles II*, London Longmans, 1934.

Burghclere, Lady Winifred. *George Villiers, Second Duke of Buckingham, 1628–1687*, London, John Murray, London, 1903.

Cartwright, Julia. *Madame*, New York, E P Dutton, 1901.

— *Sacharissa, Some Account of Dorothy Sidney, Countess of Sunderland, Her Family and Friends 1617–1684*, London Seeley & Co, 1901.

Chapman, Hester W. *Great Villiers – A Study of George Villiers Second Duke of Buckingham*, London, Secker & Warburg, 1949.

Childs, John. *The Army of Charles II*, London, Routledge & Kegan Paul, 1976.

Christie W D (ed.). *Letters addressed from London to Sir Joseph Williamson*, London, Camden Society, 1874.

Cibber, Colley. An *Apology for the Life of Mr Colley Cibber, Comedian*, London, John Watts, 1740.

Clark, Andrew (ed.), *Life and Times of Anthony Wood, antiquary of Oxford 1632–1695 described by Himself*, Oxford, Oxford Historical Society, 1891–1900.

Cooper, William D (ed.). *Savile Correspondence*, London, Camden Society, 1858.

Cronin, Vincent. *Louis XIV*, London, Collins, 1964.

De Beer, E S, (ed.). *The Diary of John Evelyn*, Oxford, Oxford University Press, 1959.

Dean, C G T. *The Royal Hospital Chelsea Hutchinson*, London, 1950.

Dick, Oliver Lawson. *Aubrey's Brief Lives*, Harmondsworth, Peregrine Books, 1962.

Fane, Sir Francis. *Commonplace Book.* Shakespeare Library.

Farley-Hills, David (ed.). *Rochester – The Critical Heritage*, London, Routledge & Kegan Paul, 1972.

Fell-Smith, Charlotte. *Mary Rich, Countess of Warwick*, London, Longmans, 1901.

Fraser, Antonia. *King Charles II*, London, Mandarin, 1996.

Genest, John. *Account of the English Stage from the Restoration in 1660 to 1830*, London, HE Carrington, 1832.

Gilbert, G D, (ed.). *Memoirs of the Court of England in 1675 by Marie Catherine Baronne D'Aulnoy*, London, The Bodley Head, 1913.

Gilmour, Margaret. *The Great Lady – A biography of Barbara Villiers*, New York, Alfred A Knopf, 1941.

Goodwin, Gordon (ed.). *Memoirs of Count Grammont by Count Anthony Hamilton*, Edinburgh, John Grant, 1908.

Gray, Robert. *The King's Wife*, London, Secker & Warburg, 1990.

Greene, Graham. *Lord Rochester's Monkey*, London, The Bodley Head,

1974.

Greer, Germaine. *John Wilmot, Earl of Rochester,* Horndon, Northcote House, 2000.

Hamilton, Anthony. *Memoirs of the Count de Grammont,* London Swan Sonnenschein.

Hamilton, Elizabeth. *The Illustrious Lady, A biography of Barbara Villiers,* London, Hamish Hamilton, 1980.

Harbage, Alfred (revised by S Schoenberg). *Annals of English Drama 975–1700,* London Methuen, 1964.

Harris, Brice. *Charles Sackville,* New York, Lemma, 1972.

Hartmann, Cyril Hughes. *Charles II and Madame,* London, Heinemann, 1934.

— *La Belle Stuart,* London, Routledge, 1924.

Hartmann, Cyril Hughes (ed.). *Games and Gamesters of the Restoration by Charles Cotton,* Port Washington Kennikat, 1971.

Hartnoll, Phyllis. *A Concise History of the Theatre,* London Thames & Hudson, 1974.

Hartnoll, Phyllis, (ed.). *The Oxford Companion to the Theatre,* Oxford University Press, 1951.

Haswell, Jock. *James II,* London, Hamish Hamilton, 1973.

Haydon, Peter. *The English Pub – A History,* London, Robert Hale, 1994.

Hayward, Arthur L. (ed.). *A Complete History of the Lives and Robberies of the Most Notorious Highwaymen by Captain Alexander Smith,* New York, Bretano's.

Hayward, Arthur L. (ed.). *Tom Brown's Amusements, Serious and Comical,* London, George Routledge, 1927.

Hibbert, Christopher. *Highwaymen,* London, Weidenfeld & Nicolson, 1967.

Highfill, P et al (eds.). *Biographical Dictionary of Actors, Actresses, Musicians, Dancers, Managers and Other Stage Personnel in London 1660–1800,* USA, Southern Illinois University Press, 1973.

Hill, C P. *Who's Who in Stuart Britain,* London, Shepheard Walwyn, 1988.

Hopkins, Graham. *Nell Gwynne – A Passionate Life,* London, Robson Books, 2000.

Hopkirk, Mary. *Queen Over the Water, Mary Beatrice of Modena Queen of James II,* London, John Murray, 1953.

Hutton, Ronald. *Charles II,* Oxford, Clarendon, 1989.

Imbert-Terry, H M. *A Misjudged Monarch,* London, Heinemann, 1917.

Jusserand, J J. *A French Ambassador at the Court of Charles II,* London, T Fisher Unwin, 1892.

Kaye, W. *The Romance & Adventures of the Notorious Colonel Blood,* Manchester, John Heywood, 1903.

Kenyon, John. *The Popish Plot*, London, Heinemann, 1972.

Lamb, Jeremy. *So Idle a Rogue – the Life and Death of Lord Rochester*, London, Allison & Busby, 1993.

Lanchorne, Dr. *Letters Supposed to have passed between M de St Evrémond and Waller*, Baltimore, Coale & Tumas, 1809.

Langbaine, Gerard. *An Account of the English Dramatic Poets*, London 1691.

Latham R & Matthews W. (eds.). *The Diary of Samuel Pepys*, 10 vols, London, HarperCollins, 1995.

Lee, Matthew Henry (ed.). *Diaries and Letters of Philip Henry*, London Kegan Paul, Trench, 1882.

Lennep, William van, et al (eds.). *The London Stage, Part One 1660–1700*, USA, University of Illinois Press, 1961.

Love, H (ed.). *Penguin Book of Restoration Verse*, Harmondsworth, Penguin, 1978.

Luttrell, Narcissus. *A Brief Historical Relation of State Affairs from September 1678 to April 1714*, Oxford University Press, 1857.

Lyle, R C. *Royal Newmarket*, London, Putnam & Co, 1945.

Lyson, Daniel. *Historical Account of the Parishes of Middlesex not included in the Environs of London*, London, T Cadell, 1800.

Macaulay, Thomas. *History of England*, London, 1850.

MacQueen-Pope, W. *Theatre Royal Drury Lane*, London, W H Allen, 1945.

Margoliouth, H M (ed.). *Marvell's Poems and Letters*, Oxford University Press, 1952.

Marvell, Andrew. *The Works of Andrew Marvell*, Ware, Wordsworth, 1995.

Masters, Brian. *The Mistresses of Charles II*, London, Blond & Briggs, 1979.

Milhous, J & Hume R (eds.). *A Register of Theatrical Documents 1660–1737*, Carbondale, Southern Illinois University Press, 1991.

— *Roscius Anglicanus*, London, The Society for Theatre Research, 1987.

Miller, John. *James II – A study in Kingship*, London, Methuen, 1989.

Nicol, Allardyce. *British Drama: an Historical Survey from the Beginnings to the Present*, London, George G Harrap, 1925.

Nicolson, Majorie Hope. *The Conway Letters, The correspondence of Anne, Viscountess Conway, Henry More, and their friends, 1642–1684*, Yale University Press, 1930.

Norman, Charles. *Rake Rochester*, London, W H Allen, 1955.

Norrington, Ruth. *My Dearest Minette*, London, Peter Owen,1996.

North, Roger. *Lives of the Norths*, London, G Bell, 1972.

Norton, Lucy. *The Sun King and His Loves*, London, Folio Society, 1982.

Ogg, David. *England in the Reign of Charles II*, Oxford, Clarendon, 1963.

Ollard, Richard. *Clarendon and His Friends*, New York, Atheneum, 1988.

— *Pepys A Biography*, London, Hodder & Stoughton, 1974.

Petherick, Maurice. *Restoration Rogues*, London, Hollis & Carter, 1951.

Picard, Liza. *Restoration London*, London, Weidenfeld & Nicolson, 1997.

Pike, Clement Edwards (ed.). *Selections from the Correspondence of Arthur Capel Earl of Essex 1675–1677*, London, Camden Third Series, 1913.

Pinto, Vivian de Sola. *Sir Charles Sedley 1639–1701*, London, Constable, 1917.

— *Enthusiast in Wit*, London, Routledge & Kegan Paul, 1962.

Pope, Walter. *Memoires of M du Vall*, London, 1670.

Redwood, John. *Lord Rochester and the Court of Charles II*, History Today, May 1974, pp. 342–7.

Rush, Philip. *The Book of Duels*, London, Harrap, 1964.

Sergeant, Philip W. *My Lady Castlemaine*, Boston, Dana Estes, 1911.

Sharp, Jane. *The Midwives Book*, London, Simon Miller, 1671.

Sheffield, John. *Buckingham's Miscellanea*, London, Haworth Press, 1933.

Singer, S W (ed.), *Rev. Joseph Spence, Anecdotes, Observations, and Characters, of Books and Men*, Carbondale, Southern Illinois University Press, 1964.

Smith, David Nichol (ed.). *Characters of the Seventeenth Century*, Oxford, Clarendon, 1918.

Stackhouse, Thomas, (ed.). *Bishop Gilbert Burnet History of His Time*, London, Everyman, 1979.

Stow, John. *Survey of London, Strype's edition*, London, Whitaker, 1842.

Summers, Montague. *The Playhouse of Pepys*, New York, Humanities Press, 1964.

— *The Restoration Theatre*, London, Macmillan, 1934.

Sydney, William Connor. *Social Life in England*, London, Ward & Downey, 1892.

Taylor, John Russell (ed.). *Penguin Dictionary of the Theatre*, London, Penguin, 1966.

Thompson, Edward Maunde (ed.). *Correspondence of the Family of Hatton*, London, Camden Society, 1878.

— *Letters of Humphrey Prideaux*, London, Camden Society, 1835.

Thomson, George Malcolm. *The First Churchill*, London, Secker & Warburg, 1979.

Thomson, Gladys Scott. *Life in a Noble Household 1641–1700*, London, Jonathan Cape, 1937.

Treglown, Jeremy (ed.). *The Letters of John Wilmot, Earl of Rochester*, Oxford, Blackwell, 1980.

— *Spirit of Wit – Reconsiderations of Rochester*, Oxford, Blackwell, 1982.

Verney, Margaret M (ed.). *Memoirs of the Verney Family*, London, Longman, Green & Co, 1907.

Vieth, David M (ed.). *The Complete Poems of John Wilmot, Earl of Rochester*, New Haven, Yale University Press, 1979.

Walker, John. *The Queen Has Been Pleased – The Scandal of the British Honours System*, London, Sphere, 1987.

Weales, Gerald (ed.). *The Complete Plays of William Wycherley*, New York, University Press, 1967.

Weber, Harold. *The Restoration Rake-Hero*, Madison, University of Wisconsin Press, 1986.

Weinreb, B & Hibbert, C (eds.). *The London Encyclopaedia*, London, Macmillan, 1983.

Wheatley, D. *The Private Life of Charles II*, London, Hutchinson, 1933.

Wheatley, H B. *Historical Portraits*, London, Bell, 1897.

Wilson, J H (ed.). *The Rochester-Savile Letters 1671–1680*, Columbus, Ohio State University Press, 1941.

— *A Rake and His Times*, New York, Farrar, Straus & Young, 1954.

— *All the King's Ladies – Actresses of the Restoration*, USA, University of Chicago Press, 1958.

— *Mr Goodman the Player*, USA, University of Pittsburgh Press, 1964.

— *The Court Wits of the Restoration – An Introduction*, USA, Princeton University Press, 1948.

Younghusband, Major-General Sir George. *The Jewel House*, London, Herbert Jenkins, 1921.

Zimbardo, Rose A. *At Zero Point – Discourse, Culture and Satire in Restoration England*, Lexington, University Press of Kentucky, 1998.

Zimmerman, Father B. *Carmel in England: A history of the English Mission of the Discalced Carmelites 1615–1849*, London, Burns & Oakes, 1899.

Index

Constant Delights